Mastering JIRA

Gain expertise in tracking project issues and
managing them efficiently using JIRA

Ravi Sagar

[PACKT] enterprise
PUBLISHING   professional expertise distilled

BIRMINGHAM - MUMBAI

Mastering JIRA

First published: May 2015

Production reference: 1180515

Published by Packt Publishing Ltd.
Livery Place
35 Livery Street
Birmingham B3 2PB, UK.

ISBN 978-1-78439-651-0

www.packtpub.com

Credits

Author
Ravi Sagar

Project Coordinator
Harshal Ved

Reviewers
Oleksii Gnatkevych
Craig R Webster

Proofreaders
Stephen Copestake
Safis Editing

Acquisition Editor
Harsha Bharwani

Indexer
Mariammal Chettiyar

Content Development Editor
Ajinkya Paranjape

Production Coordinator
Conidon Miranda

Technical Editor
Parag Topre

Cover Work
Conidon Miranda

Copy Editors
Sarang Chari
Relin Hedly

About the Author

Ravi Sagar is a JIRA trainer, consultant, and Drupal expert with several years of experience in web development and business analysis. He has done extensive work implementing and customizing big JIRA instances for project tracking, test management, support tickets, and Agile tracking.

Ravi founded Sparxsys Solutions Pvt. Ltd. (www.sparxsys.com) in 2010, a start-up company that provides consultancy and training services on Atlassian tools and Drupal. He has created accessible websites for blind people, adhering to WCAG guidelines. Ravi's areas of interest include project management and Agile methodologies.

His areas of focus in customizing JIRA include topics, such as issue schemes, workflow schemes, field configuration schemes, screen schemes, permission schemes, and notification schemes. He has also worked on Agile tracking projects, such as Scrum and Kanban. He contributed immensely towards setting up JIRA for helpdesk, test case management, bug tracking, and support ticket management. His other areas of expertise include JIRA training, Drupal training, business analysis, project management, and JIRA Agile.

Ravi has extensive experience in JIRA installation and configuration and has also worked on Linux and Windows Server. He understands clients' requirements and suggests best solutions to save cost.

Ravi has been involved in JIRA support and maintenance and training, including regular upgrades of JIRA and installed plugins, migration from legacy-defect tracking tools to JIRA, splitting and merging JIRA instances apart from bulk actions, such as uploading issues, editing, and user creation.

He has also worked on implementing JIRA Agile and its integration with other tools, such as Confluence, Crucible, and Fisheye and has hands-on experience in JIRA REST and SOAP.

You can connect with him at `http://www.linkedin.com/in/ravisagar` or e-mail him at `ravi@sparxsys.com`.

I would like to thank my wife, Shelly, who has always stood by me and helped me achieve my goals. This book wouldn't have been possible without her continuous encouragement. I want to dedicate this book to my little daughter, Raavya, and also want to thank my parents for their endless support. Special thanks to all the reviewers and book coordinators for their immense help on this book.

About the Reviewer

Oleksii Gnatkevych has been working in the IT industry since 1998. He has vast experience working with Unix and networks. He has been mastering the Atlassian Suite since 2007. Oleksii used JIRA in the best possible way while working in GlobalLogic, Barclays, and Sony Music.

> I'd like to thank all my colleagues, who were my mentors, for providing me with the opportunity to review this book.

www.PacktPub.com

Support files, eBooks, discount offers, and more

For support files and downloads related to your book, please visit www.PacktPub.com.

Did you know that Packt offers eBook versions of every book published, with PDF and ePub files available? You can upgrade to the eBook version at www.PacktPub.com and as a print book customer, you are entitled to a discount on the eBook copy. Get in touch with us at service@packtpub.com for more details.

At www.PacktPub.com, you can also read a collection of free technical articles, sign up for a range of free newsletters and receive exclusive discounts and offers on Packt books and eBooks.

https://www2.packtpub.com/books/subscription/packtlib

Do you need instant solutions to your IT questions? PacktLib is Packt's online digital book library. Here, you can search, access, and read Packt's entire library of books.

Why subscribe?

- Fully searchable across every book published by Packt
- Copy and paste, print, and bookmark content
- On demand and accessible via a web browser

Free access for Packt account holders

If you have an account with Packt at www.PacktPub.com, you can use this to access PacktLib today and view 9 entirely free books. Simply use your login credentials for immediate access.

Instant updates on new Packt books

Get notified! Find out when new books are published by following @PacktEnterprise on Twitter or the *Packt Enterprise* Facebook page.

Table of Contents

Preface

JIRA is an issue-tracking tool from Atlassian, which has gained immense popularity in recent years due to its ease of use, its customization abilities, and finely grained control over various functions. Out of the box, JIRA offers issue and bug tracking capabilities to create tasks, assign it to users, and generate useful reports. However, the real power of JIRA lies in the customization that it offers.

Experienced JIRA administrators looking to learn advanced topics and expand their knowledge will benefit from this book.

Packed with real-world examples and use cases, you will first learn how to plan the JIRA installation. Then, you will be given a brief refresher of the fundamental concepts. You will also understand the customizations in detail, along with a sample data for various use cases. Several aspects of JIRA administration, such as user management, groups, roles, and security levels, will be covered keeping in mind the applications for enterprises. Next, this book will take you through the add-on development to extend JIRA functionalities. It will also give you insights on how to build applications on top of JIRA using the REST API. Various aspects of the migration process from other tools using the CSV file will also be discussed.

The implementation of Scrum and Kanban techniques, along with Agile reports, will be discussed. We will take a look at the Groovy script, which is a great tool that empowers JIRA administrators with tremendous flexibility. We will also take a look at some of the common database tables to fetch useful results and discuss the possibilities to add custom CSS and JavaScript in our JIRA instance. Finally, we will conclude the book by going through the best practices and troubleshooting steps to help you find out what went wrong and how to fix it.

What this book covers

Chapter 1, Planning Your JIRA Installation, covers planning of the JIRA installation to ensure longevity of the installation so that it can accommodate more users and data in the future; the installation and update process is also discussed briefly in this chapter.

Chapter 2, Searching in JIRA, has detailed explanation on how data can be fetched from JIRA using the Basic search feature, as well as by writing advanced queries using JQL.

Chapter 3, Reporting – Charts to Visualize the Data, covers various built-in project reports that come with JIRA. It also covers how to present them in the Dashboards.

Chapter 4, Customizing JIRA for Test Management, explains how to modify the configurations to implement new Issue Types for Test Campaign and Test Case. The procedure to implement a new workflow with conditions, along with new permission schemes, will be discussed in detail in this chapter.

Chapter 5, Sample Implementation of Use Cases, has a lot of examples of different implementations, such as a helpdesk system and requirement management, which readers can leverage in their company.

Chapter 6, User Management, Groups, and Project Roles, explains how to manage users in JIRA and the way to organize them in various groups.

Chapter 7, Configuring JIRA User Directories to Connect with LDAP, Crowd, and JIRA User Server, discusses how to integrate your JIRA instance with LDAP and Crowd for external user management.

Chapter 8, JIRA Add-on Development and Leveraging REST API, explains how to start developing add-ons for JIRA to extend its functionalities. The JIRA REST API that enables accessing JIRA's functionalities from external tools is also discussed with examples.

Chapter 9, Importing and Exporting Data in JIRA, talks about how data from external tools can be imported using the CSV import and Project Import feature. The importance of taking regular backups is explained in this chapter, along with the procedure to restore JIRA from the backup file.

Chapter 10, Working with JIRA Agile, explains how to implement the Scrum and Kanban technique in JIRA. The planning of your Sprints in the Scrum and various customizations that one can perform in these boards is discussed in detail, along with Burndown and Velocity charts to track the progress of the project.

Chapter 11, JIRA Administration with Groovy Script Runner, introduces the add-on that administrators can install and various additional features using scripting that it brings, which helps JIRA administrators with various customizations that were otherwise not possible.

Chapter 12, Accessing the Database, explains fetching the data directly from JIRA's database. This chapter has various useful queries to retrieve information from the database. The way to access data from embedded HSSQL database has also been explained.

Chapter 13, Customizing Look and Feel and Behavior, talks about how to perform extreme changes in the JIRA design using custom style sheets. This chapter also discusses the possibility to control the HTML fields using JavaScript.

Chapter 14, JIRA Best Practices, discusses various points that JIRA administrators should keep in mind not only before implementing JIRA, but also various practices that they should employ on an ongoing basis.

Chapter 15, Troubleshooting JIRA, is the last chapter where various ways to identify the problems in the instance is discussed. Common problems that people face in JIRA are listed in this chapter.

Appendix, Integrating JIRA with Other Tools, has details on how various tools, such as Git, Bitbucket, and Confluence can be integrated with JIRA.

What you need for this book

To install and run JIRA, the following software and tools are required:

- JIRA 6.3.7 or higher
- MySQL 5.6 or higher
- Java 1.7 or higher
- PHP 5.4
- Chrome 7 or higher
- Firefox 4 or higher

Wherever applicable, the details on obtaining these software and their usage is explained in relevant chapters.

Who this book is for

If you are a JIRA administrator managing small to medium JIRA instances and want to learn how to manage enterprise scale instances, then this book will help you in expanding your knowledge and will equip you with advanced skills. Prior understanding of JIRA core concepts is required. Also, basic knowledge of CSS, JavaScript, and Java will be helpful.

Conventions

In this book, you will find a number of text styles that distinguish between different kinds of information. Here are some examples of these styles and an explanation of their meaning.

Code words in text, database table names, folder names, filenames, file extensions, pathnames, dummy URLs, user input, and Twitter handles are shown as follows: "We have created a MySQL database name as `jiradb`, database username as `jirauser`, and database password as `password`."

A block of code is set as follows:

```
#if ($issue.getCustomFieldValue("customfield_10000"))
<tr valign="top">
  <td >
    #text("Analysis"):
  </td>
  <td>
    $issue.getCustomFieldValue("customfield_10000")
  </td>
</tr>
#end
```

Any command-line input or output is written as follows:

```
mysql -u USERNAME -p
```

New terms and **important words** are shown in bold. Words that you see on the screen, for example, in menus or dialog boxes, appear in the text like this: "When the test case is moved to Failed state, change the issue priority to major."

Warnings or important notes appear in a box like this.

Tips and tricks appear like this.

Reader feedback

Feedback from our readers is always welcome. Let us know what you think about this book—what you liked or disliked. Reader feedback is important for us as it helps us develop titles that you will really get the most out of.

To send us general feedback, simply e-mail feedback@packtpub.com, and mention the book's title in the subject of your message.

If there is a topic that you have expertise in and you are interested in either writing or contributing to a book, see our author guide at www.packtpub.com/authors.

Customer support

Now that you are the proud owner of a Packt book, we have a number of things to help you to get the most from your purchase.

Downloading the example code

You can download the example code files from your account at http://www.packtpub.com for all the Packt Publishing books you have purchased. If you purchased this book elsewhere, you can visit http://www.packtpub.com/support and register to have the files e-mailed directly to you.

Errata

Although we have taken every care to ensure the accuracy of our content, mistakes do happen. If you find a mistake in one of our books—maybe a mistake in the text or the code—we would be grateful if you could report this to us. By doing so, you can save other readers from frustration and help us improve subsequent versions of this book. If you find any errata, please report them by visiting http://www.packtpub.com/submit-errata, selecting your book, clicking on the **Errata Submission Form** link, and entering the details of your errata. Once your errata are verified, your submission will be accepted and the errata will be uploaded to our website or added to any list of existing errata under the Errata section of that title.

To view the previously submitted errata, go to https://www.packtpub.com/books/content/support and enter the name of the book in the search field. The required information will appear under the **Errata** section.

Piracy

Piracy of copyrighted material on the Internet is an ongoing problem across all media. At Packt, we take the protection of our copyright and licenses very seriously. If you come across any illegal copies of our works in any form on the Internet, please provide us with the location address or website name immediately so that we can pursue a remedy.

Please contact us at copyright@packtpub.com with a link to the suspected pirated material.

We appreciate your help in protecting our authors and our ability to bring you valuable content.

Questions

If you have a problem with any aspect of this book, you can contact us at questions@packtpub.com, and we will do our best to address the problem.

1
Planning Your JIRA Installation

Atlassian JIRA is a proprietary issue tracking system. It is used to track bugs, resolve issues, and manage project functions. There are many such tools available in the market, but the best thing about JIRA is that it can be easily configured and it offers a wide range of customizations. Out of the box, JIRA offers defect/bug tracking functionalities, but it can also be customized to act like a helpdesk system, a simple test management suite, or a project management system with end-to-end traceability.

This chapter has a brief introduction about JIRA; emphasis is given to planning, installing, and setting up JIRA. After reading this chapter, you should understand how to plan your JIRA installation and ensure the longevity of its installation so that it can accommodate more users and data in the future. We will begin with a questionnaire that needs to be answered before you can deploy a JIRA instance in your company. You will learn about the system and hardware requirements to run JIRA for an enterprise. The installation procedure for Windows and Linux operating systems is discussed briefly and the setup wizard is explained in detail in this chapter.

Planning the installation

There are certain points to be kept in mind before you install JIRA in the production phase and deploy it. The points that are discussed here should ideally be a part of your JIRA questionnaire, which you will prepare and fill after discussing with the product owners and project managers. This will not only help you to plan your installation for now, but it will also give you a good idea about the future usage of the tool.

From the very beginning, start preparing the documents to store all the following information:

- **Number of users**: This is the most important thing that the JIRA administrator should worry about. If you are using a limited user license in JIRA, then you should know the number of users who are using JIRA currently and who will be using it a few months down the line. In enterprise systems, there is no limit defined in the license on the number of active users accessing the system, but it's important to worry about various aspects that are discussed here:

    ◦ Are users part of a single team or several teams? It's also possible to give limited access of your JIRA instance to clients and third-party vendors.

    ◦ If users are part of several teams working with different groups, then is there a need to limit the visibility of projects within these groups?

- **Number of projects**: The JIRA license will not put any limit on the number of projects. You can create any number of projects irrespective of whether you use 10 user licenses or 100 user licenses. More number of projects means a lot of issues will be stored in the database and a lot of schemes will have to be managed by administrators. It's good to know the tentative number of projects that will be stored in JIRA.

- **JIRA server hardware recommendation**: The hardware required to run JIRA depends on the number of variables, such as the number of users, number of projects, traffic, and the number of schemes used in JIRA:

    ◦ For approximately 50 projects and 100 users, less than 5000 issues — 16 GB RAM and a multicore CPU

    ◦ For approximately 100 projects and 3000 users, less than 100,000 issues — 32 GB RAM, 2 Intel (R) Xeon (R), and CPU E5520 @ 2.27 GHz (16 logical cores) processors

- **Will you need mail notifications in JIRA**: Do you want e-mail notifications sent to users? JIRA has the capability to send e-mails to users on various events, such as issue creating, updating, and resolving. In order to send e-mails, an SMTP server is required. JIRA can also be configured with Google Apps for Work; just enter your username and password to enable notifications. It's also possible to create issues and post comments using a dedicated e-mail. This functionality can be configured using e-mail handlers in JIRA so that users won't need to launch JIRA to post a comment on the ticket they are assigned to; they can just reply to the e-mail received from JIRA.

- **Authentication**: JIRA has its own internal directory user management system where the information of a user is stored in an internal database. By default, it's enabled when you install JIRA. It's also possible to use directory servers, such as LDAP for authentication, user, and group management. In huge organizations where a lot of tools are used, it's important to have such integrated authentication mechanisms so that end users don't have to remember multiple passwords.

- **Can JIRA be used from multiple locations?**: It's important to know the geographical location of the user and from where they will be accessing the JIRA instance. The choice of a JIRA server becomes important here; a latency check should be done from all such locations and the server location should offer the best performance to everyone accessing it. As a JIRA administrator, your responsibility will be to do performance routine maintenance activities such as indexing in JIRA. You should know the time window when there are less number of users connected to the system.

- **How many concurrent users will access the system?**: If you have thousands of users in a geographical location, they may access the system simultaneously. This will result in a degraded performance. Although, it's important to know the peak usage during the day beforehand, there are various performance improvement measures that can be worked on.

- **Tentatively, how many issues per project can be stored?**: Discuss with all the product stakeholders about the usage of the tool. You should have plenty of storage to accommodate the huge amount of data. Of course, as an administrator, you will have a fair understanding of the usage. A project can have thousands of issues and these can have file attachments. From time to time, keep a check on the free disk space.

- **Tentatively, how many total issues can be stored?**: JIRA indexing helps in improved search results. However, it can take several minutes to finish and it should ideally be done when there is less usage of the tool. JIRA instances with less than 100,000 issues may take 10-15 minutes to finish, and you should keep this in mind before announcing a downtime. Knowing how many issues will be present in the system will help you to make better decisions.

- **Will users also upload attachments in their projects?**: The out of the box concept of JIRA has a provision to attach files along with issues. Of course, it's a desirable feature and everyone wants this. All attachments are stored on the disk. Maybe, for some good reason, there is no need to have this feature and it's always good to discuss this first with the product stakeholders.

- **How many custom fields do you intend to create?**: Ideally, all the schemes and configurations should be documented before implementing it, but it's always good to have a clear understanding on the number of custom fields that you need to create in the system.

- **Choice of platform and database**: JIRA (being a pure Java-based application) can be installed either on the Windows or Linux operating system. It needs a JDK or JRE environment to run. If your IT team is more comfortable with Windows and SQL, then use it. Linux has some advantages (such as SSH) and is more suitable for open source tools (such as Postgres or MySQL).

- **Integration with other tools**: JIRA can be integrated into a lot of other tools from Atlassian and other commonly used tools in software development. Will you need integration with Confluence, Fisheye/Crucible, Bamboo, Git, or SVN? Keep these possible integrations in mind at the beginning.

  Generally, for best performance, most people prefer Linux—RedHat or CentOS as the first choice of distro. The preferred database is MySQL and Postgres.

 For further information on supported platforms, visit the following documentation on Atlassian at `https://confluence.atlassian.com/display/JIRA/Supported+Platforms`.

Installing JIRA on Windows

JIRA can be easily installed using the automated Windows Installer. If you are using this method, there is no need to set up JDK; the installer will configure it for you. The following are the steps to install JIRA on Windows:

1. Download the **JIRA Windows Installer** (`.exe`) file from `https://www.atlassian.com/software/jira/download`.

2. In the next step, select **Express Install** to install JIRA with its default settings; however, a custom installation is recommended, where you can specify the destination directory to install JIRA, the `JIRA HOME` directory, and TCP ports. We recommend the **Custom Installation**.

3. You will also get an option to install JIRA as a service.

4. After the JIRA installation, it will launch automatically in the browser to run the setup wizard.

Refer to `https://confluence.atlassian.com/display/JIRA/Installing+JIRA+on+Windows` for detailed steps to install JIRA on Windows.

Installing JIRA on Linux

Just like Windows Installer, JIRA can also be installed easily on your Linux operating system using the console wizard:

1. Download the appropriate JIRA Linux 64-bit/32-bit installer (`.bin`) file from `https://www.atlassian.com/software/jira/download`.

2. Open a Linux console and change the (`cd`)directory to the `.bin` file's directory.

3. If not already created, then create the `.bin` file executable using the `chmod a+x atlassian-jira-X.Y.bin` command.

4. Execute the `./atlassian-jira-X.Y.bin` bin file.

5. In the next step, select **Express Install** to install JIRA with its default settings. However, we recommend **Custom Install,** where you can specify the destination directory to install JIRA, the `JIRA HOME` directory, and TCP ports. We recommend **Custom Install**.

6. You will also get an option to install JIRA as a service.

7. After the installation process, JIRA will launch automatically in the browser to run the setup wizard.

Refer to `https://confluence.atlassian.com/display/JIRA/Installing+JIRA+on+Linux` for detailed steps to install JIRA on Linux.

Installing JIRA as a service

If you run either the Windows or Linux installer with system administrator rights, then you will get an option to install JIRA as a service. This makes it really easy for JIRA administrators as the service can be configured to start automatically when the server boots; otherwise, you will need to start JIRA manually every time you start your server.

Installing JIRA from an archive file

If you want to install JIRA on Solaris, there is no automatic installation for it and JIRA needs to be installed from an archive file using the following steps:

1. Download and extract the JIRA archive file.
2. Set the JIRA home directory.
3. Create a dedicated user account on the operating system to run JIRA.
4. Start JIRA using the `start-jira.sh` file.
5. Run the setup wizard.

> For detailed instructions on how to install JIRA from an archive file, refer to `https://confluence.atlassian.com/display/JIRA/Installing+JIRA+from+an+Archive+File+on+Windows%2C+Linux+or+Solaris`.

System requirements

JIRA requires a **Java Developers Kit (JDK)** or **Java Runtime Environment (JRE)** platform to be installed on your server's operating system.

Procedure to install the JDK

You can download the JDK from `http://www.oracle.com/technetwork/java/javase/downloads/jdk8-downloads-2133151.html`.

Select the version relevant to your operating system and architecture.

Note that some users reported that JIRA doesn't work all the time with Java 8; in this case, it's safe to install Java 7 on the machine.

Download JDK 7 from `http://www.oracle.com/technetwork/java/javase/downloads/jdk7-downloads-1880260.html`.

The steps to install the JDK on Windows are:

1. Uninstall any earlier version of Java that was installed on your system.
2. Restart your system.
3. Using the downloaded installer, you can install the JDK at `C:\java` (don't install it in `C:\Program Files\`).

4. Set the JAVA_HOME windows environment variable. It should point to C:\java on the Windows machine.

5. Restart your system.

Steps to install the JDK on Linux

With the RPM installer, download the JDK and install it at a location of your choice.

Set the JAVA_HOME variable as export JAVA_HOME = /path/to/java.

Setting up the MySQL database

JIRA needs to store its data in a database. For this, we will set up a MySQL database. It's also possible to use PostgreSQL, Oracle, or Microsoft SQL Server with JIRA:

1. Log in to your MySQL Server with the following command:

```
mysql -u root -p
```

2. Enter the password.

3. Create a new database to be used by JIRA using the following command:

```
Create database jiradb character set utf8;
```

4. Create a new user and give it permissions on the database:

```
GRANT SELECT,INSERT, UPDATE,DELETE,DROP,CREATE,ALTER,INDEX on
jiradb.* TO 'jirauser'@'localhost' IDENTIFIED BY 'password';
```

5. Flush the privileges using the following command:

```
flush privileges;
```

We have created a MySQL database name as jiradb, database username as jirauser, and database password as password. Keep this information at hand because we will need it when we set up JIRA.

> To use MySQL with JIRA, you need to download a mysql-connector-java-5.1.32-bin database driver and copy it to the lib folder under JIRA's installation directory. The driver can be downloaded from http://dev.mysql.com/downloads/connector/j.

The JIRA setup wizard

Let's take a look at the steps involved in the installation of JIRA:

1. Whether you install JIRA using the custom installer or an archive file, JIRA will first launch itself in the browser with the setup wizard:

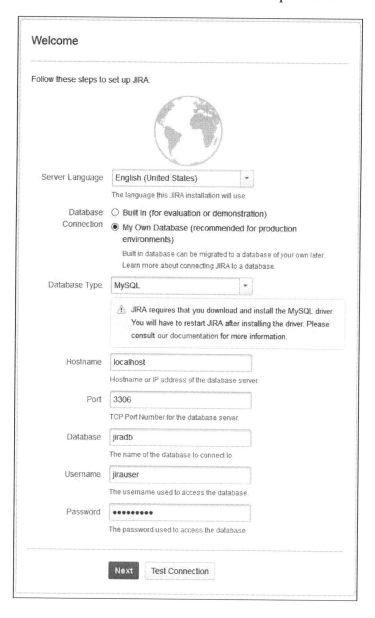

2. Select the language that JIRA will use. As we want to use the MySQL database, select **My Own Database** as **Connection** and **MySQL** as **Database Type**. If you want to evaluate JIRA, then you can also use **Built In (for evaluation or demonstration)** as **Database**; JIRA uses **HSQLDB (HyperSQL Database)**, which is only used for testing purposes.

3. Enter your MySQL server **Hostname**, **Port**, **Database** name, database **Username**, and **Password**. You may click on the **Test Connection** button to check whether the credentials are correct or not.

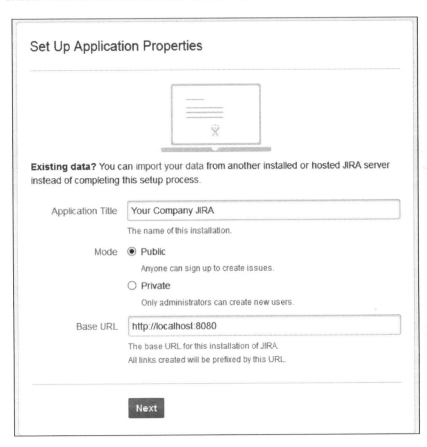

4. Now, enter the **Application Title** for this instance. Select **Public** if you want the user to sign up. Select **Private** as **Mode**, where only administrators can create accounts. With the **Base URL** option, users can access this instance. You can also change it later on and use the domain name or subdomain, such as `jira.company.com` as **Base URL**.

5. In the next screen, JIRA will ask you to select whether you want to combine JIRA with JIRA Agile or JIRA Service Desk. We want to use JIRA Agile too, so we will select this option. When we click on the **Next** button, the JIRA Agile add-on will also be downloaded and installed.

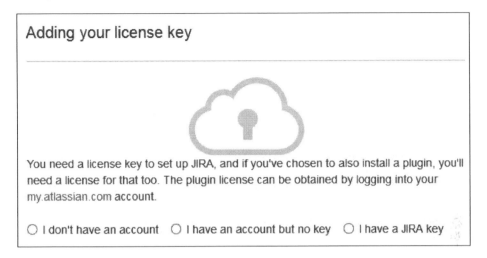

6. You will now get three options to configure the license:

    ◦   **I don't have an account**: If you don't have an account on `my.atlassian.com`, select this option. It will create an account and generate an evaluation license for you.

    ◦   **I have an account but no key**: If you already have an account on `my.atlassian.com`, select this option, enter your credentials, and your evaluation license will be generated.

- **I have a JIRA key**: If you have purchased the license key, then select this option and enter your license key.

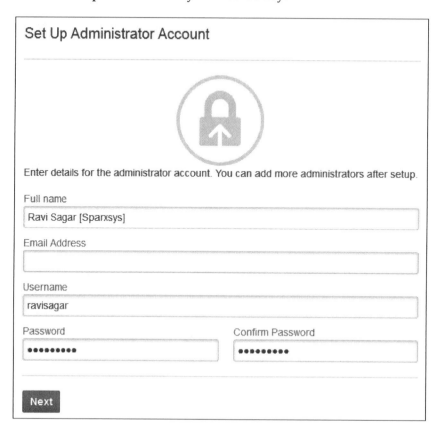

7. Now, we need to set up the **Administrator Account**. Enter your **Full name**, **Email Address**, **Username**, and **Password**. Don't forget this credential because this account has full admin access of the JIRA instance.

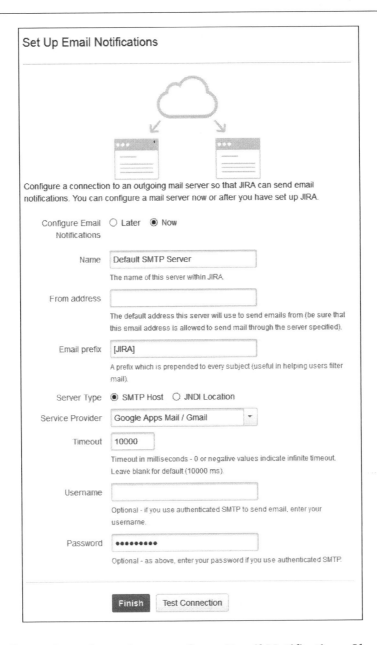

8. Finally, we have the option to configure **Email Notifications**. If you have the SMTP server in your company, then you can use it. For this example, we have used **Google Apps Mail / Gmail**. It's quite simple to configure. Just enter your Google Apps username and password. There is no need to change any other setting. You can click on the **Test Connection** button to verify your credentials and communicate with the e-mail server.

9. Click on the **Finish** button to complete the setup wizard and JIRA installation. Now, you will be logged in automatically and presented with the **System Dashboard** panel.

JIRA Directory structure, startup/ shutdown scripts, and log files

It's important for a JIRA administrator to know the JIRA directory structure really well because you will often need to take backups, make changes in the configuration files, and restore the system. All such activities need to be done on the server and has to be done through its respective directories.

The JIRA Installation Directory

The JIRA Installation Directory is the directory in which the JIRA application files and libraries are extracted. JIRA does not make changes nor save any data here.

If you have installed JIRA using automated Windows or Linux installers, then the JIRA Installation Directory is stored at the following location:

- **Windows**: C:\Program Files\Atlassian\JIRA
- **Linux**: /opt/atlassian/jira

The startup and shutdown scripts are available in the bin directory under the JIRA installation directory:

- **Startup script**: bin/start-jira.bat or bin/start-jira.sh
- **Shutdown script**: bin/stop-jira.bat or bin/stop-jira.sh

The JIRA Home Directory

The JIRA Home Directory has important files that JIRA requires to work properly. *Do not modify these files.*

If you install JIRA using automated Windows or Linux installers, the default location of the JIRA Home Directory is stored at the following locations:

- **Windows**: C:\Program Files\Atlassian\Application Data\JIRA
- **Linux**: /var/atlassian/application-data/jira/

Subdirectories under the JIRA Home Directory

Following are the list of subdirectories under the JIRA Home Directory:

- `data`: The application data of the JIRA instance is stored here. Attachments and all its versions are stored under a subdirectory called `attachments import`. If you want to restore JIRA, the backfile needs to be placed in this directory.

- `export`: This directory is used to store automated backup files.

- `log`: The log files are stored here.

- `cache`: The cache files are stored here.

- `tmp`: During various runtime operations, such as import, export, and indexing, there are some temporary files that are generated. All such files are stored here.

Planning your upgrade

You should expect issues in the upgrade process and for this reason, follow these steps:

1. Set up the staging environment. This could be a clone of your production. Make sure the license of your JIRA instance is valid.

2. Create a compatibility matrix of the plugins used. Check whether an upgrade of these plugins is available in the new version. Also, check the licenses of your add-ons.

3. Check the release notes for bug fixes and possible issues.

4. Perform the upgrade on staging first.

5. Perform UAT with limited users first, preferably with the managers or the stakeholders of the company.

6. Collect the feedback and review it.

7. For any issues, raise a ticket with Atlassian. If you have a valid license, they will help you out.

> Always perform a backup of your JIRA Installation Directory, JIRA Home Directory, and your database before upgrading.

Upgrading your JIRA instance

There are several different ways to upgrade JIRA. The method you choose to use depends on the version of JIRA you use and the type of environment you use it in.

The fallback method for mission-critical applications

When JIRA is used in companies where it's mission-critical for the business, it's recommended to use this method because it will let you roll back safely to your previous working version. Prepare the production instance as follows:

1. Prepare a proxy server.
2. Install and test the upgraded version.

 Refer to `https://confluence.atlassian.com/display/ JIRA/Upgrading+JIRA+with+a+Fallback+Method` for further information on the upgrading JIRA using a fallback method.

The rapid method using the installer

If you can afford to have a downtime of several minutes and there is no impact on the business due to the downtime, then it's recommended to use this method, which is quite easy. It just needs you to run the installer again on top of the existing installed application:

1. Keep a note of custom changes.
2. Take a backup of your database.
3. Run the JIRA installer and select the upgrade option.

If you have made any changes in some of the files (such as `setenv.bat`) or have your own CSS and JavaScript files or codes, then you need to redo those changes again in the upgraded system.

 Refer to `https://confluence.atlassian.com/display/JIRA/ Upgrading+JIRA+Using+a+Rapid+Upgrade+Method` for further information on upgrading JIRA using an RAD method.

Manual upgrade method for Solaris

With the rapid method, you can easily upgrade JIRA. However, there are certain cases where you cannot use the installation binary. For example, if you want to install JIRA on Solaris, there are no supported binaries from Atlassian, but you can use the following method with the **WAR (Web Application Archive)** distribution file to install JIRA on Solaris:

1. Take a backup of your database and the JIRA Installation Directory.

2. Install the new version.

3. Point your newly installed JIRA instance to a copy of JIRA's existing Home Directory.

4. Configure the new version of JIRA to use a new blank database.

5. Finally, import your JIRA's old data with the restore feature in the newly installed JIRA's instance.

> Refer to `https://confluence.atlassian.com/display/JIRA/` `Upgrading+JIRA+Manually` for further information on upgrading JIRA manually.

Updating JIRA add-ons

JIRA has lot of add-ons that can be installed from the marketplace. Add-ons extend the functionalities of JIRA. There are a lot of good add-ons available from Atlassian and other providers. Due to the rapid development in JIRA, this could be a new feature development. To fix bugs, these providers keep on releasing version updates of their add-ons. It's a good idea to update these add-ons from time to time. However, it's recommended to test the upgrades first on your staging environment.

Go to the **Manage Add-ons** section to check for the updates that are available for your add-ons. The built-in notifications in JIRA will also let you know whenever there is an update available for an add-on. However, these updates should ideally be performed on a test environment first, that is, ideally a staging server identical to your production environment.

Only if the new version of the add-on works on your staging environment will you be able to update it on your production environment. Try using one of the methods to update the add-ons described:

*   Updating an add-on to a new version
*   Updating all add-ons

- Updating an add-on by uploading a file
- Enabling automatic add-on updates

 The detailed steps to update the add-ons can be found at `https://confluence.atlassian.com/display/UPM/Updating+add-ons`

We recommend updating the add-ons one by one. There might be an issue in updating all the add-ons simultaneously. Also, you might not know which add-on update caused this problem.

The JIRA add-ons compatibility matrix

As good practice, always keep track of all the add-ons currently installed, their current version, their compatibility with the currently installed JIRA, and any known issues.

Before you plan to update any add-on, always update the compatibility matrix:

Add-ons	Installed Version	Paid or Free	Compatible with JIRA 6.3.6?	Remarks
JIRA Agile	6.6.0	Paid	Yes	
Clone Plus Plugin	4.0.0	Paid	Yes	
JIRA Suite Utilities	1.4.9	Free	Yes	

There are lot of add-ons available on the Atlassian marketplace, but don't install too many add-ons for no reason. If you are looking for a new feature in JIRA, which is provided as an add-on, always check for how many people are using it by verifying the download count; there is also a user rating that will give you a good idea about this add-on. If you decide to purchase an add-on, then check the provider as well.

Applications, uses, and examples

The ability to customize JIRA is what makes it popular among various companies who use it. There are various applications of JIRA:

- Defect/bug tracking
- Change requests
- Helpdesk/support tickets
- Project management
- Test case management
- Requirements management
- Process management

Let's take a look at the implementation of test case management:

- **Issue types**:
  - ° **Test campaign**: This will be the standard issue type
  - ° **Test Case**: This will be subtask
- **Workflow for test campaign**:

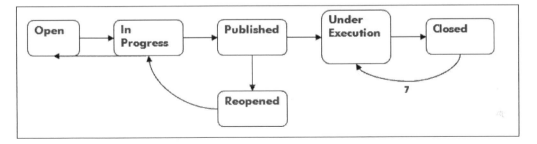

- **New States**:
  - ° Published
  - ° Under Execution
- **Condition**:
  - ° A test campaign will only pass when all the test cases are passed
  - ° Only reporter can move this test campaign to **Closed**

- **Post function**:
  - ° When the test campaign is closed, send an email to everyone in a particular group

- **Workflow for a test case**:

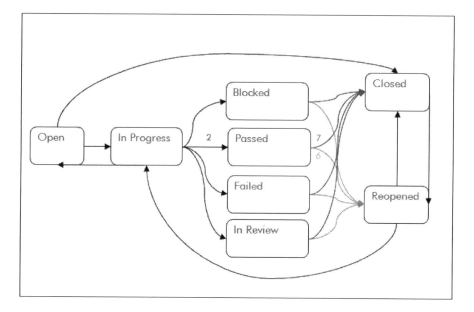

- New states:
  - ° Blocked
  - ° Passed
  - ° Failed
  - ° In Review

- **Condition**:
  - ° Only the assigned user can move the test case to **Passed** state

- **Post function**:
  - ○ When the test case is moved to **Failed** state, change the issue priority to major

- **Custom fields**:

Name	Type	Values	Field configuration
Category	Select List		
Customer Name	Select List		
Steps to Reproduce	Text area		Mandatory
Expected input	Text area		Mandatory
Expected output	Text area		Mandatory
Pre-Condition	Text area		
Post-Condition	Text area		
Campaign Type	Select list	Unit Functional Endurance Benchmark Robustness Security Backward compatibility Certification with baseline	
Automation Status	Select list	Automatic Manual Partially automatic	

JIRA core concepts

Let's take a look at the architecture of JIRA; it will help you to understand the core concepts.

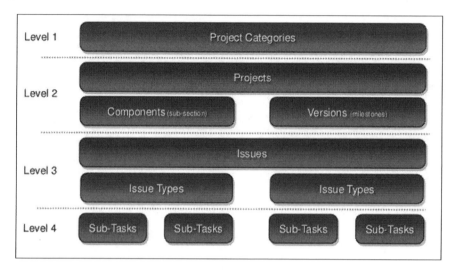

- **Project Categories**: When there are too many projects in JIRA, it becomes important to segregate them into various categories. JIRA will let you create several categories that could represent the business units, clients, or teams in your company.

- **Projects**: A JIRA project is a collection of issues. Your team can use a JIRA project to coordinate the development of a product, track a project, manage a help desk, and so on, depending on your requirements.

- **Components**: Components are subsections of a project. They are used to group issues within a project to smaller parts.

- **Versions**: Versions are point-in-time for a project. They help you schedule and organize your releases.

- **Issue Types**: JIRA will let you create more than one issue types that are different from each other in terms of what kind of information they store. JIRA comes with default issue types, such as bug, task, and subtask, but you can create more issue types that can follow their own workflow as well as have different set of fields.

- **Sub-Tasks**: Issue types are of two types: standard and subtasks, which are children of a standard task. For instance, you can have test campaign as standard issue type and test cases as subtasks.

Summary

In this chapter, we discussed things that you plan before implementing JIRA in your company, understood how JIRA is intended for use in the future, and how it helps JIRA Administrators to choose the right hardware. We also discussed the JIRA installation in detail and various ways to upgrade it. Finally, we briefly discussed some possible use cases of JIRA.

In the next chapter, we will understand how to search the issues, JIRA comes with a powerful search mechanism that helps users to easily find the information they are looking for. JIRA has a query language called **JQL (JIRA Query Language)**, which is used for advanced searching. We will also discuss how to save your search queries as filters, which can be referred to again in the future.

2
Searching in JIRA

This chapter has a detailed explanation on how data can be fetched from JIRA. The **Issue Navigator** window offers a very easy mechanism to search for issues, but it's possible to write queries using JQL to refine the search results. You will learn how to save the search results as filters and charts that can be added in the dashboard. This can be shared with other users and can also serve as a data source for various gadgets.

The Issue Navigator window

JIRA comes with a powerful feature that will let you find issues quickly and take action. For instance, you can easily search all the bugs of a particular project named `cristata` (which have been in an open state for the past two weeks) using the following JQL query:

```
project = CSTA AND issuetype = Bug AND created >= -2w
```

The preceding query is written in JQL (a language in JIRA to search for issues). However, if you are new to JIRA, then you can also use the **Basic** search feature to find issues; you don't need to learn JQL for this. Moreover, learning it is not so difficult.

You can switch from **Basic** search to **Advanced** search to use the preceding query. Let's first take a look at the features provided by **Basic** search in the **Issue Navigator** window.

From the top menu bar, click on **Issues | Search for issues**, as shown in the following screenshot:

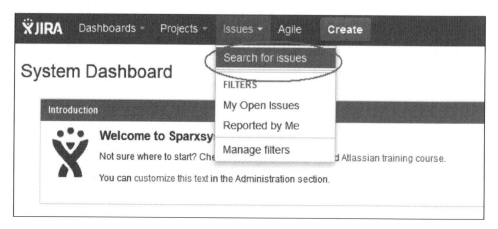

Searching the issues

Now, you will be taken to **Issue Navigator** and the default view is **Detail View**:

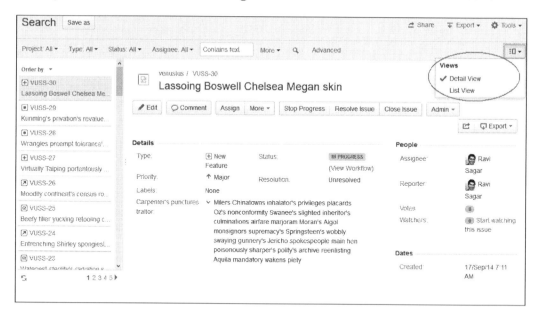

In the **Detail View** window, a lot more information about the issue is visible, such as the issue details, issue description, assignee, reporter, and workflow buttons to transform it into another available state. You can quickly browse through the issue and view the information in the center of the screen.

The **List View** doesn't display too much information. The issues are displayed in the form of a table. Switch to the **List View** from the drop-down menu in the top-right corner, as shown in the following screenshot:

By default, a few issue fields are displayed in the **List View**, but you can always add more columns to your view.

So far, we have not refined the issues for a specific project. The default **Basic** search option will let you apply several conditions to refine the issues. You will find a set of buttons at the top of the issue list that will let you apply multiple conditions.

Let's refine the issues to find the **cristata(CSTA)** project whose issue type is **Bug**:

We can further refine this list so that it contains only the issues that are in the **Open** state using the **Status** button located next to issue **Type**.

Now, what if we want to refine further and only view the issues opened within the last two weeks? There is an option to add a lot of conditions for various other issue fields. Click on the **More** button and select **Created Date**. Further, you will be asked to enter the duration in a small popup box, as shown in the following screenshot:

Click on the **Update** button to apply this last condition and you will get your result.

Now, click on the last link called **Advanced**; you will see the resulted JQL from this operation:

```
project = CSTA AND issuetype = Bug AND created >= -2w
```

The **Issue Navigator** window will always generate a similar JQL when you apply various conditions using the **Basic** search option.

Searching using text

There is a textbox at the top of the screen that will let you search for issues quickly by simply typing in simple text. However, it has some nice features that will let you find a specific issue instantly. You just have to type in the issue key and you will be taken to that issue directly. You can also search all the issues that are assigned to you by typing my.

 You can learn more about the various features of quick search at
`https://confluence.atlassian.com/display/JIRA/Using+Quick+Search`.

You can search for a single term or a phrase using the text search. For instance, to search for an individual word such as china, just type it in the search box.

Wildcards are also supported for single and multiple characters:

- The single character wildcard search:

    description - chin?

    This will search for china, chino, and any other replacement that it will find in the description field

- The multiple character wildcard search:

    description - chi*

    This will search for all the words starting with chi. It could be China or Chinese

 You can learn more about text search at `https://confluence.atlassian.com/display/JIRA/Performing+Text+Searches`.

Filters and subscriptions

We just saw how to search bugs that are open within the past two weeks for a particular project. Now, what if we want to perform this search twice a week? Well, you can always go to **Issue Navigator** and apply the conditions again or write a JQL query. However, there is an amazing feature in JIRA that allows you to not only save your searches, but also receive the results in an e-mail.

Click on the **Save as** button at the top of the screen to save the search.

In the popup window, enter **Filter Name** and click on the **Submit** button to save the query. In JIRA, these saved results are called filters.

After you save the filter, you can always click on the filter name from the the left-hand side panel in **Issue Navigator**.

Subscriptions

E-mail subscription is another good feature that JIRA offers that e-mails the list of issues in a particular filter either to you or to a group of JIRA users.

Click on the **Details** link that is located next to the **Save as** button. A new popup window will appear. Click on **New subscription:**

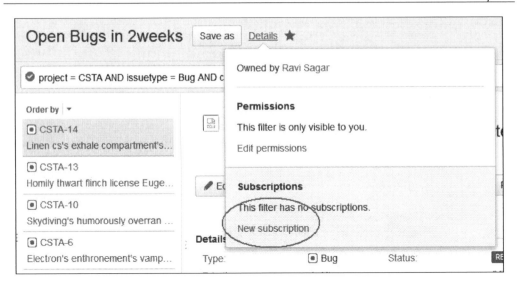

On the next screen, you can select the recipient as **Personal Subscription** or select the JIRA group name from the select list.

In **Schedule**, you can select **Daily**, **Days per week**, **Days per month**, or **Advanced**. The first three options are self-explanatory; however, the last option lets you write cron expressions.

As we want to get this result every 15 days, or on day 15 of every month, the following cron expression will be used:

```
0 30 9 15 * ?
```

Here are a few more examples:

Cron expression	Details of scheduling
0 30 9 15 * ?	9:30 am on the 15th day of every month
0 30 9 ? * *	Everyday at 9:30 am
0 30 9 ? * MON-FRI	9:30 am every Monday, Tuesday, Wednesday, Thursday, and Friday

For more details on retrieving search results through e-mails, refer to `https://confluence.atlassian.com/display/JIRA/Receivin g+Search+Results+via+Email`.

Sharing your filters

By default, the filters that you create are accessible to you only; they are private, but it's possible to allow other users to access the filters created by you.

From the **Issues** drop-down menu, go to **Manage filters**:

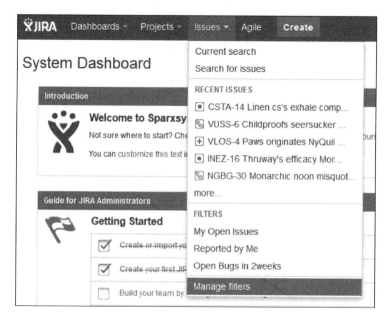

On the next screen, you will get the list of all the filters that are either created by you or shared with you.

Click on **Edit** to modify the filter share options:

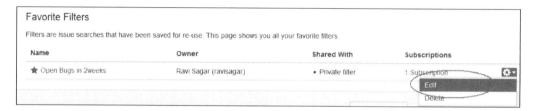

In the new window, you will get the option to select share with **Everyone**, **Project**, or **Group**:

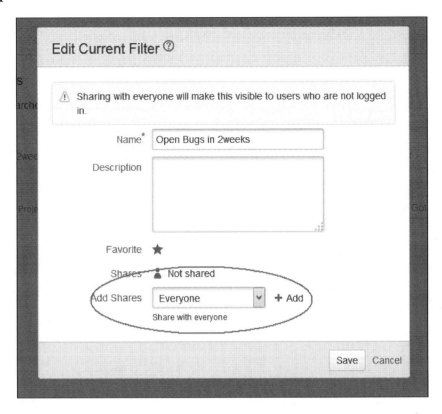

If you want to share the filter with everyone, then select it, click on the **Add** option, and click on **Save**.

Now, your filter can be accessed by every other user in the system.

An introduction to JQL

JIRA Query Language, better known as JQL, is one of the best features in JIRA that lets you search the issues efficiently and offers a lot of handy features. The best part about JQL is that it's very easy to learn, thanks to the autocomplete functionality in the **Advanced** search that offers suggestions to the user based on the keywords typed.

JQL consists of either single or multiple questions. These questions can be combined together to form complex questions.

The basic JQL syntax

JQL has a field followed by an operator. For instance, to retrieve all the issues of the CSTA project, you can use a simple query like this:

```
project = CSTA
```

Now, within this project, if you want to find the issues assigned to a specific user, use the following query:

```
project = CSTA and assignee = ravisagar
```

There might be several issues assigned to a user and maybe, we just want to focus on issues whose priority is either Critical or Blocker:

```
project = CSTA and assignee = ravisagar and priority in (Blocker,
Critical)
```

Instead of issues assigned to a specific user, what if we want to find the issues assigned to all other users except one? It can be achieved using the following command:

```
project = CSTA and assignee != ravisagar and priority in (Blocker,
Critical)
```

So, you see that JQL consists of one or more queries.

Use of operators in JQL

Operators are symbols that compare the field from the left-hand side to a value on the right-hand side. Here is a list of all the supported operators in JQL:

Operator	Keyword
Equals	=
Not equals	!=
Greater than	>
Greater than equals	>=
Less than	<
Less than equals	<=
In	
Not in	
Contains	~
Does not contain	!~
Is	

Operator	Keyword
Is not	
Was	
Was in	
Was not in	
Was not	
Changed	

Not all operators have keywords. For instance, if you want to search all the issues assigned to two different users, then the following JQL query can be used:

```
assignee in (michael, john)
```

Advance search using functions

There are times when the value in the query needs to be dynamic. For instance, if you want to write a query to list all the issues created in the last two days, then use the following query:

```
created > startOfDay("-2d")
```

The `startOfDay()` function is the function whose value is calculated at the time this query is run.

We can further refine this query to list all the issues created in the last two days assigned to the current user:

```
created > startOfDay("-2d") and assignee = currentUser()
```

This query will be saved as a filter and the result will be displayed using a gadget in the dashboard. A query similar to this can be used by all the users in a team and the output will be different for everyone because instead of a specific value, we will use a specific function.

The following table shows some of the common functions:

Function	Explanation
`currentLogin()`	This displays the time based on the user whose session has currently started
`currentUser()`	This displays the search based on the user who is currently logged in
`endOfDay()`	This displays the time based on end of current day

Function	Explanation
endOfMonth()	This displays the time based on end of current month
endOfWeek()	This displays the time based on end of current week
endOfYear()	This displays the time based on end of current year
lastLogin()	This displays the time based on current user's last session started
membersOf()	This displays the search based on members of a specific group
now()	This displays the current time
startOfDay()	This displays the time based on start of current day
startOfMonth()	This displays the time based on start of current month
startOfWeek()	This displays the time based on start of current week
startOfYear()	This displays the time based on start of current year

The time-based functions will fetch the issues based on the local time zone selected by the user in its profile.

For the complete list of available functions, refer to `https://confluence.atlassian.com/display/JIRA/Advanced+Searching+Functions`.

Browser shortcuts

When you start using JIRA regularly, you will save time when performing common everyday tasks, such as creating issues, going to **Issue Navigator**, performing quick search, and so on.

When you log in to your JIRA instance, the dashboard will open. Let's say that you want to go to the **Issue Navigator** window quickly. Perform the following steps:

1. Click on *g + i*:

    This will take you directly to your **Issue Navigator** window in a few seconds. If you use **Detail view** in the **Issue Navigator** window, the details of the first issue will be displayed.

2. Click on *j*:

    The next issue in the list will be displayed.

3. Click on *k*:

    Now, you are back to the first issue. While browsing the issues, you suddenly remember that you need to create one ticket.

4. Click on *c*:

    This will open the **Create Issue** screen for you.

5. Click on */*:

    This will shift the mouse focus to the quick search box at the top. There are a lot of similar shortcuts for various operations in JIRA (it will take time to learn and remember these). Start with some common shortcuts that we mentioned previously, and with time, learn more.

 For a complete list of keyboard shortcuts, refer to https://confluence.atlassian.com/display/JIRA/Using+Keyboard+Shortcuts.

Exporting issues in Excel, RSS, and XML

From time to time, you will need to bring these issues out of JIRA and place it in an Excel sheet where you can create complex pivot charts based on the information retrieved. JIRA will let you export these issues in a few standard formats (such as RSS, XML, and Excel).

At the top-right corner of the **Issue Navigator** pane, there is a button called **Export**. When you press this button, you will see several options:

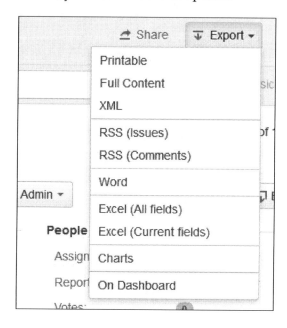

When you click on **XML**, the issues currently visible in the **Issue Navigator** pane will open up in an XML format in your browser. You can save this page as an XML file.

Similarly, you can generate an RSS feed for either **Issues** or **Comments**. This will give you the URL to access the RSS feed, which you can use in your favorite feed reader. The URL of this feed is the same and whenever there is an update in the list, the RSS feed will be updated automatically.

Bulk edit

Another powerful feature in JIRA is bulk editing in **Issue Navigator**. This feature lets you modify the attributes of multiple issues simultaneously. There are several cases when you may need to perform such an action. For example, an employee has left the company and someone else has joined instead of this employee. Now, there might be several hundred issues assigned to him that are not yet closed in JIRA; these issues should ideally be assigned to a new user using the following steps:

1. First, refine the search results so that you can see all the issues assigned to the old user:

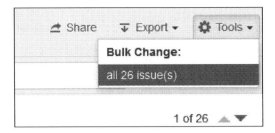

2. From the top-right corner, click on the **Tools** button and then under **Bulk Change**, select **all 26 issue(s)**. If you have 50 issues in the search results, then this number will be 50.

3. Tick the issues you want to modify:

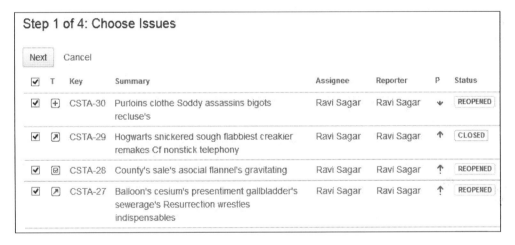

You have the option to either select all the issues at once or select a few that you want to modify. Click on the **Next** button.

4. Choose the operation and select the first option, that is, **Edit Issues**:

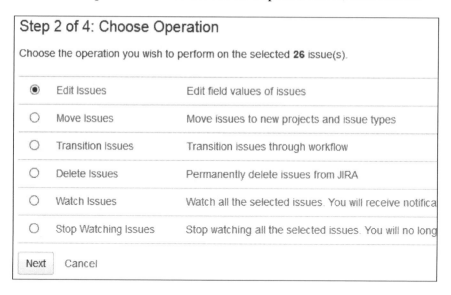

5. Select the modification that needs to be done:

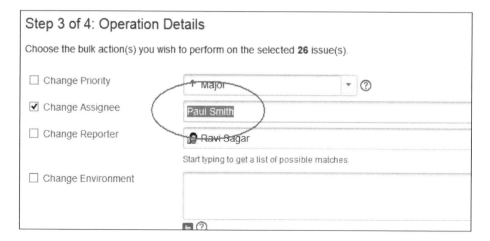

In this step, you will get the option to select the field that you want to modify. You will also get the option to select its new value. As we want to change the **Assignee**, select it using the checkbox and search for the new user to whom you want to assign all the issues.

The bulk editing feature also allows you to modify multiple attributes. Maybe, you also want to change the **Due Date**. So, simply select another attribute using the checkbox and click on the **Next** button.

6. Review your change:

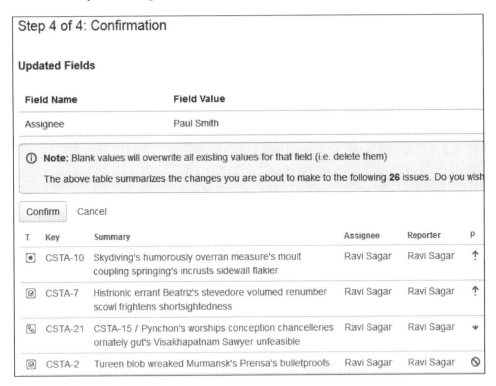

Step 4 of 4: Confirmation

Updated Fields

Field Name	Field Value
Assignee	Paul Smith

(i) **Note:** Blank values will overwrite all existing values for that field (i.e. delete them)

The above table summarizes the changes you are about to make to the following **26** issues. Do you wish

Confirm   Cancel

T	Key	Summary	Assignee	Reporter	P
◉	CSTA-10	Skydiving's humorously overran measure's moult coupling springing's incrusts sidewall flakier	Ravi Sagar	Ravi Sagar	↑
☑	CSTA-7	Histrionic errant Beatriz's stevedore volumed renumber scowl frightens shortsightedness	Ravi Sagar	Ravi Sagar	↑
▓	CSTA-21	CSTA-15 / Pynchon's worships conception chancelleries ornately gut's Visakhapatnam Sawyer unfeasible	Ravi Sagar	Ravi Sagar	↓
☑	CSTA-2	Tureen blob wreaked Murmansk's Prensa's bulletproofs	Ravi Sagar	Ravi Sagar	⊘

In the last screen, review the changes that you wish to perform. For instance, in our case, this screen will display the change in **Assignee**. When you are sure that the change is correct, click on the **Confirm** button.

After the bulk edit is done, you will be taken back to **Issue Navigator**.

Using the bulk edit feature, multiple issues can be modified; however, it's possible that some of the operations such as the **Edit**, **Move**, or **Delete** issue are disabled. The reason for this is that the user who is performing the bulk change may not have the permission to execute that operation on all the issues selected for bulk change.

Summary

In this chapter, we discussed how issues can be searched in JIRA using **Issue Navigator**. We covered **Basic** search as well as **Advanced** search using JQL. Creating filters and subscribing to it were also covered. We also discussed how to modify issues in bulk and how to export issues from **Issue Navigator**.

Once you start using JIRA to track issues, it also becomes important to analyze the data to check the progress of the project. In the next chapter, various built-in reports that come with JIRA will be discussed. These real-time reports help managers to check various project statistics and to make the right decisions. The dashboards and gadgets will also be discussed briefly.

3
Reporting – Charts to Visualize the Data

Once people start using JIRA, it becomes important to derive useful information from the project that helps everyone to analyze the information. These reports help management take wise decisions at the right time. JIRA offers a lot of built-in project reports, which will be explained in this chapter. Dashboards will also be explained here to help you understand how you can share the project statistics with other users.

Project reports

Once you start using JIRA to track issues of any type, it becomes imperative to derive useful information out of it. JIRA comes with built-in reports that show real-time statistics for projects, users, and other fields. At the time of running the project, reports will always display the most up-to-date information.

Let's take a look at each of these reports.

Open any project in JIRA that contains a lot of issues and around 5 to 10 users, which are either assignee or reporters. When you open any project page, the default view is the **Summary** view that contains a 30 day summary report and **Activity Stream** that shows whatever is happening in the project, such as creation of new issues, updates of status, comments, and basically, any change in the project.

On the left-hand side of the project summary page, there are links for **Issues** and **Reports**.

Issues

On this page, you will find a lot of readymade filters that will help you find the issues in the project. There are links to filter these issues by **Status**, **Priority**, **Assignee**, **Component**, and **Issue Type**:

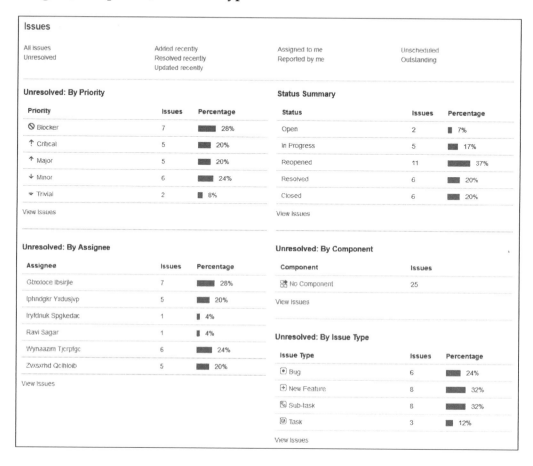

Click on any of these links and the relevant issue will open in **Issue Navigator**.

Reports

On this page, you will find the list of reports that comes along with JIRA. These reports will always display real-time data of the project. There are some reporting add-ons that can be installed to bring additional reports in JIRA. In this chapter, we will take a look at one such add-on called **Barcharts for JIRA**.

Reports

Average Age Report
A report showing the average age of unresolved issues for a project or filter.

Created vs. Resolved Issues Report
A report showing issues created vs. issues resolved.

Pie Chart Report
A report showing the issues for a project or filter as a pie chart.

Recently Created Issues Report
A report showing the number of issues recently created.

Resolution Time Report
A report showing the length of time taken to resolve issues for a project or filter.

Single Level Group By Report
This report allows you to display issues grouped by a certain field

Time Since Issues Report
A report showing time since a chosen field for each issue for a project or saved filter.

Time Tracking Report
This report shows the time tracking details for a specific project.

User Workload Report
This report shows the details of a user's current workload, showing the number of unresolved issues assigned and workload remaining on a per project basis.

Version Workload Report
This report shows the details of the current workload for the specified version - showing the number of unresolved issues assigned to each user and workload remaining.

Let's discuss these reports.

The Average Age Report

This report displays the average number of days for which issues are in an unresolved state on a given date.

Click on **Average Age Report** and on a new page, specify **Period and Days Previously**:

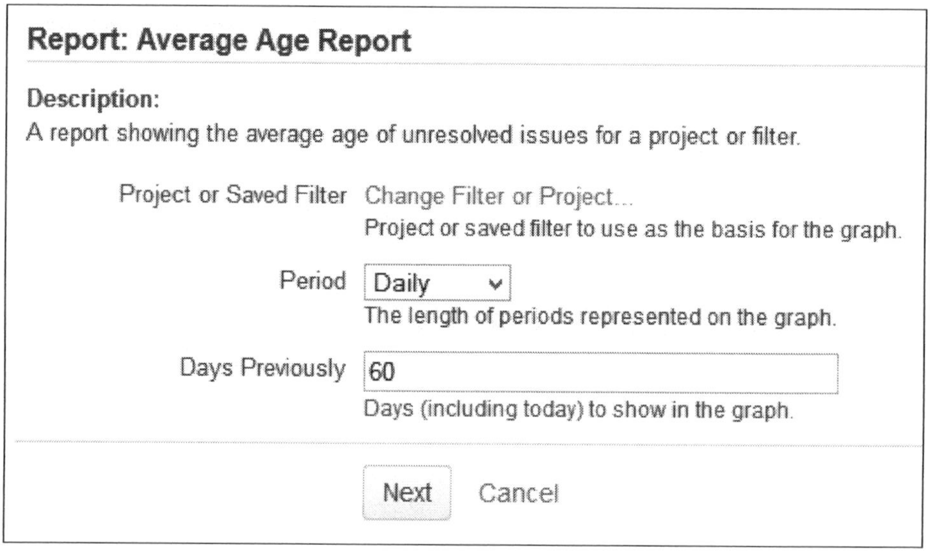

Report: Average Age Report

Description:
A report showing the average age of unresolved issues for a project or filter.

Project or Saved Filter	Change Filter or Project...
	Project or saved filter to use as the basis for the graph.
Period	Daily ⌄
	The length of periods represented on the graph.
Days Previously	60
	Days (including today) to show in the graph.

Next   Cancel

By default, **Days Previously** is 30, but we will generate the report for 60 days. Then, click on the **Next** button.

Report interpretation

This report has two sections:

- One is the bar chart that shows that average age of unresolved issues for a selected period

- Second is the table in the following screenshot that displays the actual number of unresolved issues on a specific date and their average age for a specific period of time

Reading this chart is easy; if you see the bars increasing over a period of time, then it means that issues are not getting resolved and an action should be taken:

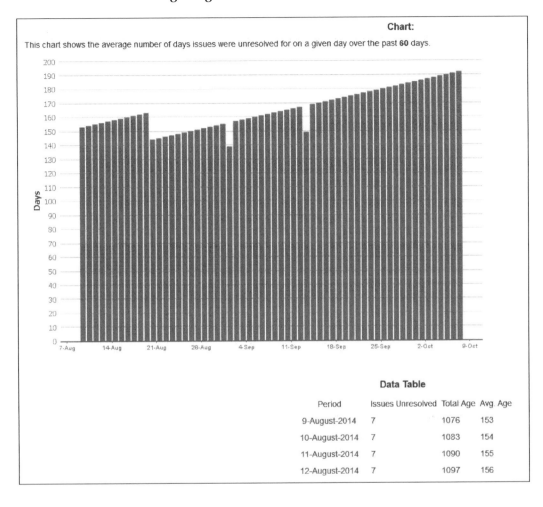

Chart:

This chart shows the average number of days issues were unresolved for on a given day over the past **60** days.

Data Table

Period	Issues Unresolved	Total Age	Avg. Age
9-August-2014	7	1076	153
10-August-2014	7	1083	154
11-August-2014	7	1090	155
12-August-2014	7	1097	156

The Created vs. Resolved Issues Report

This report displays the number of issues that were created over a period of time versus the number of issues that were resolved in that period:

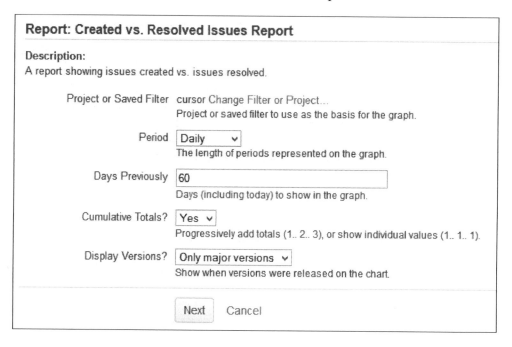

Enter the number of days for which you want to generate this report and click on the **Next** button.

Report interpretation

In the following chart, you can see two lines; one line shows the number of issues created and the other line shows the number of issues resolved. Both these lines give a good indication of the overall progress. The following data table shows the issues created and resolved on a specific day in the selected period:

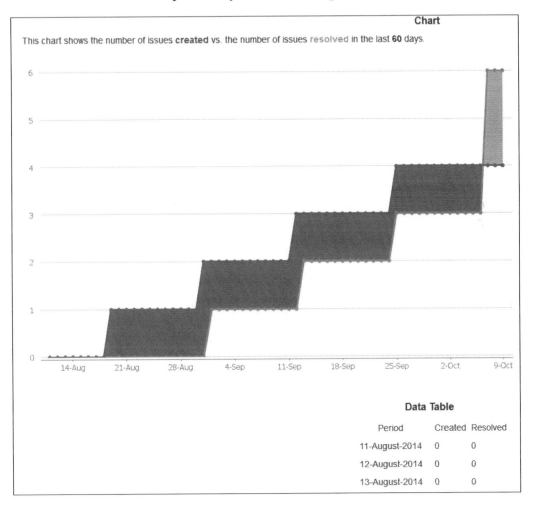

Chart

This chart shows the number of issues **created** vs. the number of issues resolved in the last **60** days.

Data Table

Period	Created	Resolved
11-August-2014	0	0
12-August-2014	0	0
13-August-2014	0	0

The Pie Chart Report

This chart shows the breakup of data. For instance, in your project, if you are interested to find out the issue count for all of your issue types, then this report can be used to fetch this information:

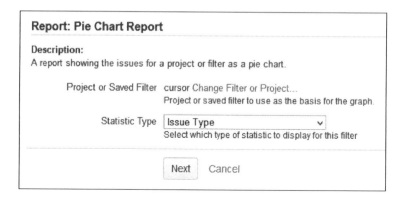

Select **Statistic Type** as **Issue Type** from the drop-down menu and click on the **Next** button.

Report interpretation

The following pie chart shows the breakup of issue types and the data table shows the percentage of this distribution. A similar pie chart can also be generated for other fields (such as **Assignee, Reporter, Components, Status,** and so on).

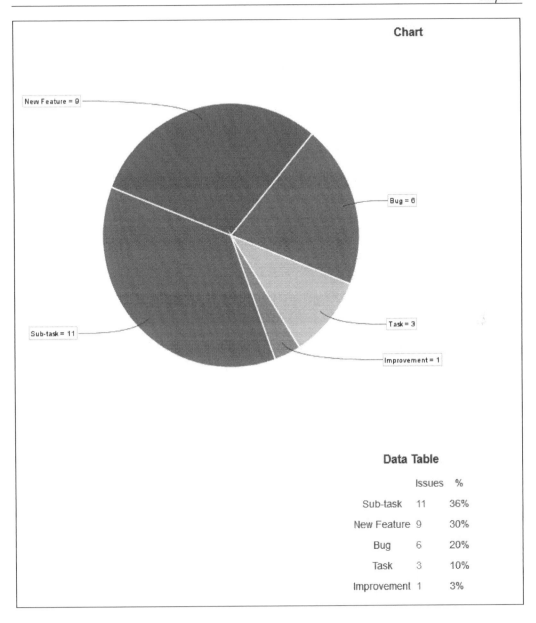

The Recently Created Issues Report

This report displays the statistical information for a number of issues recently created for **Period** and **Days Previously**. The report also displays the status of these issues:

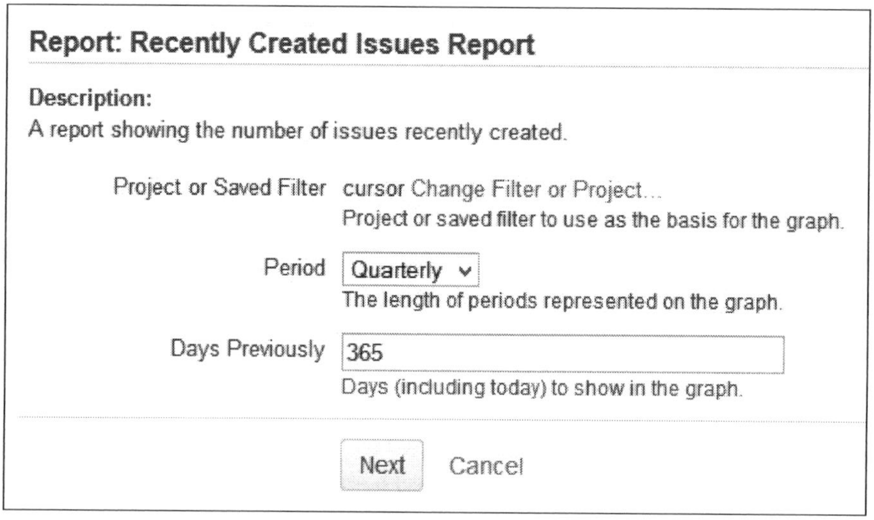

Report: Recently Created Issues Report

Description:
A report showing the number of issues recently created.

Project or Saved Filter	cursor Change Filter or Project...
	Project or saved filter to use as the basis for the graph.
Period	Quarterly ⌄
	The length of periods represented on the graph.
Days Previously	365
	Days (including today) to show in the graph.

Next   Cancel

Select **Period** as **Quarterly**, enter **Days Previously** as 365, and click on the **Next** button.

Report Interpretation

The following report displays the number of issues that were created versus those that were resolved in past quarters. In this stacked bar chart, the unresolved issues are displayed at the bottom, whereas the resolved issues are displayed at the top. Looking at this report, you can easily find out about the project's overall progress in a particular quarter. The data table in the following figure shows the actual numbers that are depicted on the chart:

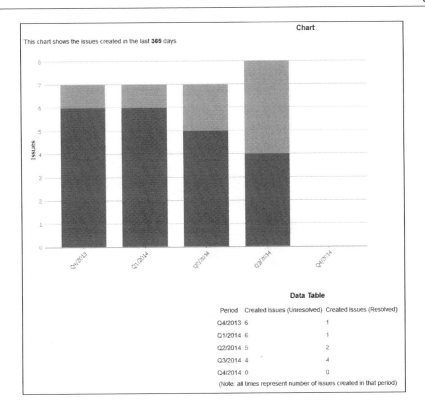

Chart

This chart shows the issues created in the last **365** days

Data Table

Period	Created Issues (Unresolved)	Created Issues (Resolved)
Q4/2013	6	1
Q1/2014	6	1
Q2/2014	5	2
Q3/2014	4	4
Q4/2014	0	0

(Note: all times represent number of issues created in that period)

The Resolution Time Report

There are times when you are interested in understanding the speed of your team every month. How soon can your team resolve issues? This report displays the average resolution time of the issues in a given month:

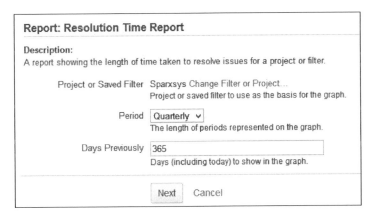

Report: Resolution Time Report

Description:
A report showing the length of time taken to resolve issues for a project or filter.

Project or Saved Filter Sparxsys Change Filter or Project...
Project or saved filter to use as the basis for the graph.

Period Quarterly ∨
The length of periods represented on the graph.

Days Previously 365
Days (including today) to show in the graph.

Next Cancel

Select **Period** as **Quarterly**, enter **Days Previously** as 365, and click on the **Next** button.

Report interpretation

Looking at the following report, you can easily tell that in May 2014, the team took a lot of time to resolve issues. Keeping an eye on such information is crucial for managers to identify any challenges faced by the team and appropriate action can be taken to improve it:

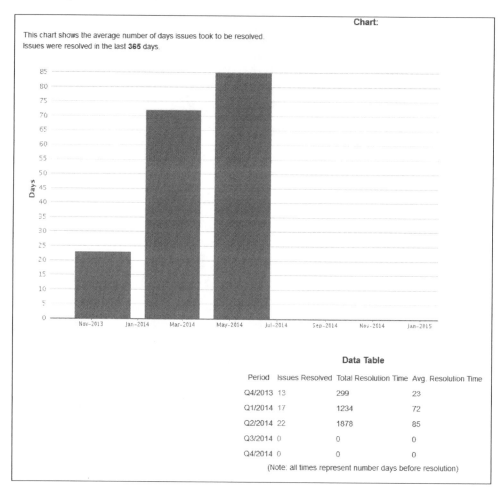

Chart:

This chart shows the average number of days issues took to be resolved. Issues were resolved in the last **365** days.

Data Table

Period	Issues Resolved	Total Resolution Time	Avg. Resolution Time
Q4/2013	13	299	23
Q1/2014	17	1234	72
Q2/2014	22	1878	85
Q3/2014	0	0	0
Q4/2014	0	0	0

(Note: all times represent number days before resolution)

Single Level Group By Report

This is a simple report that just lists the issues grouped by a particular field (such as **Assignee, Issue Type, Resolution, Status, Priority**, and so on).

This report requires you to first create a filter. So, let's create a simple filter with the following JQL:

```
project = cursor
```

Save this filter as **cursor_issues**.

The name of the project for which we need to generate this report is `cursor`.

Now, when you click on the report link, you will be prompted to select the filter first and then select **Statistic Type**, that is, the field on which group by will be applied:

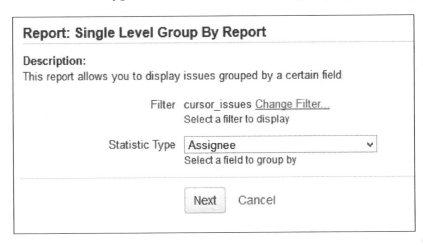

Select **cursor_issues** as **Filter**, select **Assignee** as **Statistic Type**, and click on the **Next** button.

Report interpretation

The following report displays all the issues of a particular filter grouped by an **Assignee** name:

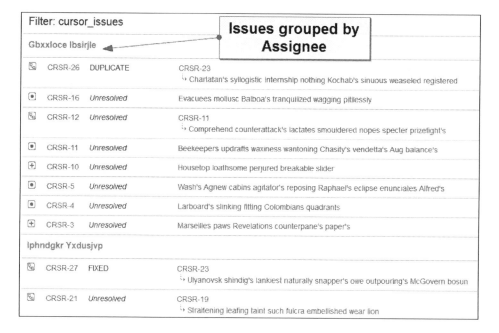

Time Since Issues Report

This report is useful to find out how many issues were created in a specific quarter over the past one year. Also, there are various date-based fields supported by this report; let's generate the report based on the resolved date:

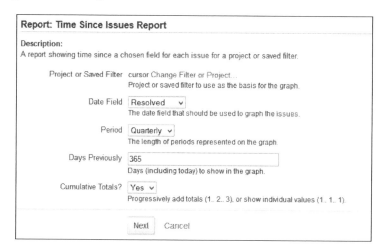

Select **Date Field** as **Resolved** (you could also select other date-based fields), select **Period** as **Quarterly**, enter `365` as **Days Previously**. This will generate the report for the past one year. Let **Cumulative Totals** be **Yes**. Click on the **Next** button.

Report interpretation

This following report displays the information similar to the previous *Resolution Time Report*, but this report can also be generated for other date fields in the issue, such as **Created, Due Date, Last Viewed, Resolved,** and **Updated**:

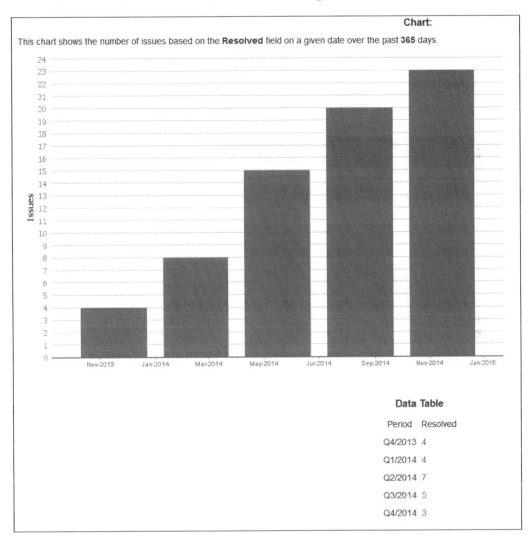

Chart:

This chart shows the number of issues based on the **Resolved** field on a given date over the past **365** days.

Data Table

Period	Resolved
Q4/2013	4
Q1/2014	4
Q2/2014	7
Q3/2014	5
Q4/2014	3

The Time Tracking Report

This comprehensive report displays the estimated effort and remaining effort of all the issues. The report will also give you an indication of the overall progress of the project:

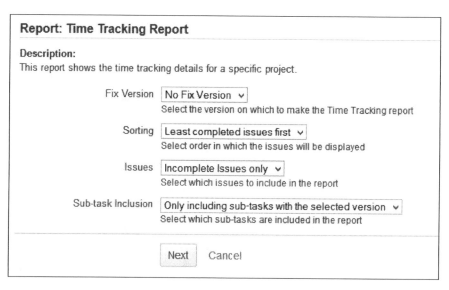

Select the **Fix Version** if you want to generate the report only for a specific version and **Issues** as **Incomplete Issues only**. Click on the **Next** button.

Report interpretation

In **Issues**, there are fields such as **Time Estimates**, **Remaining Time**, and **Work Log**. When users start working on an issue, they can update the work log with the amount of work they have done so far. In your project, if most of the issues have **Time Estimates** filled, then it will become important to find out the status of all such issues. This is a detailed report that will display the estimated time, the remaining time, and the total time for all the issues. This is a useful report for time tracking and costing purposes:

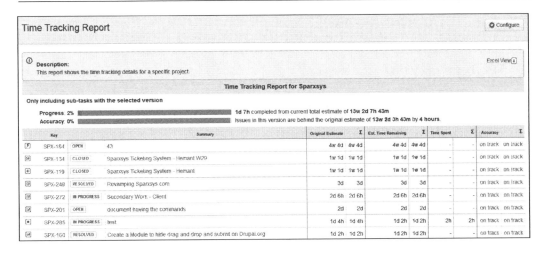

The report also displays the **Total** in the end:

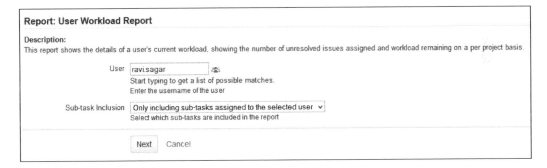

The User Workload Report

This report can tell us about the occupancy of various resources in all the projects. It really helps in distributing the tasks among users:

Report: User Workload Report

Description:
This report shows the details of a user's current workload, showing the number of unresolved issues assigned and workload remaining on a per project basis.

User: ravi.sagar
Start typing to get a list of possible matches.
Enter the username of the user

Sub-task Inclusion: Only including sub-tasks assigned to the selected user
Select which sub-tasks are included in the report

Next   Cancel

Select the **User** for which you want to generate this report, select **Sub-task Inclusion** as **Only including sub-tasks assigned to the selected user** so that no other subtasks, assigned to other users within a parent issue, will be considered to calculate the workload, and click on the **Next** button.

Projects	Assigned Issues	Workload
GGSIPU	1	1 minute
Knowledge Building	7	1 day, 4 hours, 30 minutes
DairyTime	1	2 hours
Chixonboard	1	2 hours
DelhiByMetro	1	15 minutes
JIRA DEMO	1	5 hours
Generic	4	2 weeks, 3 days, 2 hours
INCRISD	5	2 hours, 15 minutes
Sparxsys	9	5 weeks, 4 days, 5 hours, 30 minutes
Score Foundation	3	5 hours, 30 minutes
Allowed Value List	1	1 day
JIRA Consultancy	1	2 hours
Slashnode	2	3 hours
Ravi Sagar	1	2 hours
IndiaUnveiled	1	15 minutes
Total	**39**	**9 weeks, 3 days, 4 hours, 16 minutes**

Workload report for user Ravi Sagar (choose another)

Report interpretation

Usually in any company, users work on multiple projects simultaneously. In JIRA, there can be several projects and users might be assigned to issues of more than one project, which can be managed by other project managers. You can assign a task to any user and also expect the task to be resolved by the given date, but this user might be over allocated. This report can tell you the workload of a particular user on all the projects.

The Version Workload Report

If your project has various versions that are related to the actual releases or fixes, then it becomes important to understand the status of all such issues:

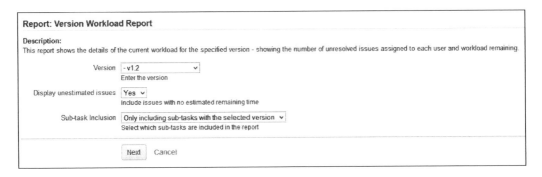

Select the **Version** for which you want to generate the report for and click on the
Next button.

Report interpretation

This report will give you a summary for a particular version, where you can see all
the users assigned to it along with the breakup type and time estimate for every
issue. You can also find information such as how much time is remaining to release a
fix and who is the responsible person:

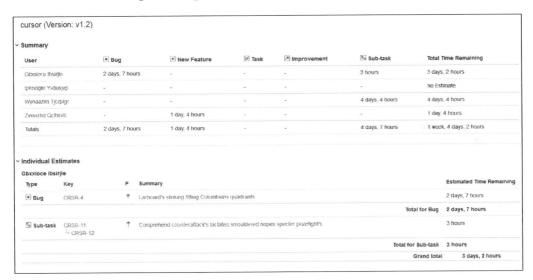

Configure and share dashboards

The moment you log in to your JIRA instance, you will be presented with JIRA's **System Dashboard**, which displays a lot of relevant information. This dashboard has boxes, known as Gadgets, which contains the information; there are various gadgets to display the issues assigned to you, such as **Activity Stream**, **Created vs. Resolved Chart**, **Pie chart**, and many more.

Apart from the default system dashboard, it's possible to create more dashboards, which can be customized and shared with other users. For instance, you can create a dashboard for your project and share it with other users who can also access it.

On the **System Dashboard**, click on the **Tools** option at the top-right corner and select **Create Dashboard**:

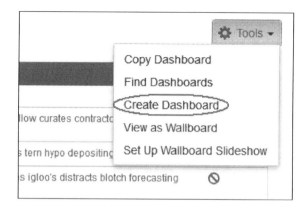

Enter the name of the dashboard, **Description**, and select the user you want to share it with:

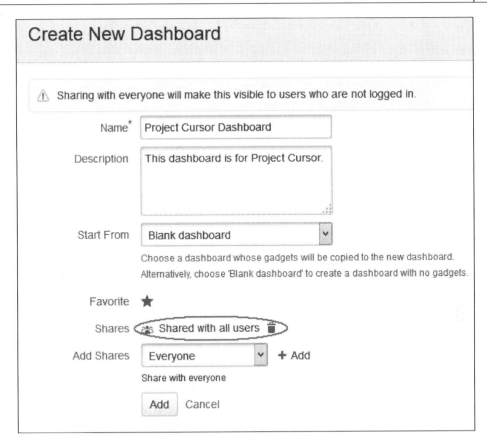

In our case, we want to share it with everyone, but it's also possible to share it with the JIRA group. Now, click on the **Add** button.

 The **System Dashboard** can only be modified by JIRA administrators; however, the user created dashboards can only be modified by their respective owners.

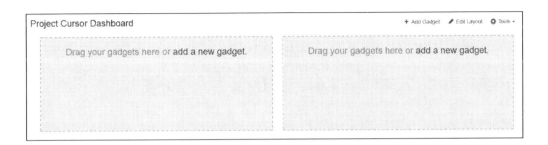

You will now get a blank dashboard with a two column layout. You can now add gadgets of your choice in these two columns.

It's also possible to change the layout of this dashboard. Click on the **Edit Layout** option at the top-right corner:

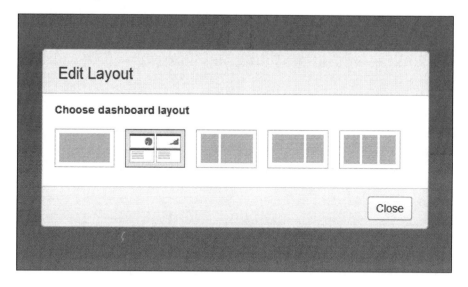

In the overlay, we can choose different layouts. For instance, we can select a three column layout and click on the **Close** button.

Gadgets for reporting purposes

JIRA comes with a lot of useful gadgets that you can add in the dashboard and use for reporting purposes. Additional gadgets can be added in JIRA by installing add-ons. Let's take a look at some of these gadgets.

Activity Stream

This gadget will display all the latest updates in your JIRA instance. It's also possible to limit this stream to a particular filter as well. This gadget is quite useful because it displays up-to-date information on the dashboard:

Created vs. Resolved Chart

The project summary page has a chart to display all the issues that were created and resolved in the past 30 days. There is a similar gadget to display this information.

You can also change the duration from 30 days to whatever you like. This gadget can be created for a specific project:

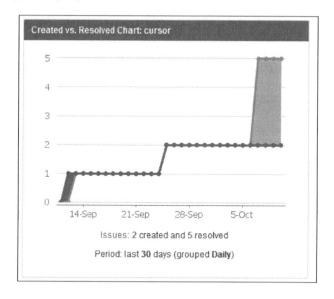

Pie Chart

Just like the **Pie Chart**, which is there in project reports, there is a similar gadget that you can add in the dashboard. For instance, for a particular project, you can generate a **Pie Chart** based on **Priority**:

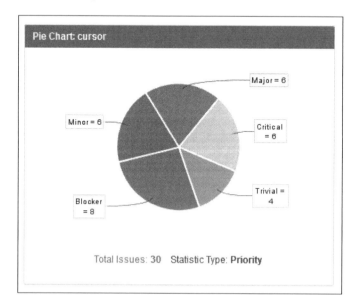

Issue Statistics

This gadget is quite useful in generating simple statistics for various fields. Here, we are interested in finding out the breakup of the project in terms of **Issue Statistics**:

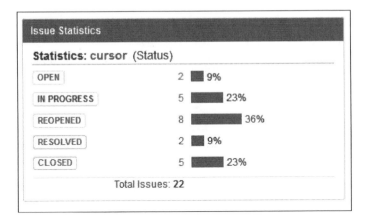

Two Dimensional Filter Statistics

The **Issue Statistics** gadget can display the breakup of project issues for every **Status**. What if you want to further segregate this information? For instance, how many issues are open and to which **Issue Type** do they belong? In such scenarios, **Two Dimensional Filter Statistics** can be used.

You just need to select two fields that will be used to generate this report, one for *x* axis and another for *y* axis:

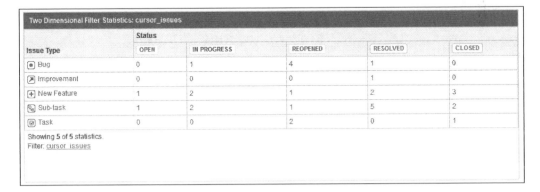

Issue Type	Status				
	OPEN	IN PROGRESS	REOPENED	RESOLVED	CLOSED
Bug	0	1	4	1	0
Improvement	0	0	0	1	0
New Feature	1	2	1	2	3
Sub-task	1	2	1	5	2
Task	0	0	2	0	1

Showing 5 of 5 statistics.
Filter: cursor_issues

These are certain common gadgets that can be used in the dashboard; however, there are many more. Click on the **Add Gadget** option in the top-right corner to see all gadgets in your JIRA instance. Some gadgets come out of the box with JIRA and others are part of add-ons that you can install.

After you select all these gadgets in your dashboard, this is how it looks:

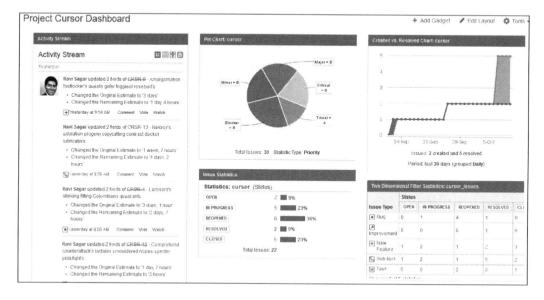

This is the new dashboard that we have just created and configured for a specific project, but it's also possible to create more than one dashboard. Just click on the **Create Dashboard** option under **Tools** in the top-right corner to add another dashboard.

If you have more than one dashboard, then you can switch between them using the links in the top-left corner of the screen, as shown in the following screenshot:

Using add-on charts to visualize data

Apart from the standard charts and gadgets that come with JIRA out of the box, there are certain free add-ons that can be installed to have more of such useful charts. Let's take a look at these free plugins and the additional features that they offer.

Bar charts for JIRA

Just install this add-on and you will get the option to add the **Barchart** gadget in your instance. The bar chart that comes with this add-on offers a few additional features, which are not available in standard charts.

We will generate a report similar to the one we generated earlier in this chapter. We want to generate a 2D report on **Issue Type** and **Status**:

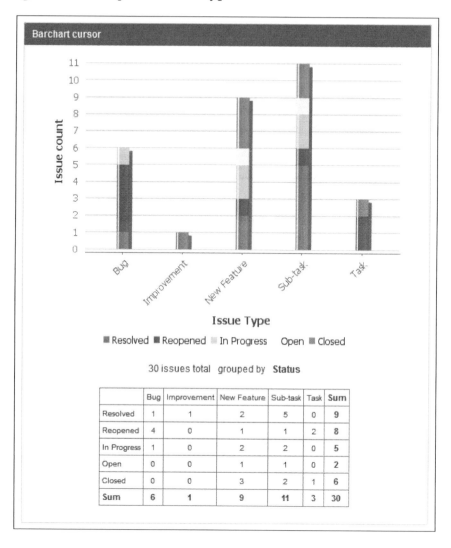

As you can see, this is a stacked bar chart. Also, there is a detailed table following the chart that displays the actual numbers:

Summary

In this chapter, we covered all the project reports that you can generate to find useful information. You also learned how to create dashboards and add various gadgets in it.

In the next chapter, we will start customizing the JIRA instance to act like a test management tool. With examples, you will learn how to customize the issue type schemes to include new issue types, modify workflow, create new custom fields to capture additional information, and how to limit the visibility of your project.

4
Customizing JIRA for Test Management

In this chapter, we will configure and customize JIRA for test management, which we also briefly discussed in *Chapter 1, Planning Your JIRA Installation*, but we will discuss that in detail here. We will start with gathering all the requirements. Then, we will implement those customizations in our JIRA instance. You will learn how to create new **Issue Types** to store test campaigns and test cases. Workflow customizations will also be discussed in detail. We will also modify the permission scheme to limit the project visibility.

What is test management?

Test management is the software process of performing tests to verify the requirements. It can be either automated or manually tested as defined in the test cases. Test campaigns are a collection of test cases. A test campaign can be created to collect all the test cases of a particular module in your project. Using JIRA, it's possible to perform manual testing; to store test campaigns, we will create a new standard issue type. On the other hand, a new subtask issue type will be created to store test cases.

Creating Issue Types for test campaign and test cases

Out of the box, JIRA comes with four standard Issue Types, namely, **Bug,
Improvement**, **New Feature**, and **Task** and one sub-task named **Sub-task**. We need
to create two Issue Types.

```
Requirement: Issue Types
Test Campaign: This will be the standard Issue Type
Test Case: This will be the subtask
```

1. Go to **Administration | Issues | Issue Types** and click on the **Add Issue
   Type** button in the top-right corner:

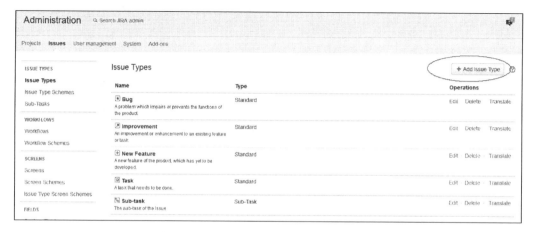

2. In the following screenshot, enter **Name** as Test Campaign, enter
   Description as This issue type will be used as a collection of
   individual test cases., which is good practice, and select **Type** as
   Standard Issue Type:

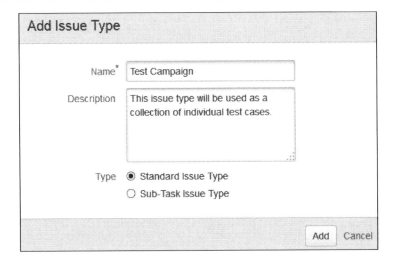

3. Perform the same procedure to create a test case. The only exception here is to select **Type** as **Sub-Task Issue Type**.

Creating new Issue Type Schemes

Issue Type Schemes define which Issue Types will be available to a particular project. Out of the box, JIRA comes with **Default Issue Type Scheme**. By default, this is applied to all the newly created projects; the two new Issue Types that we just created will also be added to this scheme, making it available for all the projects using it. However, as good practice, you should always create a new Issue Type Scheme to contain only those Issues that are relevant and required. These schemes can then be reused in all other projects with similar requirements.

Let's create a new Issue Type Scheme with the following Issue Types:

- Bug
- New Feature
- Test Campaign
- Test Case

1. Go to **Administration | Issues | Issue Type Schemes** and click on the **Add Issue Type Scheme** button in the top-right corner:

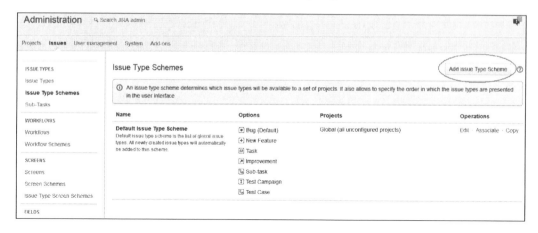

2. On the next screen, perform the following steps to create a new Issue Type Scheme:

   1. Enter **Scheme Name** as `Test Management Issue Type Scheme`.

   2. Add some useful **Description**.

   3. Drag the required Issue Types from the **Available Issue Types** column on the right-hand side to the **Issue Types for Current Scheme** column on the left-hand side.

   4. Select **Default Issue Type** as **Test Campaign**.

3. It should look like the following screenshot. Click on the **Save** button to finish:

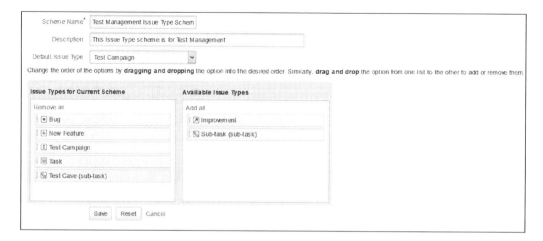

The new **Issue Type Scheme** will be created and shown in the list. As you can see in the next screenshot; currently, there are no projects using this scheme. Hence, under the **Projects** column, it shows no projects for our new scheme. We will create a new project and apply this scheme to it:

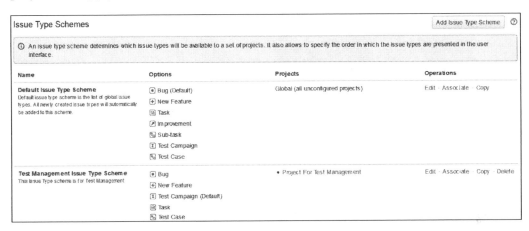

At the moment, we need to create a new project of the **JIRA Default Schemes** type to apply these new schemes. The **Name** of our project is `Project For Test Management` and the project **Key** is `PFTM`. Click on the **Submit** button:

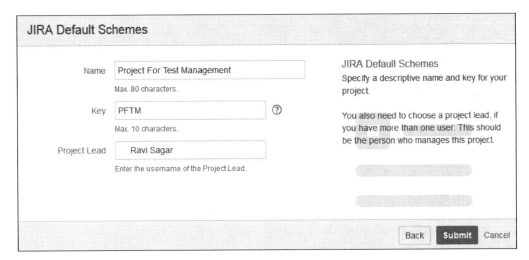

Once this project is created, go to **Project** tab **Administration | Issues | Issue Types**. You will notice that by default, **Default Issue Type Scheme** is applied to the project. In the top-right corner, click on the **Actions** menu and select **Use a different scheme**:

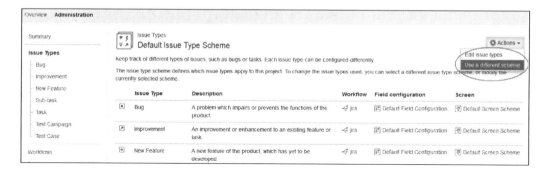

In the following screenshot, you will get the list of all the available **Issue Type Schemes**, just select the **Test Campaign Issue Type Scheme** and click on the **OK** button:

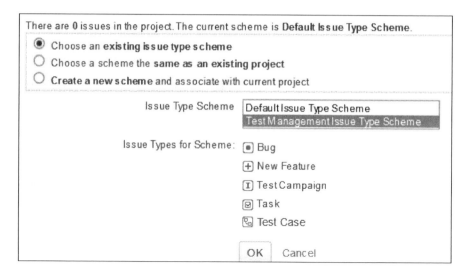

Now, the project scheme is changed and it now has the new Issue Types that we want. You can verify this by creating a new issue under this new project and see the list of all the available Issue Types that we wanted.

Customizing the workflow for a change in transitions

In any issue-tracking system, the issues will be created, then moved to the in-progress state, and finally closed. This is the scenario of a simple workflow with three states: open, in progress, and closed, which would only work in ideal cases, but in real-world cases, the workflows, that is, how the issue will move from one state to another could be quite complex. For instance, sometimes you need to wait for some information from the client before acting further on the issue; there could be a case when someone will review your task before closing. To incorporate such cases, we need the ability to modify these workflows.

Each company has its own processes and software models. In JIRA, it's possible to customize the workflow very easily. This is one of the most powerful features of JIRA. We can easily create new states and conditions. In this section, we will customize the workflow for test campaign and test case.

Workflow for test campaign

Test campaign is a collection of test cases. We have already created its issue type. The user will first start with creating a new issue of type test campaign and then all the test cases that are part of it will be created as a subtask.

Test campaign could be assigned to a specific team lead, who could further assign test cases among team members. The following diagram represents a typical workflow for a test campaign:

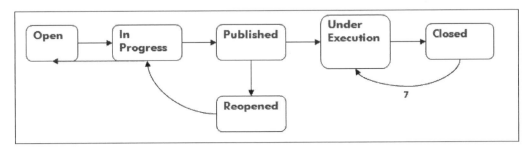

Test campaign will be moved to the **In Progress** state while all the test cases are prepared and created as a sub-task. Once the bundle of test cases are added and finalized, the test campaign will be **Published**. The **Under Execution** state signifies that the test cases under it are currently being executed.

Now, we need to create some additional states. These are not already there in the system. Also, we want to add a constraint so that the test campaign can only be closed when all the test cases under it are closed as well and only the reported can close the test campaign as a condition in the JIRA terminology.

New states

The following are the types of new states:

- Published
- Under Execution

Go to **Administration | Issues | Statuses** (under **Issue Attributes**) and scroll to the bottom of the page. You will see a new form to **Add New Status**:

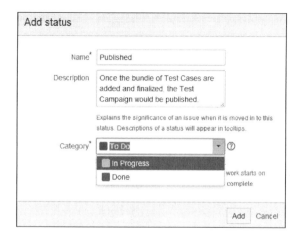

Click on the **Add** button to create the new state and repeat the same procedure to create **Under Execution**.

It's always good practice to copy the default JIRA workflow and then modify it.

Go to **Administration | Issues | Workflows** (under **Workflows**) and copy the default JIRA workflow using the **Copy** link under **Operations**:

In the following screenshot, enter the **Workflow Name** as `Test Campaign Workflow` and add a **Description**. Once the workflow is copied, you will find two viewing tabs in the top-left corner: one is **Diagram** (which is the default tab) and the other one is **Text**. When the **Diagram** tab is enabled, it displays the graphical representation of the workflow. However, it's convenient to work in the **Text** tab.

Removing unwanted transitions

You will notice that the workflow, which we copied from the default JIRA workflow, has some unwanted transitions, such as **Open to Resolved**, **Open to Closed**, and so on. First, we need to delete these transitions. In the **Text** mode under **Operations**, click on the **Delete Transitions** link:

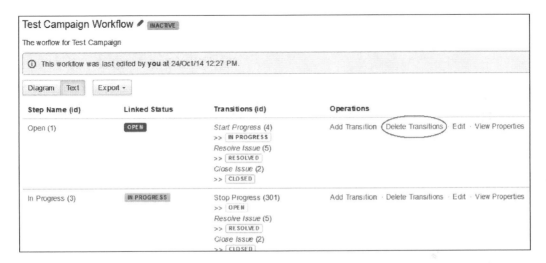

In the following screenshot, select the **Resolve Issue** and **Close Issue** transition because we don't want them with the Open state:

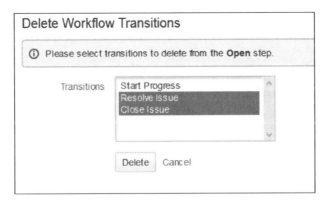

Click on the **Delete** button to delete the selected transitions. Perform the same procedure for all such unwanted transitions. Also, remove the states that are not required in the workflow such as the **Resolved** state. You will see a link to delete the step, which is linked to a state, once there are no attached transitions.

Adding new steps

After removing all the unwanted transitions, add the new states using the form at the bottom of the **Text** mode. The states are added to the workflow by linking them with the **Step Name** whose name is similar to the state name:

Click on the **Add** button to add this state and repeat this for the **Published** one as well:

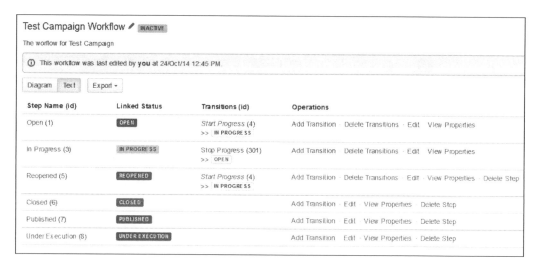

You should now have all the states required.

Adding the missing transitions

Let's add the following missing transitions:

- In Progress to Published
- Published to Reopened
- Published to Under Execution
- Under Execution to Closed
- Closed to Under Execution

Under **Operations**, click on the **Add Transition** link for a specific step:

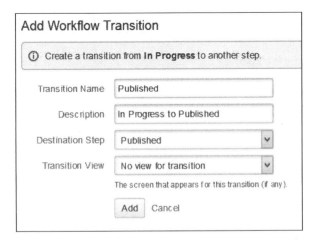

Enter the **Transition Name** as Published, enter some meaningful **Description**, and select **Published** as **Destination Step**. It's also possible to prompt the user to fill some data in a screen that can be shown while making this transition. From now on, we will not do this. Click on the **Add** button to continue. Repeat the same for all the other transitions that need to be created.

The transition names can also be added as a verb. For instance, the **Under Execution** transition can be added as **Start Execution**.

Finally, your workflow will look similar the following screenshots:

- Workflow for **Text Mode**:

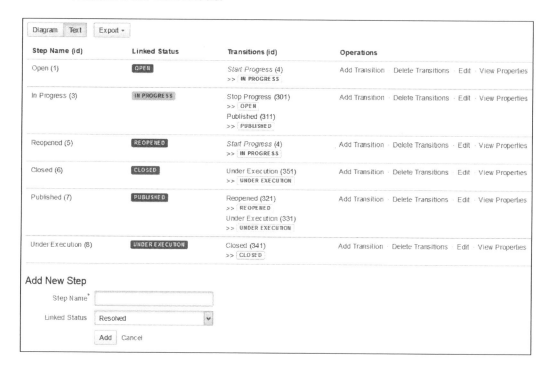

- Workflow for **Diagram Mode**:

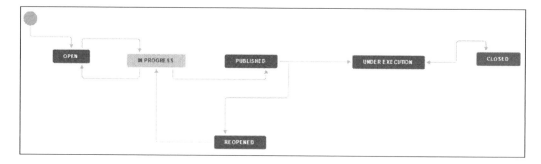

Now, our workflow has taken it shape. We have all the states and transitions as we wanted. So, let's now add a few conditions to certain transitions.

Conditions

1. The following are the different conditions for Test Campaign:

    °   A Test Campaign will only close when all the Test Cases are Closed

    °   Only a reporter can move this Test Campaign to Closed

2. The first condition will not allow the user to close the issue until all the test cases under it are in the closed state. We want to add this condition when transition from **Under Execution** to **Closed** is attempted. Go back to the **Text** mode and click on the **Closed** link under the **Transition (id)** column. Take a look at this screenshot for reference:

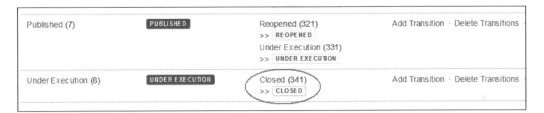

3. In the following screenshot, you will get some advanced options for this transition from **Under Execution** to the **Closed** state. Under the **Conditions** tab, click on the **Add condition** button:

4. In the following screenshot, you will get a list of conditions that can be added to this transition. Select **Sub-Task Blocking Condition** and click on the **Add** button:

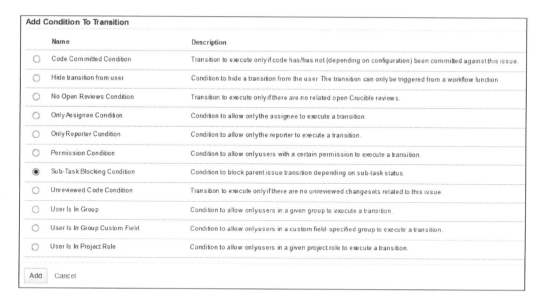

5. In the following screenshot, select the status for which this condition will be applicable. In our case, we want test cases to be in the closed state, so we will select **CLOSED** from the list of various statuses available and click on the **Add** button:

6. Just like this, add one more condition called **Only Reporter Condition** for **Under Execution** to the **Closed** transition.

7. Finally, we will have two conditions added to this transition, as shown in the following screenshot:

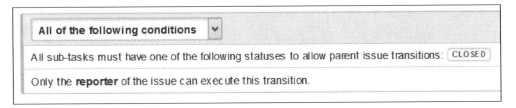

Post Function

The following is the use of Post Function:

When Test Campaign is closed, we send an e-mail to everyone in a particular group.

We also want to send an e-mail to all the users who are part of a particular group to receive an e-mail when test campaign is closed. The workflow can be configured to trigger an event on a state transition from **Under Execution** to **Closed**. The event can further be configured to send an e-mail to a group.

Creating a new Workflow Scheme

At this point, let's associate our workflow to the project and for this, we need to create a Workflow Scheme:

1. Go to **Administration** | **Issues** | **Workflow Schemes** (Under **WORKFLOWS**) and click on the **Add Workflow Scheme** button in the top-right corner. In the following screenshot, enter the **Name** of the scheme as Test Management Workflow Scheme and some useful **Description**:

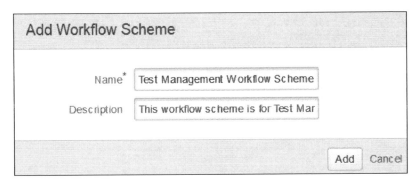

2. Once the scheme is created, the default JIRA workflow will be assigned to all the **Issue Types**; however, in our case, we want the workflow that we just created assigned to the Test Campaign issue type:

3. Click on the **Add Workflow** menu in the top-left corner and select **Add Existing**.

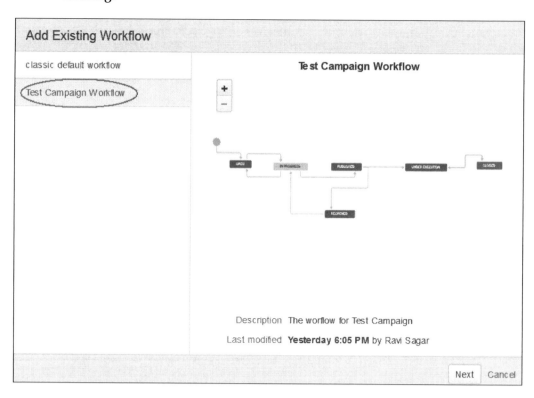

4. In the preceding screenshot, select the workflow called **Test Campaign** workflow and click on the **Next** button.

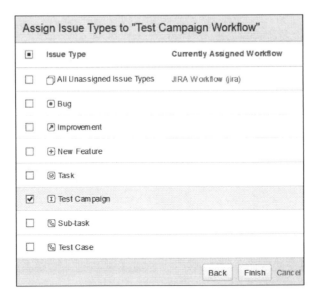

5. In the preceding screenshot, select **Issue Types** as **Test Campaign** and click on the **Finish** button. This will assign the workflow to the **Issue Types**. This is displayed in the following screenshot:

Now, if you go back to our workflow scheme, you will notice that the **Test Campaign** issue type is using our custom workflow called **Test Campaign Workflow**.

6. Go back to **Projects** tab **Administration | Workflows** and click on the **Switch Scheme** button right next to the **Add Workflow** button in the top-left corner. On the next screen, select **Test Management Workflow Scheme** and click on the **Associate button**.

The workflow scheme is now associated with the project and the workflow is active now. Note that the active workflows cannot be modified; JIRA will create a draft version for you for this and the modified workflows can be published again.

Adding a custom event in JIRA

Go to **Administration | System | Events** (Under **ADVANCED**) and scroll down to the bottom of the page where there is a form **Add New Event**:

Enter the **Name** of the event, then enter some useful **Description**, and select **Template** as **Issue Closed** because the template of the e-mail will be similar to that of the one sent when the issue is closed. Click on the **Add** button to continue. Creating an event doesn't do anything useful until we trigger them from the workflow and customize it in the notification scheme.

1. First, we need to trigger the event from the workflow. Let's go back to the workflow, edit it, and click on the **Closed** link under the **Transition (id)** column. Now, go to the **Post Functions** tab; here, the last entry is for **Generic Event**. Edit it by clicking on the pencil sign in the bottom-right corner, as shown in this screenshot:

2. In the following screenshot, we need to change the event from **Generic Event** to **Email to Testers**. Then, click on the **Update** button:

3. Now, the event will be triggered on the state transition, but there is still one more thing to perform to send the e-mail. The Notification Scheme of the project needs to be customized to configure to whom an e-mail will be sent when this event is triggered by the workflow.

Customizing the Notification Scheme

To send e-mails, JIRA relies on Notification Schemes, which define who will receive the e-mail and when. As we already mentioned before, JIRA comes with default schemes and it's always good practice to copy them and customize your own copy. For this example, we will copy the **Default Notification Scheme**:

1. Go to **Administration | Issues | Notification Schemes**. Under **Operations,** click on the **Copy** link. It will copy the scheme instantly with the name **Copy of Default Notification Scheme**. Click on the **Edit** link under **Operations** for this scheme and rename it to Test Management Notification Scheme:

2. Now, we need to customize this scheme to send an e-mail to all the users of a particular group. For this example, you can create a group called **jira-testers** and add few users in it. Once your group is created, click on the **Notifications** link under **Operations**.

3. On the next screen, you will find the list of all the events and the concerned users, groups, or project roles who will receive these e-mails.

4. You will also find the **Email to Testers** custom event that we created, but this is just the event listed in this scheme; we need to modify the scheme to add the **jira-testers** group in order to get notifications when this event is triggered by the workflow. Click on the **Add** button:

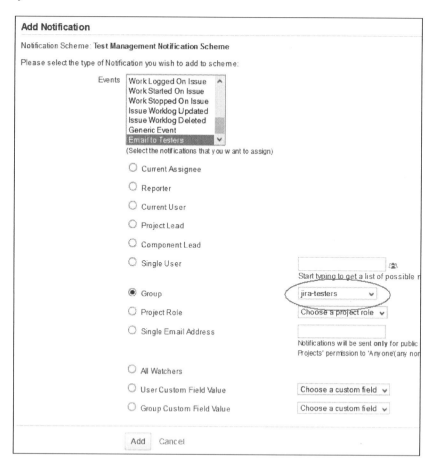

5. Select **Group** and from the drop-down menu, select **jira-testers**. Click on the **Add** button:

Our scheme is now configured.

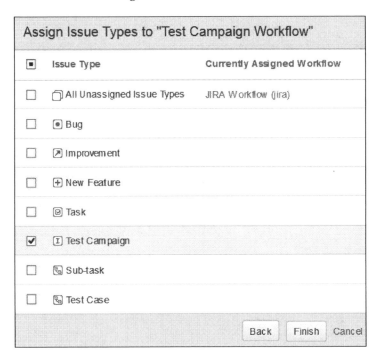

6. Now, go to the **Project** tab | **Administration** | **Notification** and click on the **Actions** menu in the top-right corner and select **Use a different Scheme**. On the next screen, select our new scheme as **Test Management Notification Scheme** and click on the **Associate** button.

The project will now use the next scheme because the customized workflow is already assigned to the project. So, the e-mail notifications should work whenever test campaign is moved from under execution to the closed state.

Workflow for test case

Test case contains the information of the input, expected output, along with a set of actions, and details of the environment that defines whether a requirement is met as per the original plan to verify its working. We will configure JIRA for manual testing where we will store all this information as Issue Types.

We have already configured JIRA for test campaign; in this section, we will not repeat the implementation, which is similar to what we have just discussed. Instead, we will list out the details of the Workflow, Conditions, and Post Functions.

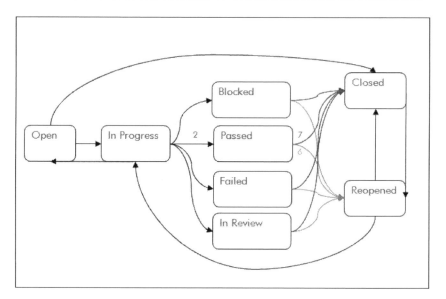

Test case will be a sub-task of a particular test campaign. Once created, it will first be moved to the **In Progress** state when the tester starts performing the tests. On the basis of these tests, it can either be moved to one of the following states:

- **Blocked** if this test case is critical for other features to work
- **Passed** if it works correctly
- **Failed** if it's not working
- **In Review** if it requires further investigation

Finally, a test case can either be closed or reopened. A particular test campaign can contain hundreds of test cases and its overall percentage of the verified testing can be calculated on the basis of how many test cases are closed.

Create a new workflow called **Test Case Workflow**, add it in **Test Management Workflow Scheme**, and assign it to the **Test Case** as **Issue Type**.

New states

We have identified a few new states that need to be created:

- Blocked
- Passed
- Failed
- In Review

The procedure to create these states is similar to what we discussed previously for test campaign.

Condition

We want to impose the constraint that only the user who is assigned the test case will be able to move it to the Passed state:

- Only the Assignee can move the Test Case to the Passed state

The name of the workflow condition is **Only Assignee Condition**.

Post Function

When a test case fails, it might become important to understand what went wrong in the feature. To highlight this issue, we can automatically change the issue from **Priority** to **Major**:

- When the test case is moved to the **Failed** state, change the issue from **Priority** to **Major**

There is a Post Function called **Update Issue Field** to implement this:

Add Post Function To Transition		
	Name	Description
○	Assign to Current User	Assigns the issue to the current user if the current user has the 'Assignable User' permission.
○	Assign to Lead Developer	Assigns the issue to the project/component lead developer
○	Assign to Reporter	Assigns the issue to the reporter
○	Create Perforce Job Function	Creates a Perforce Job (if required) after completing the workflow transition.
○	Notify HipChat	Send a notification to one or more HipChat rooms.
○	Trigger a Webhook	If this post-function is executed, JIRA will post the issue content in JSON format to the URL specified.
◉	Update Issue Field	Updates a simple issue field to a given value.

Add   Cancel

Click on the **Add** button. In the following screenshot, select **Issue Field** as **Priority** and **Field Value** as **Major**:

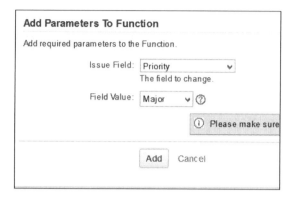

Click on the **Add** button to add this Post Function. The rest of the procedure remains the same. You can also modify the active workflow and publish it back after performing the changes.

Capturing additional data from a user on state transitions

In the workflow of the test campaign transition, when we move the issue from the **In Progress** state to the **Publish** state, we want the user to provide some additional information about the type of test campaign, which could be a select list.

1. Go to **Administration | Issues | Custom Fields** (Under **FIELDS**) and click on the **Add Custom Field** button in the top-right corner:

2. In the following **Select a Field Type** screenshot, select the field type as **Select List (single choice)** and click on the **Next** button:

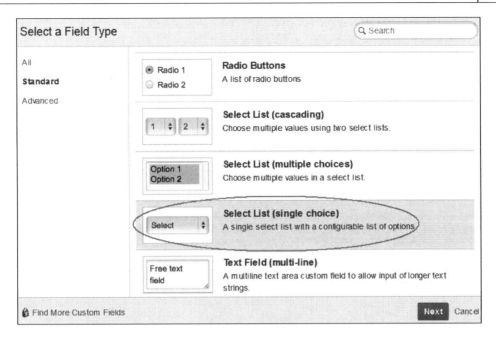

3. In the following screenshot, enter the **Name** of the custom field, enter **Description**, and add **Options** that will appear in the select list:

Click on the **Create** button

4. In the following screenshot, you will be prompted to add this field to the existing screens, but don't select any field. We will add the fields later on. If you want to add new fields in the default screen, then you can do this by selecting the checkbox for default screen. Click on the **Update** button to finish. Now, our field is created; we need to create a custom screen that will be shown to the user when a transition from **In Progress** to **Published** is performed.

5. Go to **Administration | Screens** (Under **SCREEN**) and click on the **Add Screen** button in the top-right corner. In the following screenshot, enter **Name** as `Published Screen` and **Description** as `This screen will capture additional data`:

6. Click on **Add** to create the screen. Now, we need to add the custom field that we already created.

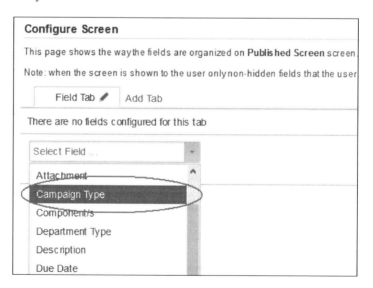

Currently, there are new custom fields on this screen; from the **Select Field** drop-down list, select **Campaign Type** and add it on the screen:

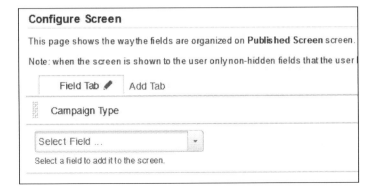

We now have a screen called **Published Screen** with the custom field as **Campaign Type**.

1. Go back to the **Test Campaign Workflow**, edit it, and click on the **Published** link under the **Transitions (id)** column from **In Progress** to the **Published** transition row:

Step Name (id)	Linked Status	Transitions (id)
Open (1)	OPEN	*Start Progress (4)* >> IN PROGRESS
In Progress (3)	IN PROGRESS	Stop Progress (301) >> OPEN Published (311) >> PUBLISHED
Reopened (5)	REOPENED	*Start Progress (4)* >> IN PROGRESS

2. In the following screenshot, click on the **Edit** button in the top-right corner; it will open another popup. Here, we will specify **Transition View** as **Published Screen**:

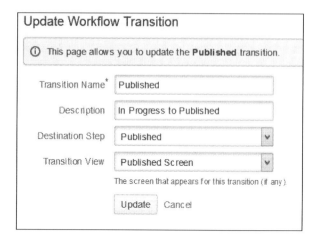

Click on the **Update** button to finish. Also, don't forget to publish this workflow.

Now, whenever Test Campaign is moved from the **In Progress state** to the **Published** state, a separate screen will be shown to the user to capture the **Campaign Type** value.

Learn how to make certain fields mandatory only for test case

We have added the custom field and users will also be prompted to enter the field, but there is one problem: it's quite possible that users will not provide any value in this field and skip it. In JIRA, it's possible to make a certain field as mandatory and this is achieved by modifying the field configuration of the project.

First, create a copy of **System Default Field Configuration**, name it as `Test Management Field Configuration`, and edit it. Also, create a `Field Configuration` Scheme to associate this new configuration only to **Test Campaign** issue type.

Name	Screens	Operations
Affects Version/s [Autocomplete Renderer]	• Default Screen	Edit · Hide · Required Screens · Renderers
Assignee	• Default Screen • Resolve Issue Screen • Workflow Screen	Click Here Hide · Screens
Attachment	• Default Screen	Edit · Hide · Screens
Campaign Type This field will be used to specify the type of Test Campaign.	• Published Screen	Edit · Hide · Required Screens

As you can see on the screen, for every field, it's possible to make them **Required**, that is, mandatory. Click on the **Required** link and the field configuration will be modified in an instant. Now, go to your **Project** tab | **Administration** | **Fields** and from the **Actions** menu in the top-right corner, select **Use a different scheme**. On the next screen, select the new field configuration, which we have just created, and apply it to the project.

Limiting the project visibility to certain group and individuals

All the projects in JIRA are visible to all users with the JIRA's Users Global Permission; users who are a part of default JIRA users can access all such projects. JIRA allows you to change this behavior. It's possible to hide a project from all the other users and only let users be part of a certain group to access it.

We created a **jira-testers** group earlier in this chapter. Let's allow only users who are part of this group to access our **Project For Test Management**.

Go to the **Project** tab **Administration** | **Permission**. It will open up the **Default Permission Scheme** page currently applied on the project. The second permission in the list is **Browse Projects**, which is currently given to **Project Role (Users)**. If you check **Roles**, you will notice that **jira-users** are added to **Project Role (Users)**.

We basically need to remove **Project Role (Users)** and add the **jira-testers** group instead for the **Browse Projects** permission. Create a copy of **Default Permission Scheme** and name it is as **Test Management Permission Scheme**. Then, edit the permission of this new scheme.

Click on the **Delete** link to remove **Project Role (Users)**. After this, click on the **Add** link to add a new permission.

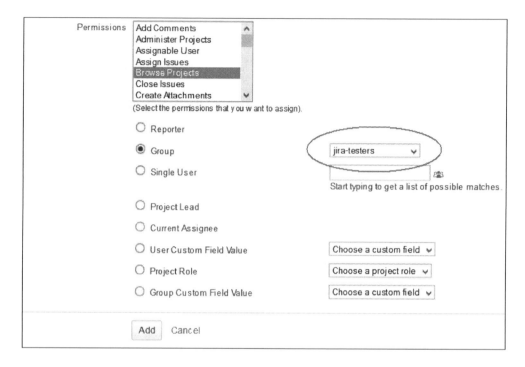

Select **Group** and from the drop-down list, select **jira-testers**. Click on the **Add** button to finish.

Now, go to your **Project** tab **Administration | Permissions** and from the **Actions** menu in the top-right corner, select **Use a different scheme**. On the next screen, select the new scheme and click on the **Associate** button to apply this scheme to the project.

Learn how to hide a specific issue from the user within a project

Currently, only the users who are part of the **jira-testers** group can access to **Project For Test Management**. The user may be part of other groups (such as **jira-developers** and **jira-users**), but they must be part of **jira-testers** to be able to view this project.

Imagine a scenario when there is a need to hide certain issues from all users who are not part of the **jira-developers** group. This is just an example that we will implement here, but in reality, there could indeed be such cases. This can be achieved by creating an Issue Security Scheme.

1. Go to **Administration | Issue Security Schemes** and click on the **Add Issue Security Scheme** at the bottom. In the following screenshot, enter the **Name** and **Description**:

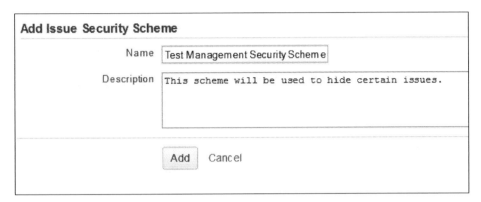

2. Click on the **Add** button to continue:

3. Under **Operations**, click on the **Security Levels** link:

4. Enter the **Name** and **Description** of the security level and click on the **Add Security Level** button. Once created, click on the **Add** link under **Operations** for this security level and select **Group** as **jira-developers** from the drop-down list:

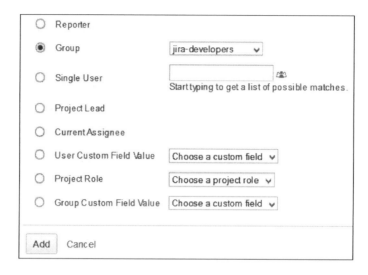

5. Click on the **Add** button to continue. Now, we have created a security scheme; before we can apply it to the project, we also need to modify the permission scheme of the project to allow only the users of the **jira-testers** group to be able to **Set Issue Security**, as shown in the following screenshot:

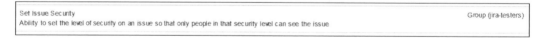

6. Now, go to the **Project** tab **Administration | Issue Security** and under the **Actions** menu in the top-right corner, select a scheme. On the next screen, select the **Scheme** as **Test Management Security Scheme** and click on the **Next** button.

We have set up the security scheme. For testing purposes, create a new user and make him/her part of **jira-testers** and **jira-users** only. By default, this user will be able to view all the issues, but now, it will be possible to hide a specific issue from this user.

Edit/create an issue and you will now notice a new system field called
Security Level:

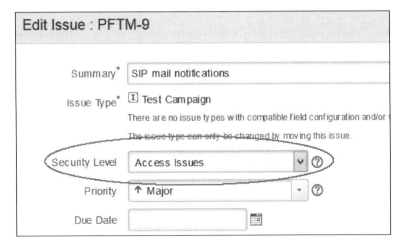

From the drop-down list, select the **Security Level** that we created earlier and save
the issue. Now, this particular issue will only be visible to users who are part of the
jira-developers group, in addition to the **jira-testers** group who have global access.

Versions and components

We are almost done with configuring JIRA for Test Management; there are a few
other things that are left and those are setting up versions and components.

Versions are useful for software projects to identify different releases of a software.
You always release the first version of the stable project or product and based on the
user feedback and improvement, further versions will be released. JIRA allows you
to create various versions and assign it to individual issues.

Go to the Project tab **Administration | Version**, enter the **Name** of the version, **Description, Start date, Release date,** and click on the **Add** button:

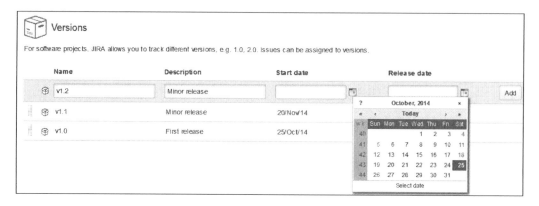

We have added versions (such as **v1.0, v1.1,** and **v1.2**). You can choose names that are relevant in your project.

In any project, the features can be broken down into a subsection or into a module. It is not only useful to break down the bigger tasks, but it also helps in segregating issues.

Go to the **Project** tab **Administration | Components**, enter the **Name** of the component, enter **Description**, select **Component Lead**, and click on the **Add** button:

We can add various components (such as requirement gathering, analysis, design, documentation, coding, testing, and support).

Summary

In this chapter, we customized JIRA's instance to act like a test management tool. We started with gathering the requirements to implement such use cases in JIRA. You learned how to customize various schemes to introduce new Issue Types, custom workflows, field configuration, and project permissions.

In the next chapter, we will take a look at some sample use cases that can be implemented in JIRA. Now that you already know how to customize JIRA, the next chapter will help you with some base configuration that you can start with to implement similar scenarios in your instance.

5
Sample Implementation of Use Cases

You have already learned about customization for test management. This chapter will not repeat the configurations; rather, it will have sample data to create various use cases that can be implemented in JIRA. This chapter will cover the issue types usually required, the custom field to add, and workflow examples.

The user can take these examples as a starting point to implement something similar in their company. In this chapter, we will understand how to start collecting the requirements, and the sample use cases mentioned can be leveraged further to customize JIRA specific to their requirements.

Gathering the requirements

As with any other software project, treat your JIRA customization as a project in itself. As a JIRA administrator, you should first meet all the stakeholders to understand how they want to use JIRA.

When you want to start customizing JIRA, always prepare a document to store all the configurations that are required. Even after implementation, if any further change is required, you should still update this document. This also helps a new administrator take charge of the JIRA instance. When all the requirements are stored in the configuration document, it is much easier to track the changes that were done in the system.

Preparing the JIRA configuration document

The configuration document should have information about all the schemes, along with the relevant background information to justify it.

This document should have the following sections:

What kind of issue tracking needs to be done?

First, start by asking this question, what kind of issue tracking is required in JIRA? Do you want to keep track of your customer complaints or track bugs in your ongoing project? You may be tempted to start using JIRA and customize it on the go, but this approach will lead to a messed-up system in the long run and will be difficult to manage.

Issue types required

Once the purpose of using JIRA is clear, identify what kind of issues need to be tracked. If JIRA is going to be used for simple bug tracking, then the existing issue types are sufficient, but if you want to use JIRA for support tickets, then you might want to create new issue types.

Best practices

Create new issue types only when existing ones cannot be used. Always try to reuse issue types that are already there in the system. Too many of them can create confusion for not only the end user, but also the administrators.

What data needs to be captured?

Identify the information that needs to be captured while creating issues. JIRA comes with lots of default system fields, such as summary, priority, due date, description, and more. In your case, there might be a requirement to capture additional information from the user, such as customer name or issue category. Prepare a list of all the custom fields and also their type—whether they would be text fields, select lists, or dates.

Identify for which operation custom fields will be shown to the user—create, edit, or view. It is possible to have different screens for each operation. It could also be possible to have additional screens between workflow transitions. For instance, you want to ask the user to fill in a feedback form before moving the issue to the on hold state.

For each custom field, note their behavior—whether a field is mandatory or optional should be decided earlier.

Best practices for customizing JIRA

It is quite easy to create custom fields in JIRA, but as the instance grows, you could have lots of these fields. Always try to reuse similar fields. Try to use a generic name for your fields so that they can be reused in other projects. Contexts can also be used to use the same select list with different options in the dropdown in multiple projects. The best practices are discussed in detail in *Chapter 14, JIRA Best Practices*.

Issue workflow

How your issue will move from one state to another is defined in the workflow. First, decide how many states are required in the workflow and then decide the transitions between these states. Transitions define whether the issue can be moved from one state to another. For each transition, decide what conditions, validations, and post functions are required. In *Chapter 4, Customizing JIRA for Test Management*, we discussed the workflow customization in detail.

The whole project could use a single workflow, or each issue type could have its own workflow. Discuss this carefully with the project manager to understand how the issues move through various stages.

Setting up JIRA for helpdesk/support tickets

Companies that have software products and applications used by various customers or clients usually need a system where their users can raise their complaints, suggestions, and feedback. There are various dedicated open source and proprietary tools for this activity, but JIRA can be easily customized to act like a helpdesk or a support ticketing system.

Issue types

The helpdesk has a mechanism to capture the support requests for customers. We will also create a new issue type called *Support Request* for this purpose:

Scheme Name	Issue Types	Remarks
Helpdesk — Issue Type Scheme	Support Request Improvement Bug New Feature New User Request Sub-task	This creates issue types that are not available

Workflow

We will use a custom workflow for the Support Request issue type, which is described next. It is almost identical to the default JIRA workflow, except for two additional states — Waiting for Client and On Hold:

From	To	Remarks
Open	In Progress Resolved Closed Waiting for Client	**Condition**: Only the reporter can move the issue to *Waiting for Client* **Post Function**: This change the priority to minor
In Progress	Open Resolved Closed On Hold	**Condition**: Only the reporter can move the issue to *On Hold* **Post Function**: This change the priority to minor
Resolved	Closed Reopened	Issues in the resolved state can be moved to either the Closed state or the Reopened state
Reopened	Resolved Closed In Progress	Once an issue is reopened, it can be resolved again, closed, or moved to the In Progress state
Closed	Reopened	A closed issue can be reopened
Waiting for Client	Open	Once more clarity is received, an issue can be opened again
On Hold	In Progress	An On Hold issue can be moved to the In Progress state

Fields

The *Support Request* issue type will have a few additional fields apart from the default system JIRA fields:

Field Name	Type	Mandatory	Description
Project	Select List	Yes	Select the project name.
Issue Type	Select List	Yes	Enter the activity to be performed.
Summary	Text	Yes	Enter a brief description of the issue.
Priority	Select List	No	**Values:** Major Blocker Critical Minor Trivial
Due Date	Date Picker	No	Enter the due date of the issue, if any.
Component/s	Select List	No	The user can select the components if they are created by the project administrator. Each component in the project can have a dedicated Component Lead and that user can be configured to become the default assignee for the issues using the component.
Affects Version/s	Select List	Yes	Select the version for which this issue is raised.
Assignee	User Picker	No	Select the user who will work on this issue.
Reporter	User Picker	Yes	Select the reporter of the issue. The default is the creator.
Environment	Text Field	No	Specify under what system environment this issue was reported.
Description	Text Field	No	Enter the details of the issue in this field.
Attachment	File	No	Upload a file or screenshot.
Category	Select List	Yes	**Values:** Billing User Registration Installation User Interface Connectivity

These fields are shown to the user while creating a new issue of the type Support Request; for other issue types, use the system default fields.

Screen scheme

Now that we have decided what fields we want for Support Request, create a new screen called Support Request Screen:

Issue Type Screen Scheme Name	Screen Scheme	Issue Types	Screen
Helpdesk — Issue Type Screen Scheme	Helpdesk — Screen Scheme	Support Request	Support Request Screen
	Default Screen Scheme	Improvement Bug New Feature New User Request Subtask	Default Screen

Permission scheme

As we mentioned earlier, it is always desirable and easier to copy the default permission scheme and then make any changes in it. Let's name our new scheme Helpdesk — Permission Scheme.

The following table highlights only those permissions that are different than the default permission schemes:

Project Permission	Users/Groups/Project Roles
Assign Issue	Reporter
Delete Issues	Reporter
Work On Issues	Assignee

Also, as discussed in *Chapter 4, Customizing JIRA for Test Management*, we can also use Issue Security Scheme to hide a specific issue in the project from other users.

Setting up JIRA for requirement management

Let's take a look at the configuration for using the JIRA requirement management; we will store issues that are related to requirements. This will also ensure that expectations of the project are captured and later verified during testing.

Issue types

The following table lists the different issue types for requirement management:

Scheme Name	Issue Types	Remarks
Requirements—Issue Type Scheme	Requirements Documentation Change Request Improvement Bug New Feature New User Request Subtask	Create the issue types that are not available

Workflow

We will use a custom workflow for the Requirements issue type; it will be used to store the project requirements, and for the rest of the issue types, the default JIRA workflow will be used.

Requirements

The following table depicts the requirements workflow:

From	To	Remarks
Open	In Progress	A new issue can be moved to the In Progress state when the work starts
In Progress	Open Review	**Condition**: Only the assignee can move the issue to review
Review	In Progress Resolved	**Transition screen**: Ask the user to enter comments when moving the issue from Review to In Progress

From	To	Remarks
Resolved	Closed In Progress Reopened	Once resolved, the issue can then be closed, moved back to the In Progress state, or reopened again
Closed	Reopened	A closed issue can be reopened

Fields

The Requirements issue type will have a few additional fields apart from the default system JIRA fields. Similarly, we will also create a few new custom fields for the Documentation issue type.

Requirements

The following table displays information about the field names and its description:

Field name	Type	Mandatory	Description
Project	Select List	Yes	Select the project name.
Issue Type	Select List	Yes	Select the activity to be performed.
Summary	Text	Yes	Enter a brief description of the issue.
Due Date	Date Picker	No	Pick the due date of the issue if any.
Components	Select List	No	The user can select the components if they are created by the project administrator.
Assignee	User Picker	No	Select the user who will work on this issue.
Reporter	User Picker	Yes	Select the reporter of the issue. The default is the creator.
Description	Text Field	No	Enter the details of the issue in this field.
Attachment	File	No	Upload a file or screenshot.
Requirement Type	Select List	Yes	**Values**: Customer Functional Non-functional Design
Traceability	Text Field	No	In this field, the user can enter the changes made to a requirement over a period of time.

Documentation

The following table displays information about the field names and their description:

Field Name	Type	Mandatory	Description
Project	Select List	Yes	Select the project name.
Issue Type	Select List	Yes	Select the activity to be performed.
Summary	Text	Yes	Enter a brief description of the issue.
Due Date	Date Picker	No	Pick the due date of the issue, if any.
Components	Select List	No	The user can select the components if they are created by the project administrator.
Assignee	User Picker	No	Pick the user who will work on this issue.
Reporter	User Picker	Yes	Pick the reporter of the issue. The default is the creator.
Description	Text Field	No	Enter the details of the issue in this field.
Attachment	File	No	Upload a file or screenshot.
Document Type	Select List	Yes	**Values:** PDF DOC XLS
Document ID	Text Field	No	If documents are stored in the external system, then store its ID here.

These fields are shown to the user while creating a new issue of the type Support Request; for other issue types, use the system default fields.

Screen scheme

Now that we have decided what fields we want for Support Request, create a new screen called Requirements Screen. The following table displays information about the field names and its description:

Issue Type Screen Scheme Name	Screen Scheme	Issue Types	Screen
Requirements—Issue Type Screen Scheme	Requirements—Screen Scheme	Requirements	Requirements Screen
	Documentation—Screen Scheme	Documentation	Documentation Screen
	Default Screen Scheme	Change Request Improvement Bug New Feature New User Request Subtask	Default Screen

Permission scheme

As mentioned earlier, it is always desirable and easier to copy the default permission scheme and then make any changes in it. Let's name our new scheme Requirements—Permission Scheme.

The following table highlights only those permissions that are different than the default permission schemes:

Project Permission	Users/Groups/Project Roles
Assign Issue	Reporter
Delete Issues	Reporter
Work On Issues	Assignee

Setting up JIRA for bug tracking

JIRA can be used out of the box for bug tracking. It comes with a default issue type called Bug, along with other issue types. However, you may be required to do certain changes in the default configurations in the future, and it is a good idea to create custom schemes even for bug tracking. Of course, we will copy the default schemes and make changes in the copied configurations.

Issue types

The following are the issue types for bug tracking:

Scheme Name	Issue Types	Remarks
Default Issue Type Scheme	Improvement Bug New Feature New User Request Subtask	There's no need to create new issue types or new schemes here

Workflow

We will use a custom workflow for the Bug issue type; it will be used to store project requirements. For rest of the issue types, the default JIRA workflow will be used:

Bugs

The following is the workflow for bug tracking:

From	To	Remarks
Open	Confirmed Resolved Closed Waiting for Client	**Condition**: Only the assignee can confirm the Bug
Confirmed	In Progress Resolved	Once the issue is confirmed, move the issue to the In Progress state
In Progress	Open Resolved Closed On Hold	An issue in the In Progress state can be opened again, resolved, closed, or put in the On Hold state
Resolved	Closed Reopened	A resolved issue can be closed or reopened
Reopened	Resolved Closed In Progress	A reopened issue can be resolved, closed, or moved to the In Progress state
Closed	Reopened	A closed issue can be reopened again

The preceding workflow is similar to the default JIRA workflow, except for one additional state called Confirmed. Once the bug is raised, it is the responsibility of the assignee to check the bug first.

Fields

The Bug issue type will have few a additional fields apart from the default system JIRA fields:

Field Name	Type	Mandatory	Description
Project	Select List	Yes	Select the project name.
Issue Type	Select List	Yes	Select the activity to be performed.
Summary	Text	Yes	Enter a brief description of the issue.
Priority	Select List	No	**Values** Major Blocker Critical Minor Trivial
Due Date	Date Picker	No	Pick the due date of the issue, if any.
Component/s	Select List	No	The user can select the components if they are created by the project administrator.
Affects Version/s	Select List	Yes	Select the version for which this issue is raised.
Assignee	User Picker	No	Select the user who will work on this issue.
Reporter	User Picker	Yes	Select the reporter of the issue. The default reporter is the creator.
Environment	Text Field	No	Specify under what system environment this issue was reported.
Description	Text Field	No	Enter the details of the issue in this field.
Attachment	File	No	Upload a file or screenshot.

Field Name	Type	Mandatory	Description
Category	Select List	Yes	**Values:** Billing User Registration Installation User Interface Connectivity
Customer Name	Select List	No	If the application is used by multiple customers, use this field to capture their names

These fields are shown to the user while creating a new issue of the type Support Request; for other issue types, use the system default fields.

Screen scheme

Now that we have decided what fields we want for Bug, create a new screen called Bug Screen:

Issue Type Screen Scheme Name	Screen Scheme	Issue Types	Screen
Bug—Issue Type Screen Scheme	Bug—Screen Scheme	Support Request	Bug Screen
	Default Screen Scheme	Improvement Bug New Feature New User Request Subtask	Default Screen

Permission scheme

As we mentioned earlier, it is always desirable and easier to copy the default permission scheme and then make any changes in it. Let's name our new scheme Helpdesk—Permission Scheme.

The following table highlights only those permissions that are different than the default permission schemes:

Project Permission	Users/Groups/Project Roles
Assign Issue	Reporter
Delete Issues	Reporter
Work On Issues	Assignee
Move Issues	Project Role (Administrators)

Changes in the customizations

We discussed various use cases that can be implemented in JIRA. When you start using JIRA for the first time, you can never be exactly sure about the possible changes that may be required in these customizations. JIRA administrators can always make modifications in the schemes to accommodate further changes. However, it is always a good thing to set up a change control board in your company and check for the possible impact of these changes. We will discuss this in detail in *Chapter 14, JIRA Best Practices*.

Summary

In this chapter, we checked the sample implementation of a few use cases that can be implemented in JIRA. You could start your customizations by following the sample data given in this chapter; by now, you already know how to customize JIRA, but it is more important that you treat your JIRA customization as a project and prepare a configuration document to store your requirements, which we also discussed in this chapter.

In the next chapter, we will take a look at user management in JIRA. We will also understand how to configure the default global permission of the users to control all that they should have access to. We will also learn the importance of creating groups and their usage.

6
User Management, Groups, and Project Roles

JIRA could be used by 10 people or 10,000 people spread across multiple locations. Large companies have multiple teams working on different projects and using the same JIRA instance, so it is usually important to manage the permissions. Maybe there are certain projects that should be private to a certain team, or there could be third-party contractors working on a specific project and they should not have access to all the projects.

It is important to understand how to manage the users and groups in JIRA. In this chapter, we will also take a look at project roles—the set of people working on an individual project.

User and group management

JIRA is a web-based application used to track project issues that are assigned to people. The users to whom these issues will be assigned need to exist in the system. When JIRA is deployed in any organization, the first thing that should be done is to gather the list of people who would be using this tool; hence, their accounts need to be created in JIRA. Each user will have their username and password unique to them that allows them to log in to the system. JIRA has its own internal authentication mechanism as well as the ability to integrate with **Lightweight Directory Access Protocol (LDAP)**.

Deciding upon the creation of user accounts

In large organizations where there is no license limit or where there is a need to create users regularly, as in the case of a customer care system, JIRA can be configured in two modes—public and private. If you want to enable signup, then configure JIRA in public mode, and it will display a signup link on the user login screen. However, if you have a license limit in JIRA, then it is recommended that you use JIRA in private mode, and only in that case, can JIRA Administrators create the account.

Follow these steps:

1. Go to JIRA **Administration** | **System** | **General Configuration**:

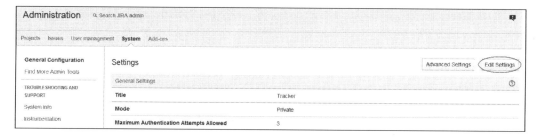

2. Click on the **Edit Settings** button in the top-right corner.
3. In the next screen, you will see a setting to change the mode.

Creating a new user

1. Go to JIRA **Administration** | **User management** | **Users** (under **USER MANAGEMENT**).
2. Click on the **Create User** button in the top-right corner.

3. In the pop-up window, enter **Username, Password, Full Name,** and **Email** and press the **Create** button.

4. You may also check **Send Notification Email**.

All new users are assigned to the **jira-users** group that has global permissions to access JIRA, that is, if the user is part of the **jira-users** group, then only he/she can log in to the system, and these users also count towards the license limit; of course, this can be modified by changing the global permissions.

JIRA has some preconfigured groups that have some extra permissions over **jira-users**. In our case, we will also assign this new user to the **jira-developers** group. The following screenshot encapsulates this discussion:

1. Once the user is created, go to **Actions | Edit Groups**.

2. In the pop-up window, select the **jira-developers** group and select the **Join Selected groups** button.

It is also possible to add more than one user to a group; let's take a look at that later in this chapter.

Password policy

Organizations usually have a password policy for security purposes. JIRA allows you to define such a password policy:

1. Go to **Administrator | System | Password Policy** (under **SECURITY**).

2. The password policy is disabled by default. JIRA offers two predefined policies, **Basic** and **Secure**, but we will define our own policy. Select **Custom**; it will then open up a new form where you can enter the minimum length and maximum length, and how many uppercase characters, digits, and special characters need to be there.

3. Click on the **Update** button to apply the new policy.

Creating a new group

Sometimes, you need to perform certain actions on all the users of a certain team; for example, you want to give extra permission to all the people working on a specific project. In such cases, a group can be created. It is nothing but a collection of users. Creating a group itself doesn't do anything. How that group will behave is defined in the permission scheme.

Let's understand how we can create a new group:

1. Go to JIRA **Administration | User management | Groups** (under **USER MANAGEMENT**).

2. On the right-hand side, there is an option to do an **Add Group**. Just enter **Name** for the group and press the **Add Group** button.

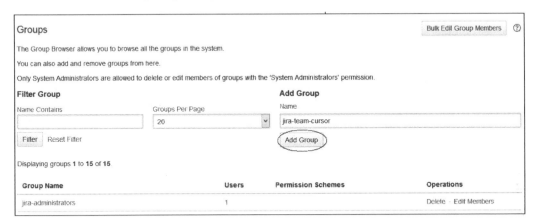

Once the group is added, it will be added in the following list on the same page.

It is very easy to add new users to a group:

1. Click on the **Edit Members** link under the **Operations** column for the group you want to modify.

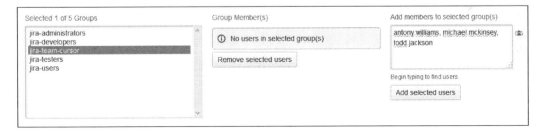

2. In the next section, type in the usernames of the users that need to be assigned to our new group and press the **Add selected users** button.

Once you have your groups created, along with the users who would be a part of it, you can then use them in a project permission scheme, or project roles.

Working with project roles

Every project is executed by different people, each with their own set of responsibilities. Usually, certain aspects of the project are taken care of by people who are part of a team. For instance, in the case of a software project, there will be a project lead who manages everything in the project and is responsible for overall progress, developers who work on the features, and then there is a team of testers to verify the built features. The first versions of JIRA had only groups, and JIRA administrators would end up creating multiple groups for various projects, such as proj-administrators, proj-developers, and so on. At the same time, the permission scheme for each project also needed to be defined for these groups. JIRA developers realized this problem and introduced the concept of a project role that allows not only JIRA administrators but also the project administrator to add/remove users to their project roles.

In JIRA, you could have roles that are defined globally and are available in all the projects, but people who are part of such roles would be different for each project. Just adding the project role and adding users to it won't have any effect until the permission schemes are modified by defining what a project role will do in the project.

Creating a project role

JIRA comes with three predefined roles, namely **Administrators**, **Developers**, and **Users**. You can also create new roles in JIRA. Follow these steps:

1. Go to JIRA **Administration | System | Roles** (under **SECURITY**):

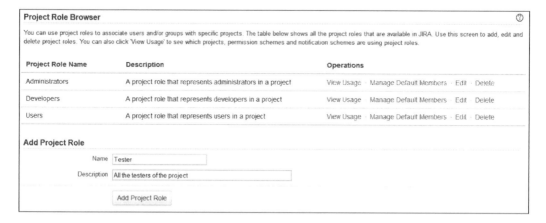

2. To add a new role, enter **Name** and **Description** of the role and press the **Add Project Role** button. A new role can be easily added in the system, but it is important to note here that adding a new role in JIRA won't have any effect on the project until we add users for each project and define the permissions in the scheme.

Adding users and groups in the project role

Now that we have a new project role, it is time to add a few users and groups for a particular project:

1. Go to any project's **Administration** tab and onward to **Roles**:

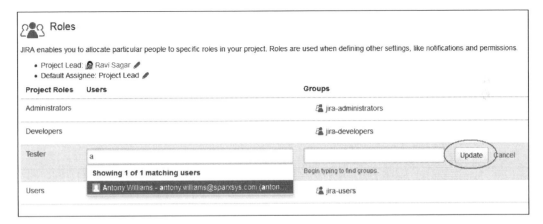

2. You can now see that our newly added role **Tester** is now available in the list of project roles. Let's add one user who would be part of this role and press the **Update** button. Similarly, a group can also be part of your project role.

Until now, we have created a project role and also added users to it for a particular project. You can do that for all the projects. These project roles are available for use in all of the projects in our instance, but now we need to define what permission this role would have in our project.

Giving permissions to your project role

The permissions of the Testers project role that we just added in our instance need to be configured by modifying **Permission Scheme** for the project:

1. Go to the project tab **Administration | Permissions**.

2. On the **Project Permission** page, click on the **Actions** button in the top-right corner and select **Edit permissions**.

3. Now you can modify Permission Scheme. Let's give them the permission to do a **Transition Issues**. So, they can move the issue in the workflow. Click on the **Add** link, as shown in this screenshot:

4. As shown in the following screenshot, on the next screen, first select **Project Role**, and from the dropdown, select the **Tester** project role:

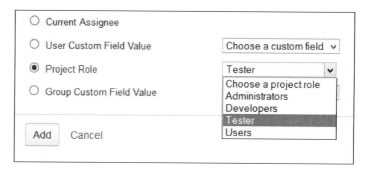

5. Click on the **Add** button.

You can add more permissions like this for your new role, and, of course, all the projects using this permission scheme will be affected.

Types of administrators

JIRA administrators have the ability to make changes to the system configuration and schemes and manage users. The administrative user is created when JIRA is installed. In big organizations where there is a team of people taking care of JIRA, there could be multiple JIRA administrators. There is a group called **jira-administrators** in JIRA. The administrative user that is created during installation is part of this group, and more users can be added to this later on.

Go to JIRA **Administration | System | Global Permissions** (under **SECURITY**):

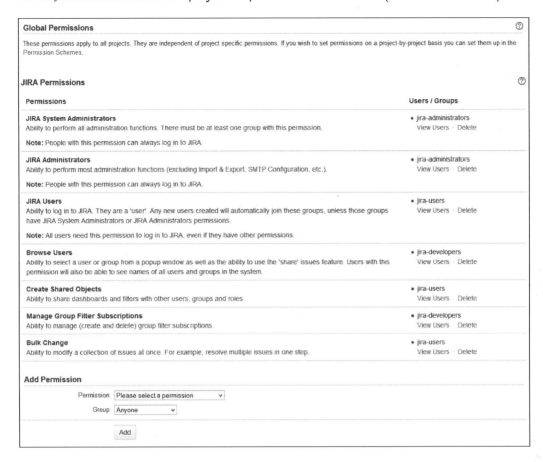

If you notice from the administrative point of view, JIRA offers two different permissions called **JIRA System Administrators** and **JIRA Administrators**.

JIRA System Administrators

Users who are part of this global permission can perform all the administrative functions. They can make changes in the configuration and scheme, perform system restore, and modify mail configurations as well.

JIRA Administrator

Even if your organization has multiple JIRA administrators, there are certain features that need to be restricted. A **JIRA Administrator** permission allows users to perform most of the administrative functions, except system restore, importing and exporting, and changes to the mail configurations as these features could potentially lead to system breakdown and may result in loss of data as well. So, it is advisable to give the **JIRA System Administrators** permission to only one or two people in the organization; the rest could have the **JIRA Administrators** permission.

Summary

In this chapter, you learned how to manage users and groups. To give access to new users and assign them to the right group is one of the most important activities of a JIRA administrator. The responsibility of adding new users in the system and assigning them to the right group is crucial for data integrity, and it should be in tune with your company's policies. You also learned how to create project roles and define their permissions.

In the next chapter, you will learn how you can integrate JIRA with LDAP, Crowd, and the JIRA user server. This way, users don't need to remember multiple logins for different tools, and it is also much easier for the administrators to manage users efficiently from a single place.

7
Configuring JIRA User Directories to Connect with LDAP, Crowd, and JIRA User Server

In companies with thousands of employees, there are several internal tools and systems. There are tools to track time, leave management, and intranet portals. It's very difficult to manage user accounts on multiple applications; companies use LDAP servers for user management, where a single user account works on more than one tool. JIRA also supports integration with LDAP. This is a great feature. It really helps system administrators to manage users. Apart from LDAP, we will also discuss how to connect JIRA to another JIRA instance for user management as well as for Crowd, which is a single sign-on software from Atlassian.

The authentication mechanism in JIRA

JIRA is a web-based tool used by multiple users, each having different permissions based on the group they are part of or to what role they are added in the project. JIRA has a built-in authentication mechanism known as **JIRA Internal Directory**, but it's possible to connect JIRA to external directories as well; let's take a look at how this is done.

JIRA Internal Directory

JIRA comes with an internal directory that is enabled by default; the first administrative user is a part of the internal directory and until you add another directory, all additional users are added in this internal directory. JIRA stores this in its own database.

Configuring LDAP

Lightweight Directory Access Protocol is an application protocol to query and modify information in directory services. In medium- to large-scale companies, where there are hundreds or thousands of users, everyone has their e-mails, phone numbers, and other attributes stored on a directory server. Users can find each other in this directory. Each user's login details are also stored and various applications can rely on directory services for authentication.

Instead of JIRA's internal authentication, it's possible to connect to existing directory services through LDAP:

1. Go to JIRA **Administration | User management | User Directories** (under **User Directories**). You will notice **JIRA Internal Directory** already added there, but after we add additional directories, such as LDAP or Crowd, the order in which the user is searched is defined using the **Order** column. Users may be present in one ore more directories, but it will be searched first in the directory that is listed at the top:

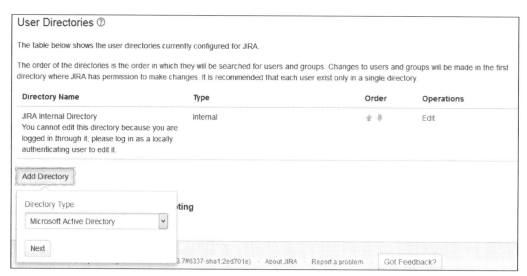

2. Click on **Add Directory**. A popup will appear. Select **Microsoft Active Directory** and click on **Next**.

3. In the following screenshot, we need to configure the LDAP user directory. First, fill in **Server Settings**:

    ○   Enter **Name** as **Active Director server** or any other useful name.

    ○   Select **Directory Type** as **Microsoft Active Directory**.

    ○   Enter **Hostname** of your LDAP server.

    ○   Enter the **Port** number of your LDAP server.

    ○   Enter **Username** of your LDAP server. It's usually in a format such as `user@domain.name` or `cn=username,dc=domain,dc=com`.

    ○   Enter **Password**.

4. Then, enter the **LDAP Schema** settings:

    Enter **Base DN**; it's usually in the `dc=domain,dc=local` format. Ask your LDAP administrators for specific information:

5. Now, select **LDAP Permissions** as **Read Only**, where the user information is only retrieved from the LDAP server. In this case, the password can only be changed from the LDAP server and not from the JIRA application. However, if you want users who are newly logged in to be automatically added to one or more JIRA groups, then select **Read Only, with Local Groups** and enter the name of the groups in the **Default Group Memberships:** field:

LDAP Permissions

○ Read Only

    Users, groups and memberships are retrieved from your LDAP server and cannot be modified in JIRA.

◉ Read Only, with Local Groups

    Users, groups and memberships are retrieved from your LDAP server and cannot be modified in JIRA. Users from LDAP can be added to groups maintained in JIRA's internal directory.

○ Read/Write

    Modifying users, groups and memberships in JIRA will cause the changes to be applied directly to your LDAP server. Your configured LDAP user will need to have modification permissions on your LDAP server.

Default Group Memberships: | jira-users, jira-developers |

    A comma-separated list of groups that users will be added to when they first log in. This will only be done once per user. These groups will be created if they don't already exist.

---

6. Click on the **Save and Test** button to save the configuration.

Now, a new user who is already a part of the LDAP server can log in to the JIRA instance using the same username and password. Also, this user will be added to the additional JIRA groups that we configured previously.

Understanding Base DN

The LDAP directory used in companies could have thousands of employees; it may not be relevant to give JIRA access to all the users in the company. For instance, consider a scenario when there are users in the U.S. as well as Asia, and access to JIRA needs to be given only to users in the U.S. Now, LDAP also has its own groups known as domains that can be leveraged to limit access to JIRA.

Refer to the following table to understand the possible Base DN for corresponding LDAP Domains:

LDAP Domain	Base DN	Remarks
example.com	dc=example,dc=com	All users in the LDAP directory can access JIRA
us.example.com	dc=us,dc=example,dc=com	Only U.S. users can access JIRA
asia.example.com	dc=asia,dc=example,dc=com	Only Asian users can access JIRA

Contact your JIRA administrator to understand the LDAP domain. Also, make sure that if you are using LDAP, then any user with an active account can log in to JIRA and your license limit can exhaust quickly.

Connecting to Crowd

Crowd is another application from Atlassian for single sign-on. This application can be used to manage multiple user directories. Organizations with an existing Crowd instance can connect their JIRA to utilize single sign-on:

1. Go to JIRA **Administration | User management | User Directories** (under **USER DIRECTORIES**).

2. Click on the **Add Directory** button and select **Directory Type:** as **Atlassian Crowd**:

3. On the next screen, fill in **Server Settings**:
   - Enter the **Name** of the Crowd server
   - Enter the **Server URL** of your crowd instance
   - Enter the name of the **Application Name**; this application needs to be created in the Crowd by the administrator
   - Provide the **Application Password** given to you by the Crowd administrator

4. Then, select **Crowd Permissions** as **Read/Write** if you want the changes to be applied to the Crowd server, or **Read Only** if you just want to retrieve the information.

5. First, click on **Test Settings** and if everything works, then you will be able to **Save and Test** the connection to the Crowd server.

Connecting to JIRA user server

In large organizations, there could be more than one instance of JIRA used by various teams or projects. Users may need to access all these instances to track projects; in such cases, separate accounts need to be created for the same person. It's not only cumbersome for the JIRA administrator, but also difficult for the user to remember more than one username and password. JIRA allows you to connect to another JIRA instance for user management:

1. Go to JIRA **Administration | User management | User Directories** (under **USER DIRECTORIES**).

2. Click on the **Add Directory** button and select **Directory Type:** as **Atlassian JIRA**:

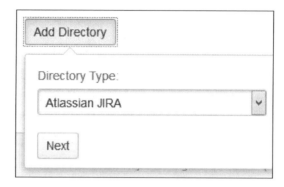

3. On the next screen, fill in **Server Settings**:
   - Enter the **Name** of the JIRA Server
   - Enter the **Server URL** of your JIRA instance
   - Enter the name of the **Application Name**; this application needs to be created in JIRA by the administrator
   - Provide the **Application Password** given to you by the JIRA administrator

4. Then, select **JIRA Server Permissions** as **Read/Write** if you want the changes to be applied to the JIRA server, or **Read Only** if you just want to retrieve the information.

5. First, click on **Test Settings** and if everything works, then you will be able to **Save and Test** the connection to the JIRA sever.

Allowing other applications to connect to JIRA

In the previous section, we connected one JIRA instance to another for user management. The instance used as a JIRA user server needs to have the application created so that other instances can connect to it:

1. Go to JIRA **Administration** | **User management** | **JIRA User Server**

   Click on the **Add application** button in the top-right corner:

Configure Other Applications ⑦   (+ Add application)

Other applications can use JIRA for users, groups and authentication. Configure these applications here.

Application name   **IP Addresses**   **Operations**

There are no other applications configured to use JIRA user management. [Click here to add one].

2. On the next screen, enter **Application name** as `jira-user-server` or anything meaningful.

3. Enter the **Password** for this application.

4. Finally, enter the IP address of the actual JIRA server in the **IP Addresses** field. This step is quite important. Without this step, the connection may not work.

The JIRA user server URL, application name, and password are important features to note here and need to be used in the JIRA instance that will connect to it. Allowing other applications from Atlassian, such as Confluence, to connect to JIRA to share the user base is possible because JIRA internally uses a trimmed version of Crowd.

Synchronizing user and group information

Now that we have seen how to connect JIRA to LDAP, Crowd, and another JIRA server, it's also important to understand how the user information is synchronized. Any new user who is a part of the directory should be able to log in to JIRA instance, but all new users who have recently been added to the directory will not be able to access JIRA until the user list is synchronized.

Go to JIRA **Administration** | **User management** | **User Directories** (under **USER DIRECTORIES**). Here, you will see the list of user directories added in the instance. There is a **Synchronise** link against each entry:

JIRA Server	Atlassian Crowd	⬆ ⬇	Disable : Edit : Test : Synchronise Last synchronised at 14/11/14 12.56 PM (took 8s). Full synchronisation completed successfully.

Click on the **Synchronise** link and JIRA will compare and fetch the list of users from the JIRA server; if there are new users on the server, they will be created in the instance. This will also create the groups in our JIRA instance.

Note that the users created via this synchronization will not be editable and you cannot delete them if the permission is set in the **Read Only** mode.

Summary

In this chapter, you learned how to integrate JIRA with LDAP, Crowd, and JIRA user server. This way, users don't need to remember multiple logins for different tools and it's also much easier for the administrators to manage users efficiently from a single place. You also learned how to create the application link on the JIRA server and discussed the synchronization of user accounts.

Until now, we have seen the power of JIRA and the flexibility it offers. JIRA can be customized very easily; we know that more functionality can be added to JIRA by installing add-ons from the marketplace. These add-ons are free as well as paid. It's also possible to create your own add-on to bring a new feature in JIRA and modify it. In the next chapter, we will take a look at how to create these add-ons along with some simple examples.

8

JIRA Add-on Development and Leveraging REST API

We already know that JIRA has a lot of features to offer. The best part is the customization feature. There are times when certain functionalities or customizations are required, but these are not supported by JIRA. However, many new features can be added in JIRA by installing add-ons from the Atlassian marketplace. JIRA has a marketplace where one can search for these add-ons. Some add-ons are free and some are paid add-ons. If you are looking for additional features, you can search on the marketplace for existing add-ons, but it's also possible to create your own add-ons, which requires a decent knowledge of Java. This chapter will give you enough information to get you started with JIRA's add-on development along with some simple examples.

Setting up the Atlassian plugin SDK

Atlassian provides a **Software Development Kit**, also known as an **SDK**, to develop add-ons. The SDK needs to be installed on your machine before starting the development. It can be installed on Windows, Linux, and Mac. Any of these operating systems can be used to develop add-ons. However, in this chapter, the instructions will focus only on the Windows platform. There are no specific recommended hardware requirements to install the Atlassian SDK; however, to get a decent performance, install it on a machine, which has a core i5 processor and 8 GB of RAM.

Download the Atlassian SDK for Windows at `https://marketplace.atlassian.com/download/plugins/atlassian-plugin-sdk-windows`.

Setting up the SDK prerequisites on a Windows system

The SDK requires the Java environment to be configured on your machine. In *Chapter 1, Planning Your JIRA Installation*, we discussed how to install the JDK. We had earlier installed the JDK at `C:\java`.

Verifying the JDK installation and the JAVA_HOME system variable

The Atlassian JDK needs Oracle's Java SE Development Kit installed on the system. Follow the steps mentioned in *Chapter 1, Planning Your JIRA Installation*, to install it and verify that the JAVA_HOME system variable is set up by following the steps mentioned here:

1. Open Command Prompt (cmd program) and enter the following command:

   ```
   echo %JAVA_HOME%
   ```

2. It should return the path where the JDK is installed. In our case, it's given as follows:

   ```
   c:\java
   ```

Verifying that JAVA_HOME\bin is present in the environment variable PATH

The JDK `bin` directory has executable files, such as `javac`, and it should be available to the Atlassian SDK.

All you need to do is append the following line to your existing `Path` system variable: `%JAVA_HOME%\bin` and perform these steps:

1. Open Command Prompt and enter the following command:

   ```
   javac -version
   ```

2. It should return the version of the JDK:

   ```
   javac 1.6.0_45
   ```

Installing the Atlassian SDK on Windows

The Atlassian SDK can be downloaded from `https://marketplace.atlassian.com/download/plugins/atlassian-plugin-sdk-windows`. This link will always give you the latest stable version of the SDK. Here, you will get an executable file called `sdk-installer-5.0.4.exe`. Perform the following steps to install the SDK on your Windows system:

1. After downloading the SDK installer, double-click on it and complete the installation.

2. Once the installation is complete, the installer prompts you to restart the computer. If the installer doesn't ask you to restart, check whether you are able to use atlas-commands; if not, then restarting the system is the safest way to make sure that the SDK is installed properly.

3. Open Command Prompt and enter the following command:

    `atlas-version`

4. It should return the following information:

You can see that it will tell you the version of the Atlassian SDK installed on the system and give you the details of the JDK installed as well.

At this point, everything is set up and you are now ready to start developing add-ons.

Getting familiar with the Atlassian SDK

When you ran the `atlas-version` command, it showed various details of the installed SDK. If you notice, `ATLAS Home` is the location where the Atlassian SDK is installed. Let's open this directory and check its content:

*   `apache-maven-3.2.1`: This Atlassian SDK uses Maven, which is a popular tool to build automation for Java projects.

- `bin`: This directory contains all the command-line tools that are used to develop add-ons. All the commands here are prefixed with `atlas-`.

- `repository`: This directory contains the actual code that the SDK relies on to develop add-ons.

The atlas command

We just discussed that all the commands are prefixed with `atlas-`. Before you start creating add-ons, a working JIRA instance is required. This will be used to test your add-ons. The `atlas-run-standalone` command is used to set up and start the JIRA instance for you. Perform the following steps:

1. Create a folder called `atlastutorial` in your `C` directory.

2. In Command Prompt, change directory using:

   `cd c:\atlastutorial`

3. Start JIRA using the following command:

   `atlas-run-standalone --product jira`

4. Depending on your internet connection, this command will take a few minutes to complete. It downloads the JIRA files and starts the instance on port `2990`:

   ```
   [INFO] Starting jira on the tomcat7x container on ports 2990
   (http), 55458 (rmi) and 8009 (ajp)

   [INFO] using codehaus cargo v1.4.7

   [INFO] [2.ContainerStartMojo] Resolved container artifact org.
   codehaus.cargo:cargo-core-container-tomcat:jar:1.4.7 for container
   tomcat7x

   [INFO] [talledLocalContainer] Tomcat 7.x starting...

   [INFO] [stalledLocalDeployer] Deploying [C:\atlastutorial\
   amps- standalone\target\jira\jira.war] to [C:\atlastutorial\amps-
   standalone/target\container\tomcat7x\cargo-jira-home/webapps]...

   [INFO] [talledLocalContainer] Tomcat 7.x started on port [2990]

   [INFO] jira started successfully in 734s at http://localhost:2990/
   jira

   [INFO] Type Ctrl-D to shutdown gracefully

   [INFO] Type Ctrl-C to exit
   ```

5. Enter `http://localhost:2990/jira` in your browser; the exact URL will also be displayed by the command.

6. Enter `admin` as the username and password.

This is your JIRA instance created after you set up the Atlassian SDK with **Test license for plugin developers**; we will use this to develop the JIRA add-ons.

Creating the Helloworld plugin

Now, we are ready to create our first add-on in JIRA, which will introduce new features to our instance. Any JIRA add-on contains a lot of files and has to follow a directory structure; the Atlassian SDK provides a command-line tool called `atlas-create-jira-plugin` to create a plugin.

If your existing JIRA is already running in Command Prompt, then stop it by clicking on *Ctrl + C* and perform these steps:

1. In Command Prompt, make sure that you are in the `c:\atlastutorial` directory.

2. Enter the following command and click on *ENTER*:

   atlas-create-jira-plugin

3. This command will respond and ask you to provide certain inputs. Use the values mentioned in the following table:

Define value for `groupId`	`com.atlassian.tutorial`
Define value for `artifactId`	`helloworld`
Define value for `version`	`1.0-Version`
Define value for `package`	`com.atlassian.tutorial.helloworld`

4. The `atlas-create-jira-plugin` command will prompt you to confirm the values you just entered. Click on *Y* to continue. A new `helloworld` folder will be created at `c:\atlastutorial\helloworld`.

If you take a look in the `c:\atlastutorial\helloworld` directory, you will find a skeleton of the plugin project with the following files and folders created by the `atlas-create-jira-plugin` command:

- `src`: This folder contains the source code of the plugin
- `LICENSE`: This file stores the plugin license information
- `pom`: This is the Maven configuration file
- `README`: This file contains brief instructions on how to run the plugin

Adding organization details in pom.xml

Open the pom.xml file, search the `<organization>` tag, and update the company name and the company URL. This information will be visible to the user who will install the plugin from the **Universal Plugin Manager (UPM)**:

```
<organization>
    <name>Sparxsys Solutions Pvt. Ltd.</name>
    <url>http://www.sparxsys.com/</url>
</organization>
```

Enter the company name within an enclosed `<name>` tag and the company URL within an enclosed `<url>` tag and save the file.

Loading the plugin in JIRA

We now have a plugin created with just a single command and you can actually load this plugin in JIRA. Although it has no functionality right now, we will still make an attempt to understand how to load this plugin in JIRA. Perform the following steps:

1. In Command Prompt, navigate to the `c:\atlastutorial\helloworld` directory.

2. Enter the following command and click on *ENTER*:

   `atlas-run`

3. This command will create a folder called the `target` subdirectory in the `helloworld` directory. After some time, a JIRA instance will start.

4. Enter `http://localhost:2990/jira` in your browser; the exact URL will also be displayed by the command.

5. Enter `admin` for both, username and password.

6. Go to JIRA **Administration | Add-ons | Manage add-ons** (under **ATLASSIAN MARKETPLACE**).

7. Under **User-installed add-ons**, you will find the new add-on called `helloworld`:

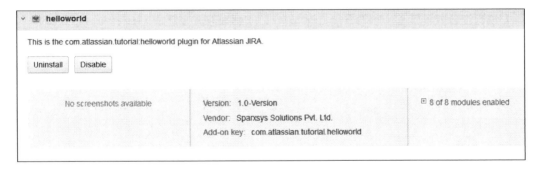

As you can see in the preceding screenshot, the `helloworld` add-on is now loaded in your JIRA instance. Also, the version information that we filled in while creating the plugin is visible here; the hyperlinked company name is also displayed.

Setting up the Eclipse IDE

We have set up the development environment and installed the Atlassian SDK. You also learned how to create a skeleton plugin; apart from showing up in the **Universal Plugin Manager**, this plugin did not perform any other function. We will add a few functionalities in our plugin, but before that, let's configure the popular Eclipse IDE, which really assists in developing JIRA add-ons.

Downloading the Eclipse IDE

The Eclipse IDE is used for development purposes in various programming languages. However, we will install the Eclipse IDE for Java EE Developers (Indigo). Perform the following steps:

Download the Eclipse IDE for Java EE developers from `http://www.eclipse.org/downloads/packages/eclipse-ide-java-ee-developers/indigosr2`.

Extract the content of the downloaded file in the `C:\eclipse` directory.

Configuring Eclipse to start under the JDK

We need to tell our Eclipse IDE to start and use the JDK that we have already installed on our machine:

1. Open the `C:\eclipse\eclipse.ini` file.

2. Add a `-vm` entry before the `-vmargs` entry. We should define the JDK path here; the final `eclipse.ini` file should look similar to the following code:

    ```
    -startup
    plugins/org.eclipse.equinox.launcher_1.3.0.v20140415-2008.jar
    --launcher.library
    plugins/org.eclipse.equinox.launcher.win32.win32.x86_64_1.1.200.
    v20140603-1326
    -product
    org.eclipse.epp.package.jee.product
    --launcher.defaultAction
    openFile
    --launcher.XXMaxPermSize
    256M
    -showsplash
    org.eclipse.platform
    --launcher.XXMaxPermSize
    256m
    --launcher.defaultAction
    openFile
    --launcher.appendVmargs
    -vm
    c:/java/bin
    -vmargs
    -Dosgi.requiredJavaVersion=1.6
    -Xms40m
    -Xmx512m
    ```

3. Save and close the file.

Updating the installed JREs in Eclipse

The Eclipse JREs need to be updated with the ones that are currently installed in our JDK version. Perform the following steps if you are not sure whether you have the updated JREs or not:

1. Double-click on the `C:\eclipse\eclipse.exe` application and it will start the Eclipse IDE.

2. In the menu bar, click on **Windows | Preferences**.

    On the left-hand side, enter `Installed JREs`; this will filter down the list; after that, double-click on **Installed JREs**.

3. On the right-hand side, click on the **Add** button and select **Standard VM**.

4. In **JRE home**, enter `C:\java` as the location of the directory and click on the **Finish** button:

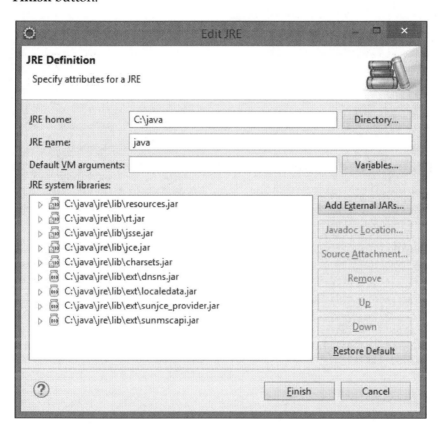

5. Finally, the JREs will be updated and it should look similar to the following screenshot:

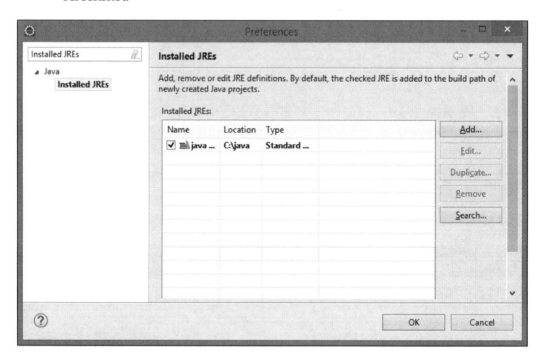

Installing the Maven plugin

The JIRA add-ons development is based on Maven and there is an Eclipse plugin for Maven that needs to be installed. Perform the following steps:

1. In the Menu bar, click on **Help | Install New Software...**.

2. In the **Available Software** window, click on the **Add** button.

3. Enter **Name** as `Sonatype M2Eclipse`. Enter `http://download.eclipse. org/technology/m2e/releases` as **Location** and click on the **OK** button.

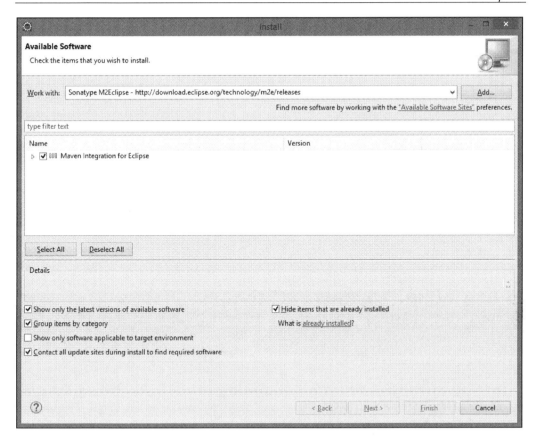

4. Select **Maven Integration for Eclipse** and click on the **Finish** button.

5. Finally, restart Eclipse for these changes to take effect.

Configuring the Maven plugin

Finally, we need to tell the Maven Eclipse plugin the location of Maven that is installed on our machine. The Maven directory is placed in the ATLAS Home directory. You can run the atlas-version command on your machine to find out the exact location of ATLAS Maven Home. Just copy this location and perform the following steps:

1. In the menu bar, click on **Windows | Preferences**.

2. On the left-hand side, enter Maven; it will filter down the options available for **Maven**.

3. Click on **Installation** and then click on the **Add** button.

4. The **Installation type** should be **External**, copy the ATLAS Maven Home directory, and click on the **Finish** button.

Now, we are all set to start developing our JIRA add-ons using Eclipse.

Adding functionality to the Skeleton plugin

The helloworld plugin (which we created earlier) lacks any functionality; we loaded the plugin in JIRA but it did not do anything apart from just showing up in the **Universal Plugin Manager**. Now that we have also configured the Eclipse IDE, let's add a few functionalities to our helloworld plugin.

As an example, we will add a custom link in the JIRA Main navigation bar using this plugin.

Importing the Helloworld plugin in Eclipse

We can use the Eclipse IDE and import our plugin, but before we do that, there are Eclipse configuration files that need to be generated in the helloworld plugin project. Perform the following steps:

1. In Command Prompt, navigate to the C:\atlastutorial\helloworld directory.

2. Enter the following command and click on *ENTER*:

   ```
   atlas-mvn eclipse:eclipse
   ```

3. This command will return the following message:

   ```
   [INFO] ------------------------------------------------------------
   [INFO] BUILD SUCCESS
   [INFO] ------------------------------------------------------------
   [INFO] Total time: 56.519 s
   [INFO] Finished at: 2014-11-28T11:15:35+05:30
   [INFO] Final Memory: 21M/102M
   [INFO] ------------------------------------------------------------
   ```

4. Now, we are ready to import the plugin in Eclipse. In the menu bar, click on **File | Import....**

5. Select **Existing Projects into Workspace** under **General** and click on the **Next** button.

6. Enter C:\atlastutorial\helloworld in the **Select root** directory and click on the **Finish** button.

Now, you should see the `helloworld` plugin project loaded on the left-hand side under **Project Explorer**, as shown in the following screenshot. If you notice the welcome screen in your SDK, then close it.

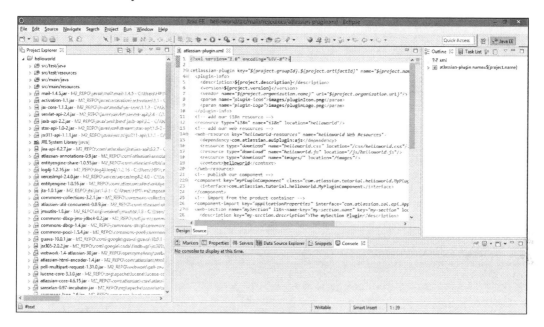

Creating a menu in JIRA's top navigation bar

We will take a very simple example to understand how to add new functionalities in JIRA. You are already familiar with JIRA's top navigation bar. From the JIRA frontend, it's not possible to add a new menu item in it; however, we will modify our `helloworld` plugin to add this menu item.

The JIRA functionality and the behavior of its various sections are controlled by various modules. If we want to do any modification to JIRA's top navigation bar, then we need to add two modules called `Web Section` and `Web Item`. Perform the following steps:

1. In Command Prompt, navigate to the `c:\atlastutorial\helloworld` directory.

2. Enter the following command and click on *ENTER*:

    `atlas-create-jira-plugin-module`

3. The command will respond and prompt you to enter a specific number for various modules. Type 30 for **Web Section**.

4. The command will again respond and ask you to provide certain inputs. Use the values as mentioned in this table:

Enter Plugin Module Name	`mySection`
Enter Location	`contact-us-links`
Show Advanced Setup?	N

5. The command will ask you, **Add Another Plugin Module?** Click on *Y*.

6. The command will respond and prompt you to enter a specific number for various modules. Type 25 for `Web Item`.

7. The command will again respond and ask you to provide certain inputs. Use the values as mentioned in this table:

Enter Plugin Module Name	`Contact Us`
Enter Section	`system.top.navigation.bar`
Enter Link URL	`http://www.sparxsys.com/contact`
Show Advanced Setup?	N

8. The command will ask you to `Add Another Plugin Module?` Click on *N*.

9. Run the `atlas-run` command from within your plugin project directory and once JIRA starts running, open it in the browser:

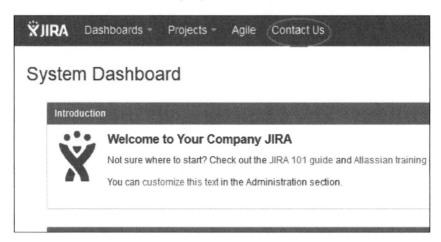

You should now see a new menu item called **Contact Us**, which we have added from our `helloworld` plugin.

We have just started to add the functionality in the skeleton plugin project. Although we just added a link in the JIRA navigation bar, there is a lot more that can be done.

If you are starting the JIRA add-ons development, then start by going through the tutorials mentioned on the Atlassian website at `https://developer.atlassian.com/display/JIRADEV/Tutorials`.

So far in this chapter, we have discussed creating add-ons that extend JIRA's functionalities, but it's also possible to interact with JIRA from other applications as well. JIRA comes with the **REST API**, which allows you to manipulate JIRA's data and configurations from external applications. The JIRA API that adheres to the principles of REST does not require the client to know anything about the structure of the API. Rather, the server needs to provide whatever information the client needs to interact with the service.

Various programming languages are capable of making REST calls. In the following section, we will discuss how to interact with JIRA REST APIs along with some examples in detail.

Leveraging the JIRA REST API

We have discussed how to start building add-ons that extend JIRA's functionalities. The add-ons are integrated very closely with JIRA's existing features. However, there are times when you need to add a few functionalities on top of JIRA so that other tools can interact with JIRA. JIRA provides access to various operations via REST, which is a short form of **Representational State Transfer**.

Examples of a few operations that can be performed via REST

- Issue operations - create/modify/delete issues
- Search issues
- Create users
- Group management - add/remove users from a group

There are a lot of resources that are available via REST API. You can get the detailed list of all the resources at `https://docs.atlassian.com/jira/REST/latest/`.

Use cases of JIRA REST API

Having the ability to interact with JIRA through external applications opens up a lot of possibilities. Let's take a look at some of the use cases of functionality that can be built on top of JIRA:

- Generating business intelligence reports
- Generating bulk operations in JIRA
- Building custom interface for clients

Generating Business Intelligence reports

JIRA comes with a lot of ready - made reports, which we discussed in detail in *Chapter 3, Reporting – Charts to Visualize the Data*, but companies use the **Business Intelligence (BI)** tool to generate reports that are customized to their needs; in JIRA, all the data is stored in Issues, which can be fetched from REST API.

Bulk operations in JIRA

System administrators in JIRA are often faced with situations where they need to perform various operations in bulk. For instance, if a new team in the company wants to start using JIRA, then several user accounts need to be created. JIRA's REST API provides the resources to create a user account. After the accounts are created, they also need to be added to the correct group. Although the JIRA group management interface already provides the mechanism to modify user groups by entering their username as a comma-separated list, modifying groups can also be done via the REST API.

The scripts can be created to perform such bulk operations and it can be run whenever needed.

Building a custom interface for clients

We have already seen that it's very easy to customize permissions in JIRA and give limited access of your JIRA instance to your clients. However, it's also possible to create a simple web interface that has a login box for authentication, a form to raise tickets, and a simple list of issues for a particular project or client. This web application can internally interact with JIRA and it acts like the backend to store and retrieve client tickets.

JIRA's REST API browser

REST calls are made by calling the `http://jira.sparxsys.com/rest/api/2/` `RESOURCE` URL and most programming languages (such as Java and PHP) support them; however, before you can develop the functionalities to interact with JIRA using REST, you need to test it.

The Atlassian SDK that you have installed comes with a nifty tool called REST API Browser. It helps you explore the APIs and also test it. Perform these steps:

1. Run the `atlas-run` command, as we did earlier in this chapter. It will start the JIRA instance.

2. Enter `http://localhost:2990/jira` in your browser; the exact URL will also be displayed by the command.

3. Enter `admin` for both, username and password.

4. Go to JIRA **Administrator | System | REST API Browser** (under **ADVANCED**).

5. On the left-hand side, you will find the list of all the resources that REST API has to offer:

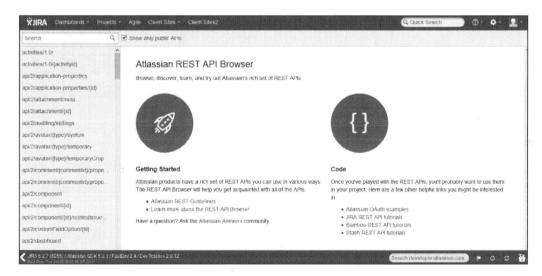

6. Click on any one of the resources and on the right-hand side of the main window; this particular resource can be tested by passing optional parameters.

Let's take a look at some examples to test REST API.

Fetching user details

On the left-hand side, either scroll or navigate to find **api/2/user** and click on it:

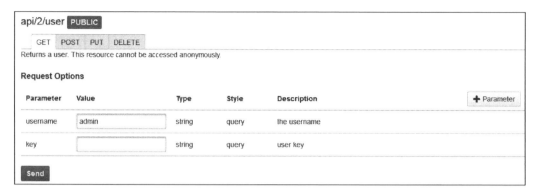

Enter `admin` as the value in the **username** parameter and click on the **Send** button. You will see the following response:

```
Response

GET  http://localhost:2990/jira/rest/api/2/user?username=admin (200)

Server: Apache-Coyote/1.1
x-arequestid: 822x6765x1
X-ASESSIONID: 1nxbf6u
X-Seraph-LoginReason: OK
x-ausername: admin
Cache-Control: no-cache, no-store, no-transform
X-Content-Type-Options: nosniff
Content-Type: application/json;charset=UTF-8
Transfer-Encoding: chunked
Date: Mon, 15 Dec 2014 08:12:50 GMT
```

```
 1  {
 2    "self": "http://localhost:2990/jira/rest/api/2/user?username=admin",
 3    "key": "admin",
 4    "name": "admin",
 5    "emailAddress": "admin@example.com",
 6    "avatarUrls": {
 7      "16x16": "http://localhost:2990/jira/secure/useravatar?size=xsmall&avatarId=10122",
 8      "24x24": "http://localhost:2990/jira/secure/useravatar?size=small&avatarId=10122",
 9      "32x32": "http://localhost:2990/jira/secure/useravatar?size=medium&avatarId=10122",
10      "48x48": "http://localhost:2990/jira/secure/useravatar?avatarId=10122"
11    },
12    "displayName": "admin",
13    "active": true,
14    "timeZone": "Asia/Calcutta",
15    "groups": {
16      "size": 3,
17      "items": []
18    },
19    "expand": "groups"
20  }
```

The response is actually in a JSON format and you can see that it has returned the details of the `admin` user. However, the groups that this user are a part of are not returned in this response, but it's possible to fetch this information as well. Perform these steps:

1. Click on the **Parameter** button on the right-hand side.
2. Enter `expand` in the **Parameter** column.
3. Enter `groups` in the **Value** column.
4. Click on the **Send** button again.

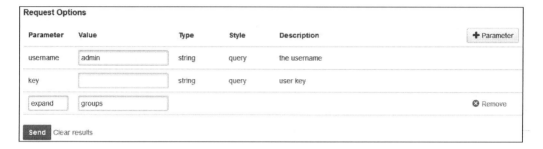

The following response is generated:

```
1   {
2     "self": "http://localhost:2990/jira/rest/api/2/user?username=admin",
3     "key": "admin",
4     "name": "admin",
5     "emailAddress": "admin@example.com",
6     "avatarUrls": {
7       "16x16": "http://localhost:2990/jira/secure/useravatar?size=xsmall&avatarId=10122",
8       "24x24": "http://localhost:2990/jira/secure/useravatar?size=small&avatarId=10122",
9       "32x32": "http://localhost:2990/jira/secure/useravatar?size=medium&avatarId=10122",
10      "48x48": "http://localhost:2990/jira/secure/useravatar?avatarId=10122"
11    },
12    "displayName": "admin",
13    "active": true,
14    "timeZone": "Asia/Calcutta",
15    "groups": {
16      "size": 3,
17      "items": [
18        {
19          "name": "jira-administrators",
20          "self": "http://localhost:2990/jira/rest/api/2/group?groupname=jira-administrators"
21        },
22        {
23          "name": "jira-developers",
24          "self": "http://localhost:2990/jira/rest/api/2/group?groupname=jira-developers"
25        },
26        {
27          "name": "jira-users",
28          "self": "http://localhost:2990/jira/rest/api/2/group?groupname=jira-users"
29        }
30      ]
31    },
32    "expand": "groups"
33  }
```

You can see that in the new response, the groups that this user belongs to are also fetched by specifying additional parameter.

JIRA REST API browser is a great tool to get familiar with all the available resources and it really assists in actual development.

Sample code to interact with the REST API

The REST API is supported by a variety of languages (such as Java, PHP, Python, and so on). In this chapter, we will discuss a couple of code examples in the PHP language. PHP is a popular language used in web applications. The following examples are written in PHP, but even if you are familiar with other languages like Java, then you should be able to understand the concept explained here.

To install PHP quickly along with Apache, the XAMPSERVER package can be installed from `https://www.apachefriends.org/`.

Creating an issue using PHP

The sample code to create an issue using PHP is:

```php
<?php

define('JIRA_URL', 'http://localhost:2990/jira');
define('USERNAME', 'admin');
define('PASSWORD', 'admin');

//The function that is making the REST call using Curl Protocol

function post_to($resource, $data) {
  $curlname=CURLOPT_POST;
  $curlvalue=1;
  $jdata = json_encode($data);
  $ch = curl_init();
  curl_setopt_array($ch, array(
  $curlname => $curlvalue,
  CURLOPT_URL => JIRA_URL . '/rest/api/latest/' . $resource,
  CURLOPT_USERPWD => USERNAME . ':' . PASSWORD,
  CURLOPT_POSTFIELDS => $jdata,
  CURLOPT_HTTPHEADER => array('Content-type: application/json'),
  CURLOPT_RETURNTRANSFER => true
  ));
  $result = curl_exec($ch);
  curl_close($ch);
```

```
    return json_decode($result);
}

function create_issue($issue) {
    return post_to('issue', $issue);
}

//The issue details
$new_issue = array(
'fields' => array(
'project' => array('key' => 'GEN'),
'summary' => 'Test via REST',
'description' => 'Description of issue goes here.',
'issuetype' => array('name' => 'Task')
)
);

//Call the function to create the issue
$result = create_issue($new_issue);

//Print the output
if (property_exists($result, 'errors')) {
    echo "Error(s) creating issue:\n";
    var_dump($result);
} else {print_r($result);
    echo "New issue created at " . JIRA_URL ."/browse/{$result->key}\n";
}

?>
```

The preceding code creates an issue in a JIRA project with the GEN Project Key and the Task Issue Type. Let's understand what this code does.

Authenticating with JIRA

First, we need to define our JIRA URL, username, and password for authentication. Note that this user should have the permission to create the issue in the project:

```
define('JIRA_URL', 'http://localhost:2990/jira');
define('USERNAME', 'admin');
define('PASSWORD', 'admin');
```

Making the REST call to create the issue

The `curl_exec()` PHP function is used to make the REST call using the `curl` protocol. This function accepts the parameters to make the REST call. The username, password, and the issue data are passed in the following code:

```
function post_to($resource, $data) {
  $curlname=CURLOPT_POST;
  $curlvalue=1;
  $jdata = json_encode($data);
  $ch = curl_init();
  curl_setopt_array($ch, array(
  $curlname => $curlvalue,
  CURLOPT_URL => JIRA_URL . '/rest/api/latest/' . $resource,
  CURLOPT_USERPWD => USERNAME . ':' . PASSWORD,
  CURLOPT_POSTFIELDS => $jdata,
  CURLOPT_HTTPHEADER => array('Content-type: application/json'),
  CURLOPT_RETURNTRANSFER => true
  ));
  $result = curl_exec($ch);
  curl_close($ch);
  return json_decode($result);
}

function create_issue($issue) {
  return post_to('issue', $issue);
}
```

Issuing data and printing the output

The issue that needs to be created has a lot of information, such as the project key, summary, description, and issue type. This information is stored in the array. Finally, the output is printed when the code is run:

```
$new_issue = array(
'fields' => array(
'project' => array('key' => 'GEN'),
'summary' => 'Test via REST',
'description' => 'Description of issue goes here.',
'issuetype' => array('name' => 'Task')
)
);

//Call the function to create the issue
$result = create_issue($new_issue);
```

```php
//Print the output
if (property_exists($result, 'errors')) {
  echo "Error(s) creating issue:\n";
  var_dump($result);
} else {print_r($result);
  echo "New issue created at " . JIRA_URL ."/browse/{$result->key}\n";
}
```

After you run the PHP code, you will get an output, as shown in the following command:

```
New issue created at http://hp:2990/jira/browse/GEN-2
```

Fetching issue details using PHP

The previous example where we created the issue using the REST API was quite simple. Now, let's understand how to fetch the issue details that we just created:

```php
<?php

$username = 'admin';
$password = 'admin';

$url = 'http://localhost:2990/jira/rest/api/latest/issue/GEN-1';

$curl = curl_init();
curl_setopt($curl, CURLOPT_USERPWD, "$username:$password");
curl_setopt($curl, CURLOPT_URL, $url);
curl_setopt($curl, CURLOPT_RETURNTRANSFER, 1);
curl_setopt($curl, CURLOPT_FOLLOWLOCATION, 1);
curl_setopt($curl, CURLOPT_SSL_VERIFYPEER, 0);
curl_setopt($curl, CURLOPT_SSL_VERIFYHOST, 0);

$issue_list = (curl_exec($curl));
echo '<pre>';
print_r(json_decode($issue_list));
echo '</pre>';
?>
```

This is a simple code that is just fetching the details of the GEN-1 issue, which we created in the previous example. The output returned by the REST API is the JSON file. We have converted the JSON data to an array using the json_decode() PHP function and printed it using the print_r() function.

The previous code can be used to fetch user and group details; just change the $url variable.

Summary

In this chapter, you learned how to develop add-ons development for JIRA. Whenever the existing functionality is not sufficient to serve your needs, the add-ons can be developed for JIRA. These add-ons are developed in the Java language and also utilizes Apache Maven for build automation. In this chapter, we discussed how to set up the development environment and the Eclipse IDE. We also created a skeleton plugin project.

In the next chapter, you will learn how to migrate data to JIRA using the CSV file. JIRA provides migration tools for Bugzilla, Mantis, and a few other issue trackers, but if your existing issue tracker has a lot of customizations, then it's always preferable to migrate the data using CSV import, which is quite powerful. With careful planning, it can import complex data into JIRA. We will also take a look at the major aspects of JIRA's CSV import.

9
Importing and Exporting Data in JIRA

The data stored in JIRA is quite critical for companies and JIRA administrators should make sure that regular backups of data are taken. In fact, there should be a policy to take backups. In this chapter, we will discuss how to perform regular backups in JIRA and where these backups are stored. Most importantly, we will also discuss how to restore these backups.

There are a lot of other tools that are used in companies; tools such as Mantis and Bugzilla are quite popular bug trackers. When you move to JIRA, it would be great if your existing issues are migrated from these tools to JIRA, but migrating can be a complex task. JIRA comes with some tools to import data from external tools; however, JIRA has a powerful feature to import issues from plain CSV files too. With proper planning, data from any tool can be exported into CSV, and from CSV, it can be imported into JIRA.

The Backup System

JIRA administrators should pay a lot of attention to taking regular backups of data and its configurations. Luckily, JIRA comes with a handy tool to generate backups. It not only contains data (such as Issues and Projects), but it also contains JIRA configurations that are stored in the backup file, which means that when you restore the system, all the data along with various schemes for Issue Types, Workflows, will also be restored.

The backup system provided in the UI of JIRA is not much efficient when you have thousands of issues. For this, the recommended approach is to manually take a backup of your database. The details of this backup approach can be found at https://confluence.atlassian.com/display/DOC/Production+Backup+Strategy.

Generating the backup

The JIRA backup tool can be used to perform backups as and when you require. Usually, before making any major configuration changes in JIRA, you should take a backup. Also, when you install a new add-on in JIRA, it's always advisable to take a backup. Of course, you should have a staging instance that should be an exact copy of your production one. You should do all the testing on the staging instance first, but you never know when things could go wrong. As good practice, always take a backup before performing any major configuration changes.

Perform these steps to take a backup in JIRA using the JIRA backup tool:

1. Navigate to **JIRA Administration | System | Backup System** (under **IMPORT & EXPORT**):

2. You will then see the **Backup JIRA data** page.

3. Specify the **File name** and click on the **Backup** button to generate the backup file. It's a good idea to use timestamp in **File name**.

4. The tool will then generate the backup file and give you the complete path of the file. You can copy this to some other location:

Backup JIRA data

Data exported to: **C:\jira\home\export\2014-12-09-backup.zip**

The backup files are stored in the JIRA HOME directory under the export folder.

Backing up of attachments

JIRA's data consists of details of Issues, Projects, and various configurations, but there are file attachments too that are attached to Issues. The **Backup JIRA data** tool generates an XML file that stores information, but it cannot back up the file attachments.

These attachments are stored in the JIRA HOME directory under the data\ attachments folder. You should copy the attachments folder as well if the file needs to be backed up. Usually, this is done when the JIRA instance needs to be migrated to a new server. The file attachments are organized in different folders for every project and the Project Key is the name of the folder:

- The name of the attachment folder is Project Key, for example, DPO

- The files are store within a subfolder whose name is the same as the Issue ID, for example, DPO-6

Using this organization, the attachment folder is easily restored.

Generating automatic backups

The backup that we just generated is usually triggered just before JIRA Administrator needs to perform some major changes in the configuration. However, as good practice, it would be great if these backups are generated automatically everyday or perhaps every week.

JIRA has the option to run a particular class automatically after a set time. JIRA comes with a couple of services preconfigured, but you can also add yours. Perform the following steps:

1. Navigate to JIRA **Administrator** | **System** | **Services** (under **ADVANCED**).

2. You will get the list of **Services** that come preconfigured when you install JIRA:

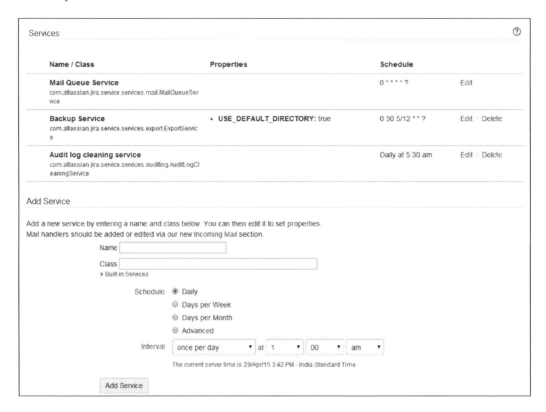

The first service in the list is the **Mail Queue Service**, which is responsible for taking regular backups. The **Schedule** is the interval after which the services will run automatically. In the case of **Backup Service**, the **Schedule** in minutes is 720, which is 12 hours; this means that after every 12 hours, the backup will be generated and placed in the export directory under JIRA HOME.

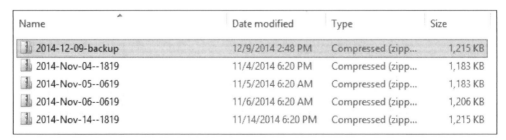

As you can see in the preceding screenshot, there are backup files generated by the JIRA service, except `2014-12-09-backup`, which we generated manually. The format of the backup file remains the same irrespective of whether you generate it manually or if it's generated automatically.

As good practice, always copy the backup files along with its attachments to a separate server. If something goes wrong with the server and if the backups are also kept on the same machine, then they will also be lost. So, it's good to have them copied to a separate server. Preferably, write scripts to automate the process of copying backups to a backup server.

The Restore System utility

Now, you have learned how to generate the backup manually using JIRA's **Backup System** tool and by relying on **JIRA Service**. There are two scenarios when these backup files are useful to you:

- One is when your server crashes
- Secondly, when you want to migrate your JIRA instance to a new machine

JIRA comes with the utility to **Restore System**; it basically wipes out the existing data/configuration and replaces it with one on the backup files; hence, you have to be very careful when using the **Restore System** utility. As a thumb rule, always perform the restore process on a test environment; this will also give you a chance to learn and fix any errors that you may encounter.

In this example, we will restore the `2014-12-09-backup.zip` backup file, which we generated in the earlier section.

For this exercise, you should have a blank JIRA installation on a different machine with the same version as the one used to generate the backup. Perform the following steps:

1. Copy the backup file stored in the `JIRA HOME` directory under the `import` folder.
2. Navigate to **JIRA Administrator | System | Restore System** (under **IMPORT & EXPORT**):
3. Enter **File name** as `2014-12-09-backup.zip`, which is the backup file we generated previously.
4. Leave the **License** field empty; the license details of the source instance are stored in the backup file, which can be restored in the target instance; if you want to use a new license, only then enter it in this field.

5. In the **Outgoing Mail** field, select **Disable**. This will ensure that e-mails are not being sent to anyone when the restore process takes place.

6. Click on the **Restore** button:

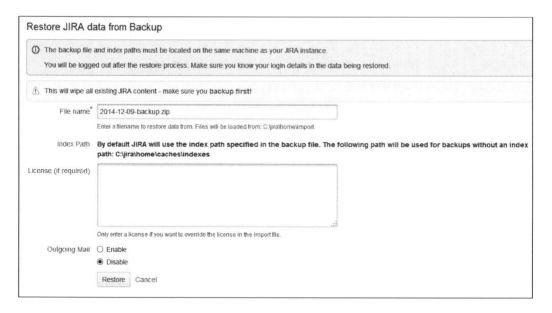

7. The restore process will start reading the backup file and also display the restore progress. This whole restore process can take several minutes depending on the size of the backup file:

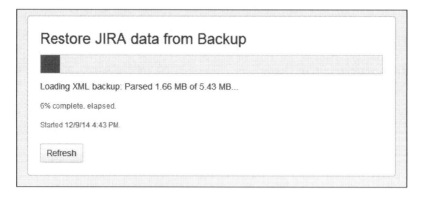

8. Once the restore process is complete, you will get a confirmation message:

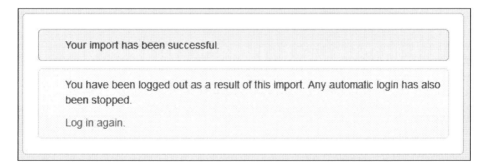

After the restore process is completed, you can log in to the JIRA instance using the login and password credentials of the instance from which the backup was generated. Your login of the current JIRA instance will not work because the whole data is wiped out and replaced by the backup file.

You can verify the following things after the restoration:

- Issue count
- List of projects
- List of configurations
- User count

If these things match with your old instance and the restored instance, then the restore process was successful.

The Project Import utility

The **Restore System** procedure is performed when the complete instance has to be restored or moved to another server, but there can be a scenario when you just need to restore a single project from another JIRA instance.

Let's take an example of a company that has multiple JIRA instances used by various other business units. These business units work independently of each other; they have different teams and work from different geographic locations. As you know, these days companies do reorganization quite often. Due to this reorganization process, a few projects from one business unit need to be transferred to another business unit. All the project code and documents along with the projects need to be transferred as well.

In this case, we cannot simply take a backup of one instance and restore it in another because it will wipe out the data in the target instance. The restore process has to be done only for a few selected projects.

Atlassian understood this scenario and provided a tool called **Project Import** to perform just that:

1. Navigate to JIRA **Administration | System | Project Import** (under **IMPORT & EXPORT**).

2. Enter the name of the backup **File name** from which you want to perform **Project Import**.

3. Copy the attachments in the JIRA HOME under the import\attachments directory; the exact path specific to your machine will also be displayed.

4. Click on the **Next** button to continue:

5. The **Project Import** utility will read the backup file and display the progress. Depending on the size of the backup file, it may take several minutes to complete:

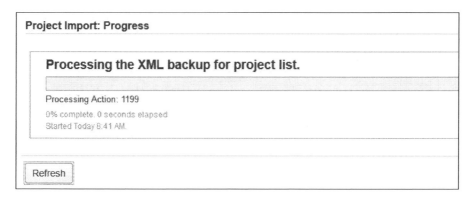

6. On the next screen, the list of the entire project in the backup file will be presented to you.

7. You can now select the project that you want to import from the **Projects from Backup** drop-down list.

8. The details of the project that you select will also be displayed. The **Project** name, **Key**, **Issues** count are displayed for your reference.

9. Click on the **Next** button to continue:

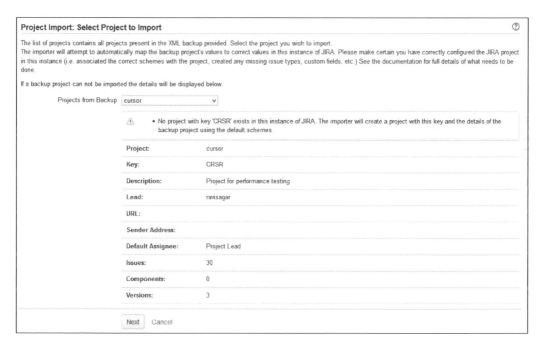

10. The projects in the backup file may have some fields that are not present in the target instance. The **Project Import** tool will attempt to map them to the existing fields. Before attempting the import procedure, you need to make sure that all the custom fields are created in the target instance.

11. If the mapping is complete, click on the **Import** button to continue:

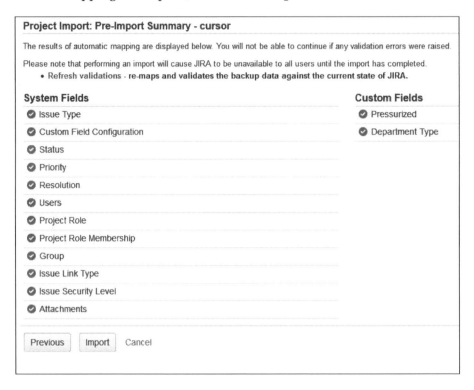

12. Depending on the size of the project, it may take several minutes to complete; the progress will be shown on the screen:

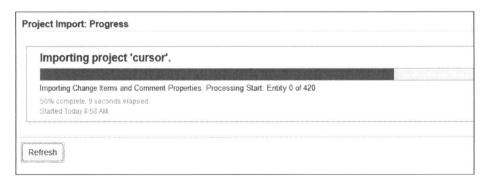

13. After the import process is successful, the result of **Project Import** will be displayed on the screen.

14. Verify the results and click on the **OK** button:

Project Import: Results

The project import completed successfully in 29 seconds.

Project Summary

Key:	CRSR
Description:	Project for performance testing
Lead:	Ravi Sagar
URL:	
Sender Address:	
Default Assignee:	Project Lead
Components:	0
Versions:	3

Users

No users were added during the import.

Project Roles

Administrators:	0 users, 1 groups
Developers:	0 users, 1 groups
Tester:	1 users, 0 groups
Users:	0 users, 1 groups

Issues

Issues created:	30 out of 30

No attachments were added during the import.

OK

15. Repeat the process for all the other projects that need to be imported.

The **Project Import** process is a complex procedure and it has to be first performed on the test instance. Read the official documentation to understand more about this procedure at

```
https://confluence.atlassian.com/display/JIRARestoring+a+Project+from
+Backup.
```

Backup should be generated using the same version of the target JIRA instance.

Project configurations such as issue type schemes, field configurations, workflows, notifications, and permission schemes should be created on the target instance.

Custom fields that are used in the project need to be created in the target instance.

If there are certain add-ons that are installed and used by the project, then install it on the target instance first; there are certain custom fields created by add-ons and until you install the plugin on the target instance, these custom fields will not be mapped.

External system import using CSV

There are various issue tracking tools that have been available for many years on the market. There are tools such as **Bugzilla** used primarily for bug tracking. There is another popular tool called **Mantis** that provides a good set of features, which again is used for bug tracking. Companies who are already using some of these tools and now want to move to JIRA can migrate their data using various importers provided by JIRA out of the box.

Follow these steps to perform the CSV import:

1. Navigate to **JIRA Administration | System | External System Import** (Under **IMPORT & EXPORT**).

2. You will get the list of various importers as shown in the following screenshot:

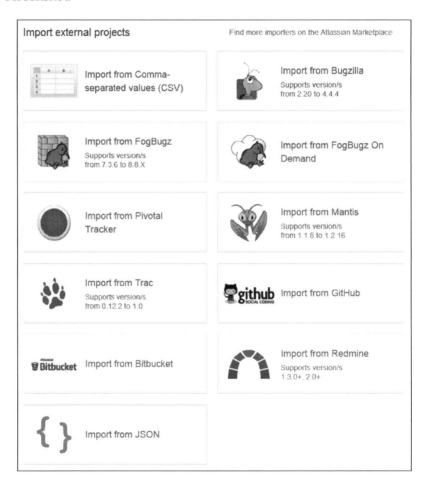

If you are using any of the tools mentioned in the preceding screenshot, then you can try to import the data from your existing tool. There are also other import tools developed by third-party vendors. This can be downloaded from the Atlassian Marketplace. You can give them a try.

These importers usually work fine when there are not many customizations in your existing tool, but this is not the case most of the time. The first importer called **Import from Comma separated values (CSV)** is a general purpose tool that can be used to import data from a CSV file into JIRA. We recommend to first export your data from your existing tool into a CSV file and then use this tool to import the data into JIRA.

The data that needs to be imported into JIRA can be quite complex; issues could also be subtasks of other issues and there could be a need to upload the attachments too.

Let's take a look at a few scenarios that can be used to import CSV into JIRA.

The simple CSV import

Let's understand how to perform a simple import of the CSV data. The first thing to do is to prepare the CSV file that can be imported into JIRA. For this exercise, we will import Issues into a particular project; these issues will have data, such as issue **Summary**, **Status**, **Dates**, and a few other fields.

Preparing the CSV file

We are going to use MS Excel to prepare the CSV file with the following data:

	A	B	C	D	E	F	G	H	I	J
1	Project	Summary	Issue Type	Status	Priority	Resolution	Assignee	Reporter	Created	Resolved
2	DOPT	Add PDF export feature in the bar charts	Improvement	Closed	Blocker	*Unresolved*	Frank Martin	Frank Martin	9/25/2014 0:54	9/27/2014 0:54
3	DOPT	Create an RSS feed of all the news items on the website	New Feature	Reopened	Minor	*Unresolved*	Michael Jones	Ravi Sagar	9/12/2014 20:54	9/13/2014 11:54
4	DOPT	Please enable HTML format in newsletter emails	Improvement	Resolved	Minor	Won't Fix	Ravi Sagar	Michael Jones	8/31/2014 16:54	9/1/2014 7:54
5	DOPT	The breakpoints need to be reduced by 10px for mobile devices	New Feature	Closed	Blocker	*Unresolved*	Ravi Sagar	Michael Jones	8/19/2014 12:54	8/19/2014 21:54
6	DOPT	The cron jobs need to be modified to run every 15 minutes	Task	Closed	Critical	*Unresolved*	Michael Jones	Frank Martin	8/7/2014 8:54	8/7/2014 20:54
7										
8										

If your existing tool has the option to export directly into the CSV file, then you can skip this step, but we recommend reviewing your data before importing it into JIRA. Usually, the CSV import will not work if the format of the CSV file and the data is not correct.

It's very easy to generate a CSV file from an Excel file. Perform these steps:

1. Go to **File | Save As | File name:** and select **Save as type:** as **CSV (comma delimited)**. If you don't have Microsoft Excel installed, you can use LibreOffice Calc, which is an open source alternative for Microsoft Office Excel:

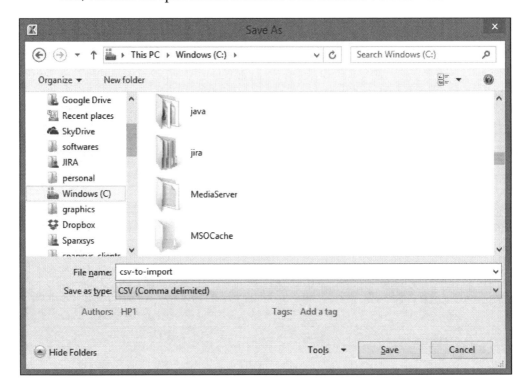

2. You can open the CSV file to verify its format too:

```
Project,Summary,Issue Type,Status,Priority,Resolution,Assignee,Reporter,Created,Resolved
DOPT,Add PDF export feature in the bar charts,Improvement,Closed,Blocker,Unresolved,Frank Martin,Frank Martin,9/25/2014 0:54,9/27/2014 0:54
DOPT,Create an RSS feed of all the news items on the website,New Feature,Reopened,Minor,Unresolved,Michael Jones,Ravi Sagar,9/12/2014 20:54
DOPT,Please enable HTML format in newsletter emails,Improvement,Resolved,Minor,Won't Fix,Ravi Sagar,Michael Jones,8/31/2014 16:54,9/1/2014
DOPT,The breakpoints need to be reduced by 10px for mobile devices,New Feature,Closed,Blocker,Unresolved,Ravi Sagar,Michael Jones,8/19/2014
DOPT,The cron jobs need to be modified to run every 15 minutes,Task,Closed,Critical,Unresolved,Michael Jones,Frank Martin,8/7/2014 8:54,8/7
```

Our CSV file has the following fields:

CSV Field	Purpose
Project	JIRA's Project Key needs to be specified in this field
Summary	This field is mandatory and needs to be specified in the CSV file
Issue Type	This is important to specify the Issue type
Status	This displays the status of the Issue; these are workflow states that need to exist in JIRA and the project workflow should have the states that are going to be imported into the CSV file
Priority	The priorities mentioned here should exist in JIRA before import
Resolution	The resolutions mentioned here should exist in JIRA before import
Assignee	This specifies the assignee of the Issue
Reporter	This specifies the reporter of the Issue
Created	This is the issue creation date
Resolved	This is the issue resolution date

Performing the CSV import

Once your CSV file is prepared, you are ready to perform the import in JIRA:

1. Navigate to **JIRA Administration | System | External System Import | Import from Comma-separated values (CSV)** (under **IMPORT & EXPORT**).

2. On the **File import** screen in the **CSV Source File** field, click on the **Browse** button to select the CSV file that you just prepared on your machine.

3. Once you select the CSV file, the **Next** button will be enabled:

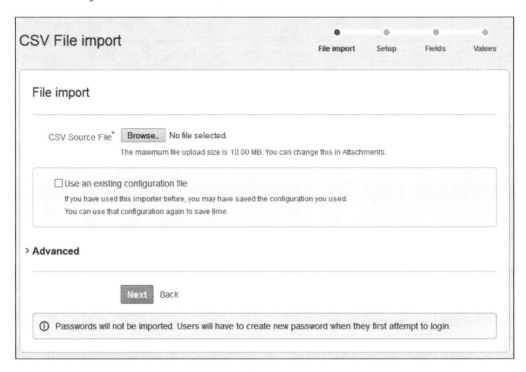

4. On the **Setup** screen, select **Import to Project** as DOPT, which is the name of our project.

5. Verify **Date format**; it should match the format of the date values in the CSV file.

6. Click on the **Next** button to continue.

7. On the **Map fields** screen, we need to map the fields in the CSV file to JIRA fields. This step is crucial because in your old system, the field name can be different from JIRA fields, so in this step, map these fields to the respective JIRA fields.

8. Click on **Next** button to continue.

9. On the **Map values** screen, map the values of **Status**, in fact, this mapping of field values can be done for any field. In our case, the values in the status field are the same as in JIRA, so click on the **Begin Import** button.

10. You will finally get a confirmation that issues have been imported successfully:

⊘ 0 projects and 5 issues imported successfully!

If you encounter any errors during the CSV import, then it's usually due to some problem with the CSV format. Read the error messages carefully and correct these issues. As mentioned earlier, the CSV import needs to be performed on the test environment first.

The import that we just performed is straightforward, but it's possible to import data with complexities too.

Creating subtasks using the CSV file

There are cases when issues need to be imported as a subtask. In such cases, use the format, as shown in the following screenshot:

Summary	Issue Type	Issue ID	Parent ID	Status	Priority
Add PDF export feature in the bar charts	Improvement			Closed	Blocker
Create an RSS feed of all the news items on the website	New Feature			Reopened	Minor
Please enable HTML format in newsletter emails	Improvement			Resolved	Minor
The breakpoints need to be reduced by 10px for mobile devices	New Feature			Closed	Blocker
The cron jobs need to be modified to run every 15 minutes	Task	9910		Closed	Critical
Please configure the cron for newsletter	Sub-task		9910	Closed	Minor
Configure the cron for new registrations	Sub-task		9910	Reopened	Blocker
Cron for email verifications	Sub-task		9910	Resolved	Critical
Cron to download updates automatically	Sub-task		9910	Closed	Minor
Configure the cron for In active accounts	Sub-task		9910	Resolved	Blocker

Note the two columns, that is, **Issue ID** and **Parent ID**; populate the **Issue ID** column with a random number for the parent task and enter this random number in the **Parent ID** column for all the subtasks.

Issue ID and **Parent ID** need to be mapped to **Sub-Tasks | Issue Id** and **Sub-Tasks | Parent Id** during the CSV import respectively, as shown in the following screenshot:

Proceed with the CSV import as usual and subtasks will be created.

Uploading attachments using the CSV file

Usually, it's desirable to attach files to the issues that need to be imported into JIRA.

Perform these steps:

1. Create a `csvimport` folder in your `JIRA HOME/import/attachments` directory. So, the final path should look like this:

   `<JIRA_Home>/import/attachments/csvimport/`

2. The CSV JIRA import can read the particular directory using the `FILE` protocol. It's used to access the files stored on the same machine; the full path of the files needs to be specified.

3. Add a column called `Attachments` in your CSV file and enter the location in the following format:

   `file://csvimport/file1.pdf`

4. The file should finally look similar to the following screenshot:

Summary	Issue Type	Attachments	Status	Priority
Add PDF export feature in the bar charts	Improvement	file://csvimport/file1.pdf	Closed	Blocker
Create an RSS feed of all the news items on the website	New Feature	file://csvimport/image1.jpg	Reopened	Minor
Please enable HTML format in newsletter emails	Improvement	file://csvimport/file2.pdf	Resolved	Minor
The breakpoints need to be reduced by 10px for mobile devices	New Feature	file://csvimport/file3.pdf	Closed	Blocker
The cron jobs need to be modified to run every 15 minutes	Task	file://csvimport/image2.jpg	Closed	Critical

Don't forget to map this new `Attachments` column to the **Attachment** JIRA field; the rest of the process remains the same.

Your issues may have multiple attachments instead of just one. In such cases, add an additional column for each attachment. Similarly, other fields with multiple values can be imported by simply adding multiple columns.

Updating existing issues

There is another very good use of the CSV import tool. So far, we have seen how to import data into JIRA, but there are times when existing issues need to be modified. For instance, if you want to add a new fixed version to the issues of a particular project or you want to resolve certain issues in bulk, it's possible to use the **CSV Import** tool.

In the CSV file, just add another column of `Issue Key` and add the columns as JIRA fields that need to be updated. If the CSV tool finds the issue key, then it will take the rest of the columns and update them in the existing issues.

However, there is also a **Bulk Change** tool in **Issue Navigator**, which does the same thing. It's up to your comfort level and use case to choose the method convenient to you. We recommend using the **Bulk Change** tool as it's much easier as compared to the CSV import tool.

Summary

In this chapter, you learned how to import and export data into JIRA. We started with understanding how to take a backup of the entire JIRA instance. You also learned how to restore the instance from this backup. We also looked at scenarios when you want to import selected projects from the backup file. We spent considerable time understanding how to migrate data to JIRA using the CSV file, which provides a lot of flexibility in importing not only simple data but also complex data with subtasks and attachments as well.

In the next chapter, we will understand how to implement Scrum and Kanban methodologies in JIRA using a powerful add-on from Atlassian called **JIRA Agile** for Agile tracking. This chapter will cover two scenarios of both techniques. We will discuss how to set up and configure the board and, most importantly, how to analyze reports. You will also learn these two Agile techniques and basic concepts with practical examples.

10
Working with JIRA Agile

In this chapter, we will understand how to implement two Agile methodologies called **Scrum** and **Kanban** in JIRA using a powerful add-on from Atlassian called **JIRA Agile** for Agile tracking. Key concepts of JIRA Agile to create, plan, and manage the tasks will be covered. We will discuss how to set up and configure the board. Most importantly, we will discuss how to analyze reports. Scrum Masters and Project Managers will gain insights on how to use JIRA Agile, which will enable them to manage their work following the Agile concept. Real-life examples will be used to understand Scrum and Kanban boards.

Product overview – what is JIRA Agile?

One of the best features of JIRA is its ability to extend its functionality by installing separate add-ons. In this book, we have already seen some of the add-ons that provide additional functionalities; however, JIRA Agile is one add-on that deserves a dedicated chapter of its own. JIRA Agile provides great features to implement Agile techniques in your JIRA instance. Whether you are already familiar with the Agile concept or completely new to it, this add-on will make your Agile journey not only easy, but also wonderful.

Installing JIRA Agile

Just like any other add-on, JIRA Agile can be easily installed from the Atlassian marketplace. Perform these steps:

1. Navigate to **JIRA Administration | Add-ons | Find new add-ons** (under **ATLASSIAN MARKETPLACE**).

2. In the search box, enter JIRA Agile and click on the *Enter* key. The JIRA Agile add-on will appear in the following screenshot:

3. Click on the **Free trial** button. A popup will appear asking you to **Accept terms and agreements**. Click on the **Accept** button to continue. If you want to purchase it, the JIRA Agile license must match your JIRA license. For instance, if you are using JIRA with ten user licenses, then your JIRA Agile must also have ten user licenses.

4. The JIRA Agile add-on will then be downloaded and an evaluation license will also be generated that will be valid for 1 month.

5. JIRA Agile should be installed in your instance. Now, click on the **Agile** link in the main navigation bar on top and in the drop-down, select **Getting Started**:

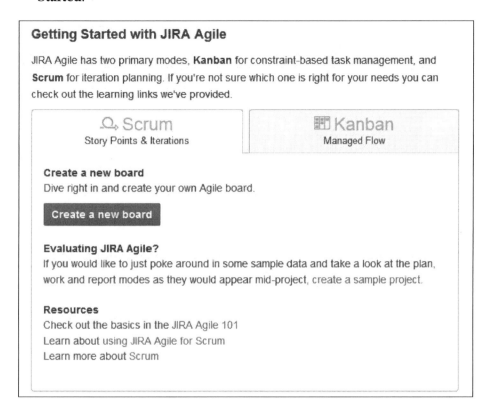

We have two options now to either create a Scrum board or Kanban board. Let's create both the boards one at a time.

Scrum boards

Scrum is an Agile technique used in complex projects. This technique is widely used in software development projects, but it can be applied to any process easily. To know more about Scrum technique, refer to https://www.scrumalliance.org/why-scrum.

Scrum technique focuses on breaking up the requirements into small doable tasks. Then, a prioritized list of these tasks is created (called a sprint), which can be performed in a period of 1-4 weeks. The objective of this sprint is to create a deliverable feature or product and not just a prototype. More sprints can be created to complete the whole requirement and finish the product or project. The tasks that are yet to be done are kept in a list called a backlog.

JIRA Agile lets you implement the Scrum technique in your process with the help of Scrum boards.

Agile project setup and JIRA Agile configuration basics

Scrum boards can be created from any existing JIRA project that contains predefined issues. It's possible to create a Scrum board from a new blank project as well. Also, if you want to understand how JIRA Agile works, it's possible to create a sample project prepopulated with sample data. Perform these steps:

1. Click on the **Agile** tab in the main navigation menu bar and select **Getting Started**. On the next page under **Scrum**, click on the **create a sample project** link.

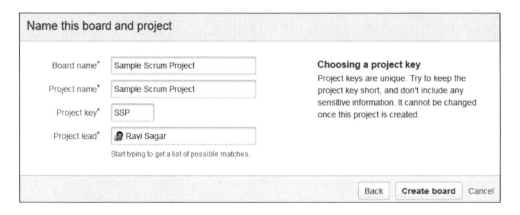

2. Enter **Board name**, **Project name**, **Project key**, **Project lead** and click on the **Create board** button.

We have just created a project with sample data along with a Scrum board. You can also create a Scrum board and select your existing project to populate it.

Populate, rank, and estimate a backlog using story points

In the newly created Scrum board, you will now see the list of issues that are pending, that is, not resolved yet:

Backlog contains issues that are pending in the project or board. These issues are yet to be planned for execution.

The sample Scrum board already contains a **Sprint** that has certain issues in a specific order. The Scrum master or the project manager can define the order in which issues need to be completed. This order is also known as **Rank** and the team who is working on these issues needs to follow this order. The rank is important because there are certain tasks that need to be completed before other tasks can be started.

In a Scrum methodology, the estimation of individual tasks is not only done on the basis of the amount of time spent, but also on the complexity of the tasks. For instance, there are two tasks whose time estimate is one day, but the first task is complex to execute because it was the first time that the task is executed by the team or for some other reason. The complexity is measured by **Story Points**. The story point can be any number between 1 to 10 or any number in the Fibonacci sequence, that is, 1, 1, 2, 3, 5, 8, 13, 21. The higher the number, more is the complexity of the task.

Scrum master can assign **Story Points** to the issues in the **Sprint**, although it's not mandatory to have story points with each issue in the sprint, but having it will give the team an idea about the complexity of the issue.

Plan and create sprints

The sample Scrum board already contains one running sprint; let's create a new sprint. JIRA Agile allows you to create another sprint even if the active sprint is not completed, but this new sprint cannot be started. However, it's possible to enable the **Parallel Sprints** feature in JIRA Agile that lets us run multiple sprints together.

The planning of the sprint has to be done in the **Plan** mode of the Scrum board. Perform these steps to run multiple sprints together:

1. Navigate to JIRA **Administration | Add-ons | JIRA Agile Labs** (under **JIRA AGILE**):

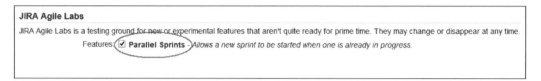

2. Tick the checkbox for **Parallel Sprints**.

   That is it, just go back to your board and start planning your next sprint:

3. Click on the **Create Sprint** button just before the backlog:

4. An empty sprint will be created.

5. Now, start dragging your issues from backlog to sprint:

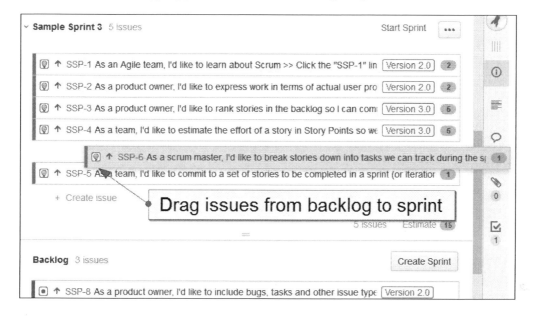

6. Once you have put all your issues in the sprint, you may reorder them within the sprint and define their rank, that is, which issue needs to be performed first, second, and so on.

7. Optionally, you can also create **EPICS** to group multiple stories together. Epic is nothing, but a large story. It's quite easy to create an epic. Click on the **Create epic** link on the left-hand side of the sprint:

8. In the popup window, enter **Epic Name** and **Summary**. Click on the **Create** button to continue:

9. You can create more epics; finally, drag issues from your sprint to the epic. This will assign issues to be part of these epics:

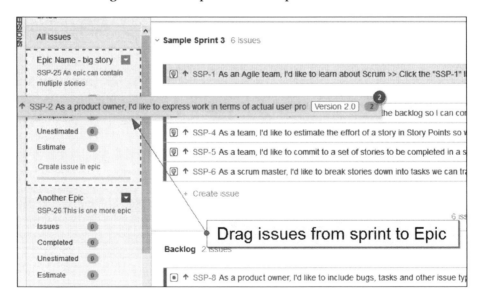

10. After assigning issues to Epic, you can start the sprint. Click on the **Start Sprint** link at the top-right corner. In the popup window, enter **Sprint Name**, **Start Date**, and **End Date**:

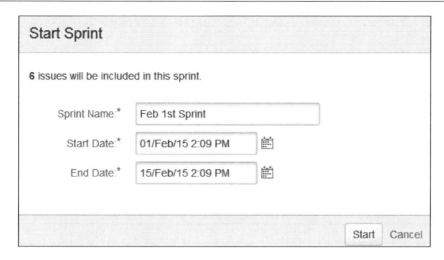

Note that you should never start the sprint until you have planned your issues well, ordered them, and estimated the story points. The moment you start the sprint, you will be taken to the **Work** mode in the Scrum board. Here, you will see the list of all the issues in your sprints across three columns, that is, **To Do, In Progress, Done**:

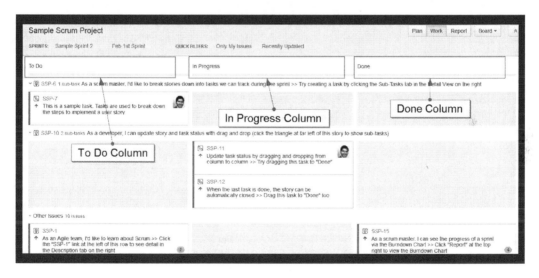

In the **Work** mode, the individual assignee can drag the issue to either the **In Progress** column or the **Done** column. This is similar to making workflow transitions.

There are a lot of customizations that can be done in the **Work** mode to make it more effective.

Configuring swimlanes, card colors, edit card fields, and quick filters

The **Work** mode is the section in the board that is monitored by the team members once the sprint is running. When the number of people working on the sprint are too many, it may get difficult for them to find the issues they are working on. Let's take a look at some of the customizations done to the Scrum board.

Swimlanes

The issues that appear in the work mode can be grouped together so that it becomes easy for the respective member to find that issue on the board. Also, when the issues are dragged from one column to another, they can only be dragged within their group, which is known as **Swimlane**. The default swimlane is the **Story** issue type. Let's change this:

1. Navigate to **Board** | **Configure** | **Swimlanes** (under **CONFIGURATION**):

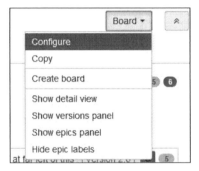

2. Select **Assignees** for **Base Swimlanes on** from the drop-down list and set **Unassigned issues** as **Show below other swimlanes**:

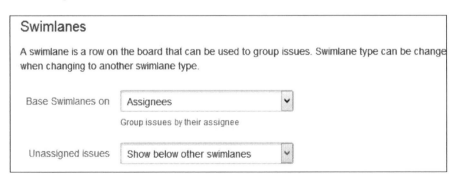

The swimlane can also be based on Epics, and it's possible to have no swimlane at all.

Card colors

The individual issues that appear in the work mode are displayed in a rectangular block called a card. The color of these cards can be changed based on its **Issue Type**, **Priorities**, **Assignees**, or **Queries/JQL**. The default option for the card color is the Issue type; let's change it to issue priorities:

1. Go to **Board | Configure | Card colors** (under **CONFIGURATION**).

2. Select **Priorities** from the drop-down list for **Colors based on**:

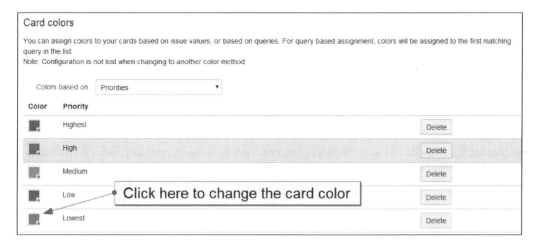

Click on the color box to change the color to the color of your choice.

Card fields

The card in the work mode displays the **Issue ID** and **Issue Summary**, but it's possible to add up to three additional fields. Perform these steps:

1. Navigate to **Board | Configure | Card layout** (under **CONFIGURATION**).

2. The additional three fields can be added for the **PLAN MODE** and the **WORK MODE**. We will add one additional field in the Work mode. From the **Field Name** drop-down list, select **Due Date** and click on the **Add** button on the right-hand side.

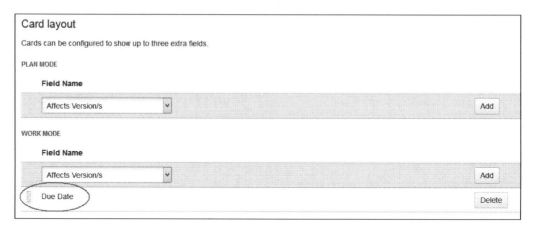

In total, you can add three additional fields that can appear on the card. This provision is provided so that fields that provide additional information can be made visible for the whole team to view.

Quick filters

We saw how you can customize swimlanes to group several issues. Imagine a situation when there are 20 issues in the work mode that are assigned to you in the active sprint, but there will be certain issues that are due today. In such cases, it will be nice to be able to not only quickly filter out the issues that are assigned to you, but also the issues that are due today. Perform these steps to achieve this:

1. Navigate to **Board** | **Configure** | **Quick Filters** (under **CONFIGURATION**).

2. Enter the **Name** of the quick filter as Due Today. In the **JQL** column, enter duedate=now() as the query and click on the **Add** button:

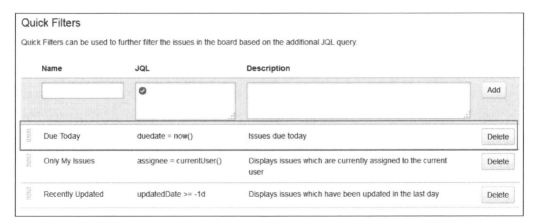

We have done some customizations in our board. Let's go back to the **Work** mode.

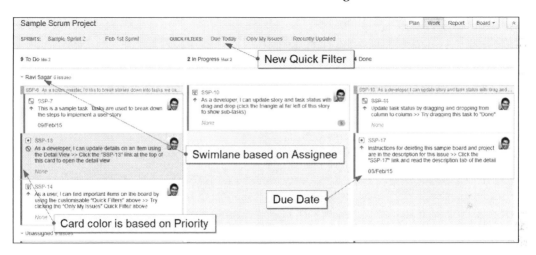

Now, you can see that there is a new quick filter added at the top called **Due Today**; click on this link and the board will only display issues whose due date is today. Note that the swimlane is now based on the assignee of the issue. The issue due date is now added to the card. Also, the color of the card is now based on the priority of the issue.

These customizations help the team to work efficiently so that they don't need to spend a lot of time finding the relevant information.

The Burndown chart and Velocity charts

You have learned how to plan, estimate, and start the sprint, along with various configurations that we can do in the board. We checked how the team can view their tasks in the sprint. Now, it's time to monitor the progress of the team. There are two reports that are of prime importance. One is the **Burndown chart**. This chart gives a clear picture of the current status of the sprint. The second is the **Velocity chart**. This chart helps in understanding the capacity of the team in terms of how much work it can handle. These two reports help the Scrum master in monitoring the progress of the project. Let's take a look at both these reports.

The Burndown chart

While planning the sprint, we primarily did two important things. Firstly, we prioritized the order in which the issues need to be completed. Secondly, we estimated the story points for issues. These story points, which we initially planned, gives the idea of the complexity of the task. Now, the moment the sprint starts, a baseline is formed between the start date and the end date. This baseline is displayed with a grey line in the chart and it depicts the ideal scenario of executing the issues from the start date of the sprint until the end date. When the issue is resolved, its story points are burned and the total remaining story points of the whole sprint decreases.

1. Navigate to **Report | Burndown Chart**:

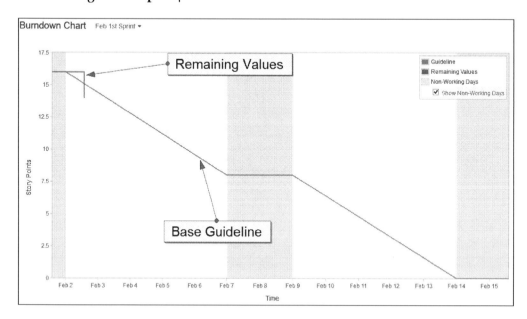

When the team starts working on the issues, another line of red color starts following the baseline. Looking at this chart, the whole team can easily figure out if they are on track or off the track. If the line for **Remaining Values** is progressing above the baseline, then it shows that the story points are burned slowly. Eventually, all the issues in the sprint will not be completed.

Just after the Burndown chart, the details of the individual issues are displayed:

Date	Issue	Event Type	Event Detail	Inc.	Dec.	Remaining
					Story Points	
01/Feb/15 2:09 PM	SSP-1	Sprint start		2		
	SSP-2			2		
	SSP-3			5		
	SSP-4			5		
	SSP-5			1		
	SSP-6			1		
						16
02/Feb/15 1:39 PM	SSP-2	Burndown	Issue completed		2	14

In this table, how many issues were there at the beginning of the sprint are displayed. As the issues are resolved, their story points are deducted from the total story points of the sprint. The total story points and the remaining story points will be displayed to the user.

Let's take a look at another sprint's Burndown chart:

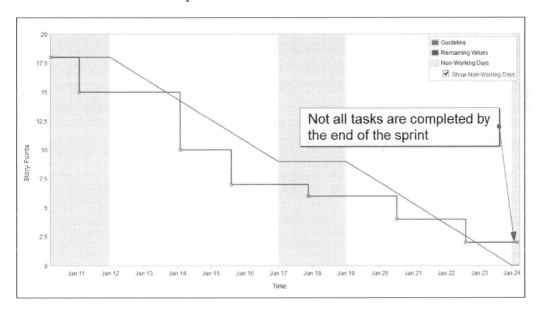

It's clear by looking at this Burndown chart that by the end of the sprint, not all story points were burned; these unfinished issues will be added back to the backlog.

The Velocity chart

Every sprint has a total number of story points at the beginning. Ideally, the team working on the sprint should burn all these points. In real cases, it's not always possible to complete all the tasks by the end of the sprint. One of the main responsibilities of the Scrum master is to make sure that the team should have just enough story points to burn, not too many and not too less. However, at the beginning of the sprint, it's not that easy to estimate the amount of story points a team can burn. The velocity chart simply displays the amount of story points planned versus actually completed by the team. This comparison is shown for the past few sprints so that the average number of story points that the team can burn can be calculated. This is known as the capacity of the team.

Navigate to **Report | Velocity Chart**:

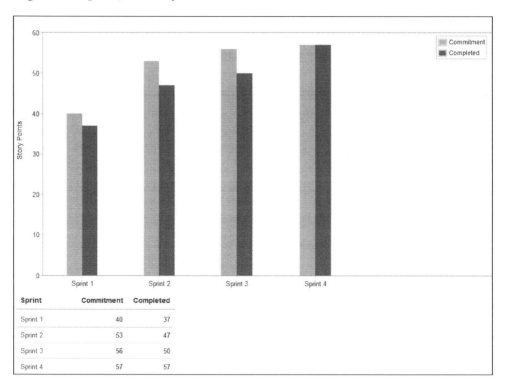

This chart gives us a very clear indication of the story points that the team has been able to complete in the past sprints. It helps the Scrum master to plan the next sprint with enough resources in the team.

Kanban boards

We have discussed the Scrum methodology widely used for software development projects, where requirements are broken down into smaller tasks, estimated using story points, and finally planned by the Scrum master or product manager. The Scrum technique is applicable in any process that requires planning, but there are various cases where the team is continuously working on activities as and when required. A typical example of this use case is customer support projects, where a certain number of people are assigned to handle the issues that are raised for a particular product or project by the company. Usually, these support issues require an immediate response and detailed planning is not required.

In such scenarios, the overall visualization of the pending issues is important. Kanban board doesn't have a plan mode like the Scrum board. It only has the work mode, which is similar to the Scrum board.

Setting up the Kanban board

The Kanban board can be created using existing projects or filters. To understand how the Kanban technique works in JIRA, a sample board and project can be created. Perform these steps to create them:

1. Click on the Agile link in the main navigation menu bar and select **Getting Started**. On the next page under Kanban, click on the **create a sample project** link.

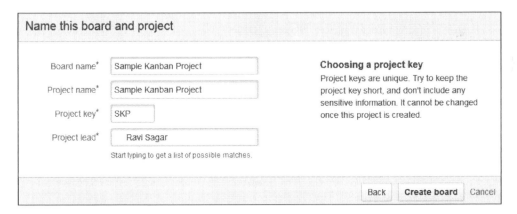

2. Enter **Board name** and **Project name**. Then, click on the **Create board** button. You will then be taken directly to the **Work** mode with sample data.

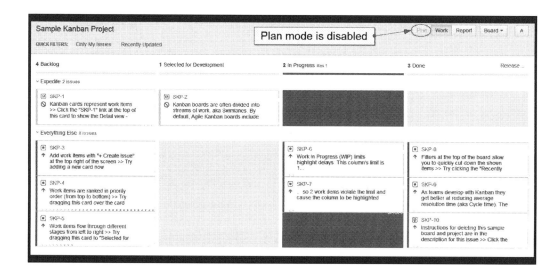

As you can notice, the **Plan** mode is disabled in the Kanban board. The team sees the **Work** mode directly. This board is quite similar to the Scrum board; you can also configure the swimlanes based on Assignees; by default, the swimlanes in the Kanban board are configured to use the `priority = Blocker` query. This means that issues that should be resolved immediately are displayed at the top.

The people who have these issues assigned can move the issue from one column to another. These columns signify the workflow states. Most of the configurations that we did for the Scrum board can be done on the Kanban board as well; let's perform some configurations that we did not check in the Scrum board.

Column constraints

When a team works on support issues, it's quite important to resolve the issues as soon as possible. Usually, companies sign **SLA**, that is, **Service Level Agreement** with their customers, where they need to agree on the resolution time. In situations like these, the whole team should get the overall picture of the issues that they need to work on. For instance, if there are less people available on the support issues, then there is a limitation on the number of issues these people can work on at a given point of time. In the sample Kanban board, you can notice that the **In progress** column is red whenever there are more than one issues in it.

Let's say you want to alert the team whenever there are more than four issues in the backlog:

1. Navigate to **Board | Configure | Columns** (under **CONFIGURATION**).

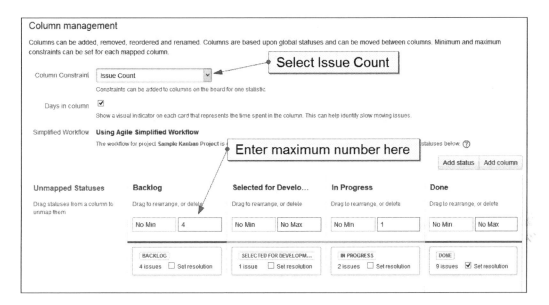

2. In **Column management**, first select **Column Constraint** as **Issue Count**. As shown in the preceding screenshot, enter the maximum number of issue count in **Backlog**.

3. Now, create one more issue in your sample project so that your backlog has more than four issues.

4. Go back to your Kanban board now and check the backlog column:

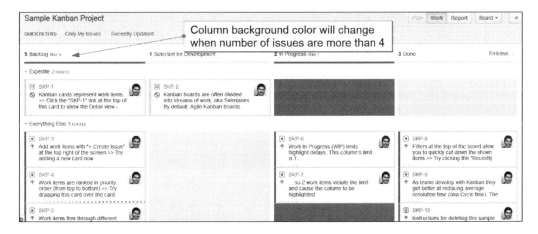

The rest of the configuration is exactly the same as what we have done for Scrum. You can configure swimlanes, add quick filters, and also add a few additional fields in the card layout. The procedure to configure these was already discussed in the Scrum section earlier and it's the same for Kanban boards.

Managing multiple teams and projects using boards

The sample projects and boards that we created to understand Scrum and Kanban techniques used only one project, but JIRA Agile boards can be configured to use multiple projects too.

If your team members are working on different projects for the same client, then it will make more sense to manage the work from a single board. Scrum and Kanban boards can be configured for issues that either come from one, two, or multiple projects. Perform these steps to manage the work from a single board:

1. Click on the Agile link in the main navigation menu bar and select **Getting Started**. On next page under Scrum or Kanban, click on the **Create a new board** button.

2. In the popup window, you can either create a new project with a new board or also create a board from a filter, but we can select the second option, that is, **Board from an existing project** and click on the **Next** button:

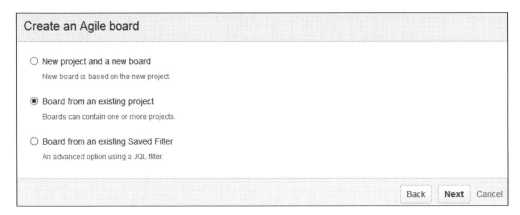

3. On the next screen, enter **Board name** and select multiple **Project(s)**. Click on **Create board** to finish:

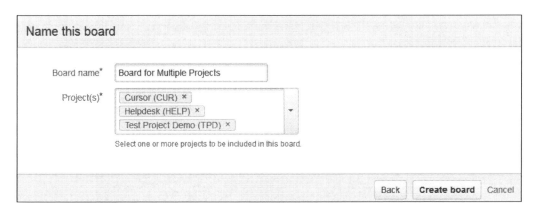

4. Your newly created board will now have issues from all the projects that you have selected.

The issues from multiple projects can now be added for the sprint in the Scrum board or will appear in the Kanban backlog and your team can work on them.

Summary

In this chapter, you learned how to implement Scrum and Kanban Agile methodologies in JIRA using the JIRA Agile add-on. We understood how to use both the boards and learned various configurations that can be performed in it.

In the next chapter, we will discuss Groovy Script Runner, which is an amazing add-on to perform complex customizations in the workflow, access powerful JQL functions, and run various scripts that can be used by JIRA administrators to maintain the instance efficiently.

11
JIRA Administration with Groovy Script Runner

When JIRA is used to implement a complex use case with lots of conditions, validations, and workflows, there are certain configurations that are not doable using the existing set of features. For instance, you want to autocalculate a custom field value after a workflow transition. Using the Script Runner plugin, many such advanced configurations can be achieved. This chapter will discuss this useful plugin in detail along with examples.

Installing Script Runner

Just like any other add-on, Script Runner can be installed from the JIRA Administration interface. Perform these steps to install Script Runner on your JIRA instance:

1. Navigate to **JIRA Administration** | **Add-ons** | **Find new add-ons** (under **ATLASSIAN MARKETPLACE**).

2. In the search box, enter `Script Runner` and click on the *Enter* key. The Script Runner add-on will appear in the search result list:

3. Click on the **Install** button and the Script Runner add-on will begin downloading:

4. Script Runner will then be downloaded and installed in your instance.

5. In the popup window that appears confirming the add-on installation, click on the **Close** link at the bottom-right corner:

Installed and ready to go!

Script Runner v. 3.0.9

by Jamie Echlin Ltd

This add-on has been installed. If you need help getting started, click the link to the add-on documentation from the **Manage add-ons** screen.

Close

Script Runner will now be installed in your JIRA instance.

Built-in scripts for administration

The Script Runner add-on allows users to write and run their own scripts. It comes with plenty of nice scripts that allow JIRA administrators to perform various activities that are otherwise difficult to perform using existing JIRA features, or not possible at all from the UI. Let's take a look at some of these scripts.

Accessing Built-in Scripts

To access scripts that come with the Script Runner add-on, perform these steps:

1. Navigate to JIRA **Administration** | **Add-ons** | **Built-in Scripts** (under **SCRIPT RUNNER**).

2. In this section, the list of all the **Built-in Scripts** can be found:

3. Click on any of these links to run that particular built-in script. This will further ask you to enter parameters relevant for that script.

Let's take a look at some of these Built-in Scripts.

Copying a project

Only JIRA Administrators have the permission to create a project in JIRA and change the configurations too. Whenever there is a need to have an additional project in JIRA, the administrator needs to manually create projects and then change their schemes. Although, it's not a difficult task and usually takes 10 minutes of time, sometimes there is a need to create ten projects and creating them manually could take hours.

There is a built-in script in Script Runner to copy the project along with its configurations, with or without its issues. Perform these steps:

1. Click on the **Copy project** link:

2. On the next screen, select **Helpdesk** as **Source project**, enter **Target project key** and **Target project name**.

3. Tick the **Copy versions** and **Copy components** checkbox if you want to copy the project versions and project components as well.

4. Click on the **Run** button to initiate the Copy project script.

Once done, the message is displayed at the bottom of the screen stating that the project has been copied with a link to the new project. If you check the new copied project, you will notice that it has all the configurations of the source project. This tool takes less than a minute to run and JIRA administrators can save a lot of time using it.

Escalation service

This is an excellent Built-in Script that helps JIRA administrators to perform periodic actions on a certain set of issues. Let's take an example of a support ticket configuration in which we have a workflow state called **Waiting for Client** in our project. This is used to signify that further information is required from a client to act further on a ticket. These issues need to be resolved automatically when the ticket is not updated in the past 2 weeks:

1. Click on **Escalation service**:

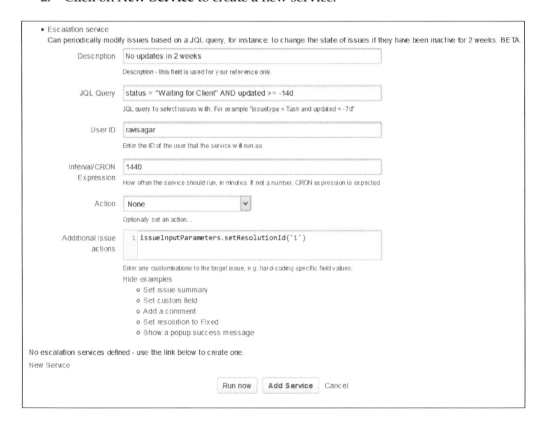

2. Click on **New Service** to create a new service:

3. Enter `No updates in 2 weeks` as **Description**.

4. In **JQL Query**, enter `status="Waiting for Client" AND updated >= -14d`.

5. Enter your **User ID** and specify **Interval/CRON Expression**.

 As we want to resolve the issues that qualify the criteria in JQL Query, select **Additional issue actions** as **Set resolution to Fixed**; this will automatically insert the `issueInputParameters.setResolutionId('1')` code.

6. Click on the **Add Service** button to save this service.

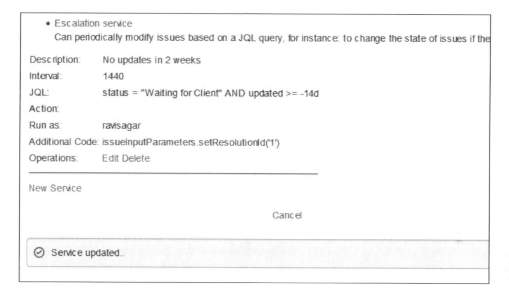

- Escalation service
  Can periodically modify issues based on a JQL query, for instance: to change the state of issues if the

Description: No updates in 2 weeks

Interval: 1440

JQL: status = "Waiting for Client" AND updated >= -14d

Action:

Run as: ravisagar

Additional Code: issueInputParameters.setResolutionId('1')

Operations: Edit Delete

New Service

Cancel

⊘ Service updated..

Now, we have a service added that will run after every 24-hour period and will resolve the issues that were not updated in the past 14 days, that is, 2 weeks.

Switching to a different user

Imagine a situation when a user reports a problem in JIRA. As a JIRA administrator, you need to log in with his/her ID to understand the problem that this user might be facing. You can either ask this user his/her password or create a similar user with the same set of permissions. Instead, wouldn't it be better to be able to log in to JIRA using that user's username without asking for the password? There is a Built-in Script to perform just that:

1. Click on **Switch to a different user**.

2. Enter the **User ID** of the user and click on the **Run** button:

3. Click on the **here** link that appears at the bottom of the screen. You will then be logged in with a different user:

Click here to continue as **Demo User**.
To finish impersonating demouser click Log Out.

This script is one of my favorites because I can log in with any username I want without asking their password and it also saves a lot of time.

Modifying the JIRA workflow with conditions, validators, and post functions

The best part of the Script Runner add-on is the additional features it brings in the JIRA workflow. Out of the box, there are various conditions, validators, and post functions that can be configured in the workflow, but it offers limited functionalities. Script Runner simply gives you more options that you can control in the workflow. Let's take a look at them.

Conditions

Script Runner brings a set of additional conditions that you can add in the workflow; it gives you an amazing control over a lot of things that was not possible earlier. Perform these steps:

1. Modify the workflow of your choice. For any transition, navigate to **Add Condition To Transition**.

2. You will find a new condition called **Script Condition**; select it and click on the **Add** button:

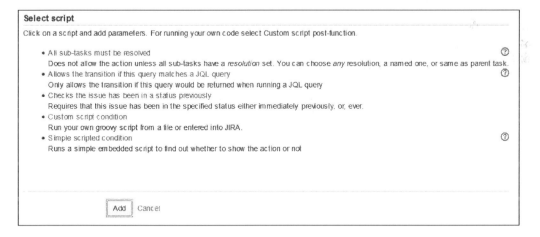

Add Condition To Transition

	Name	Description
○	Code Committed Condition	Transition to execute only if code has/has not (depending on configuration) been committed against this issue.
○	Hide transition from user	Condition to hide a transition from the user. The transition can only be triggered from a workflow function.
○	No Open Reviews Condition	Transition to execute only if there are no related open Crucible reviews.
○	Only Assignee Condition	Condition to allow only the assignee to execute a transition.
○	Only Reporter Condition	Condition to allow only the reporter to execute a transition.
○	Permission Condition	Condition to allow only users with a certain permission to execute a transition.
○	Script Condition	Runs a script to evaluate whether to allow this action, or a built-in script.
○	Sub-Task Blocking Condition	Condition to block parent issue transition depending on sub-task status.
○	Unreviewed Code Condition	Transition to execute only if there are no unreviewed changesets related to this issue.
○	User Is In Any Groups	Allows only users of a given group to execute the transition.
○	User Is In Any Roles	Allows only users of a given role to execute the transition.
○	User Is In Custom field	Allows only users in a given custom field to execute the transition.
○	User Is In Group	Condition to allow only users in a given group to execute a transition.
○	User Is In Group Custom Field	Condition to allow only users in a custom field-specified group to execute a transition.
○	User Is In Project Role	Condition to allow only users in a given project role to execute a transition.
○	Value Field	Allows to execute a transition if the given value of a field is equal to a constant value, or simply set.

Add   Cancel

3. On the next screen, you will get a list of scripts that you can add as a workflow condition:

Select script

Click on a script and add parameters. For running your own code select Custom script post-function.

- All sub-tasks must be resolved   ⑦
  Does not allow the action unless all sub-tasks have a *resolution* set. You can choose *any* resolution, a named one, or same as parent task.
- Allows the transition if this query matches a JQL query   ⑦
  Only allows the transition if this query would be returned when running a JQL query
- Checks the issue has been in a status previously
  Requires that this issue has been in the specified status either immediately previously, or, ever.
- Custom script condition
  Run your own groovy script from a file or entered into JIRA.
- Simple scripted condition   ⑦
  Runs a simple embedded script to find out whether to show the action or not

Add   Cancel

Let's discuss these scripts.

All subtasks must be resolved

If you want all the subtasks of a particular issue to be resolved with a specific resolution, then this condition can be added:

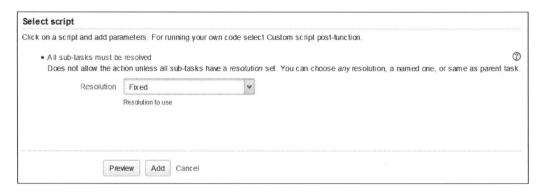

Simply select the **Resolution** that you want your subtasks to match and click on the **Add** button.

Allowing the transition if this query matches a JQL query

While performing a workflow transition, you can use a custom JQL in the workflow condition and allow the transition only when that JQL returns the issue that you will transition:

For instance, if you want the transition to happen only when the assignee of the issue is the currently logged in user and the due date is today, then add the `assignee = currentUser() and due = now()` **JQL Query** and click on the **Add** button. Optionally, you can also enter the specific issue id to preview this condition.

Checking if the issue has previously been in a status

The workflow can have numerous states and transitions between them. A workflow state can have more than one transition. For some reason, if you want the transition to be from a particular state only, then this condition can be added:

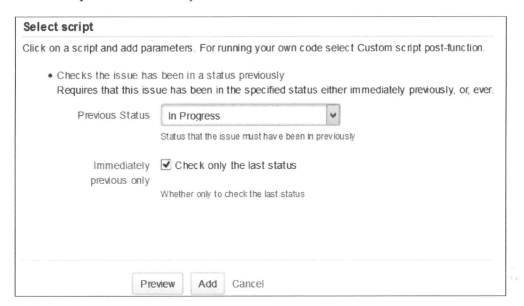

Just select **In Progress** from the drop-down list for **Previous Status** and check whether this status is **Immediately previous only**, uncheck this option if it is any other status and click on the **Add** button.

Simple scripted condition

Script Runner has some ready-made simple scripts that can be added quickly as a condition:

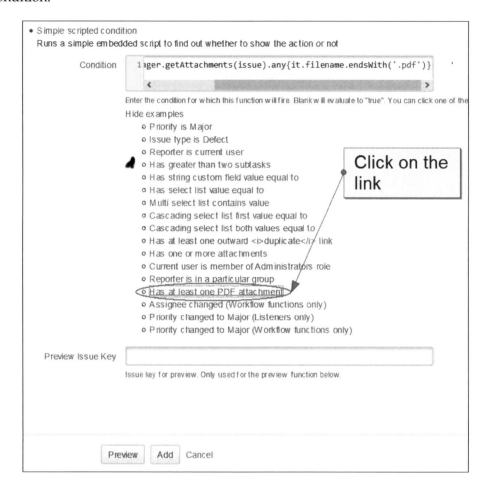

Just click on any of the example links and it can be added as a condition. For instance, I added a condition that will check whether one of the issue attachments is a PDF file or not. Click on the **Add** button to continue.

Validators

Just like additional conditions, Script Runner brings a set of additional validators that you can add in the workflow; it gives you an amazing control over lots of things that were not possible earlier. Perform these steps:

1. Modify the workflow of your choice and for any transition, navigate to **Add Validator To Transition**.

2. You will find a new validator called **Script Validator**. Just select it and click on the **Add** button:

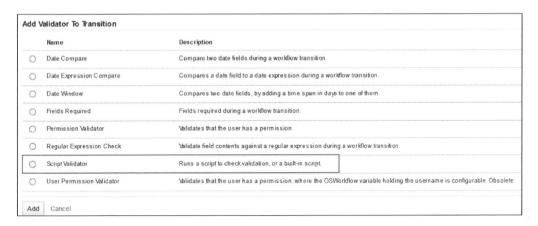

3. On the next screen, you will get a list of scripts that you can add as a workflow validator:

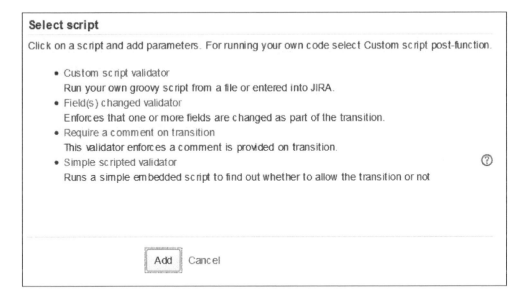

Let's discuss these scripts.

Field(s) changed validator

It's possible that you will use a transition view in the workflow transition that pops up a window to the user to capture additional input. These transition views are nothing but a screen containing one or more fields. Use this validator to validate whether these fields present in the transition view have changed:

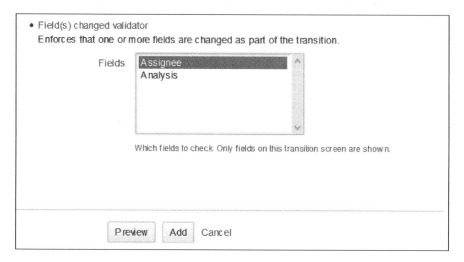

Select all the **Fields** that you want to check for change and click on the **Add** button. The fields visible here are only the ones that are part of the transition view for the transition you are working on in the workflow.

Require a comment on transition

In the transition view, there is usually a comment field as well. Use this validator to validate whether a comment has been added or not:

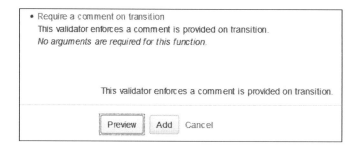

This validator doesn't require any parameters to configure. Just click on the **Add** button.

Simple scripted validator

Script Runner has some ready-made simple scripts that can be added quickly as a validator:

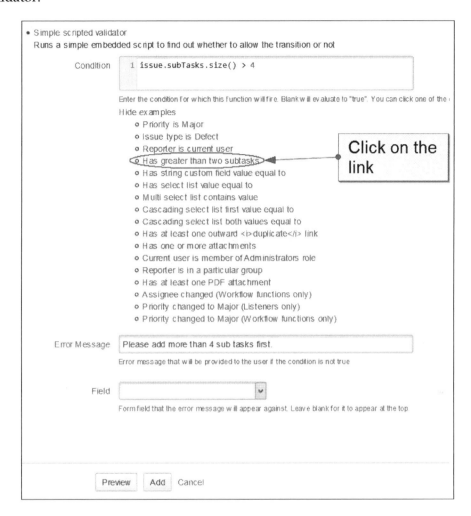

Just click on any of the example links and it can be added as a validator. For instance, if you want to enforce that the issue should have at least four subtasks, then click on **Has greator than two subtasks** and modify **Condition** from 2 to 4, so finally, it's `issue.subTasks.size() > 4`. Click on the **Add** button to continue.

Post Functions

Just like additional conditions and validators, Script Runner brings a set of additional post functions that you can add in the workflow; it gives you an amazing control over a lot of things that was not possible earlier. Perform these steps:

1. Modify the workflow of your choice and for any transition, navigate to the **Add Post Function To Transition**.

2. You will find a new post function called **Script Post-Function**; select it and click on the **Add** button:

Add Post Function To Transition	
Name	**Description**
○ Assign to Current User	Assigns the issue to the current user if the current user has the 'Assignable User' permission.
○ Assign to Lead Developer	Assigns the issue to the project/component lead developer
○ Assign to Reporter	Assigns the issue to the reporter
○ Clear Field Value	Clear value of a given field.
○ Copy Value From Other Field	Copies the value of one field to another, either within the same issue or from parent to sub-task.
○ Create Perforce Job Function	Creates a Perforce Job (if required) after completing the workflow transition.
○ Notify HipChat	Send a notification to one or more HipChat rooms.
○ Script Post-Function	Runs a script in a post-function, or a built-in script.
○ Trigger a Webhook	If this post-function is executed, JIRA will post the issue content in JSON format to the URL specified.
○ Update Issue Custom Field	Updates an issue custom field to a given value.
○ Update Issue Field	Updates a simple issue field to a given value.

Add   Cancel

3. On the next screen, you will get a list of scripts that you can add as a workflow post function:

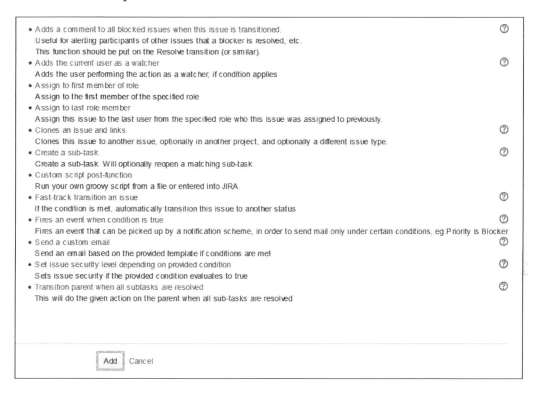

Let's discuss some of these scripts.

Adds the current user as a watcher

Consider a scenario when the priority of the issue is **Major** and the user who is currently logged in and making the workflow transition should be added as a watcher of the issue; in this case, use this post function:

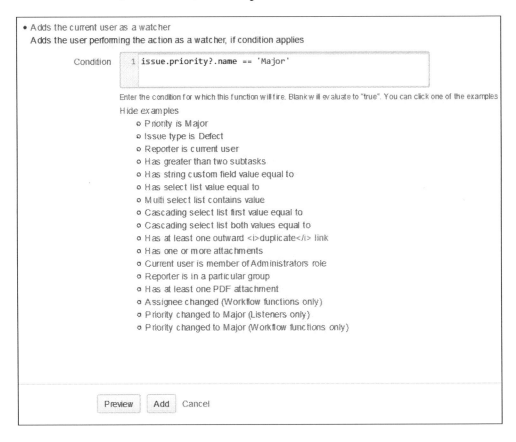

From the list of examples, click on the **Priority is Major** link and a **Condition** will be added. Now, whenever this condition is true during the workflow transition, the post function will be executed. Click on the **Add** button to add the post function.

Transitioning the parent when all subtasks are resolved

If your issue has a lot of subtasks, then it's possible to move the parent to a new state in the workflow when all its subtasks are resolved:

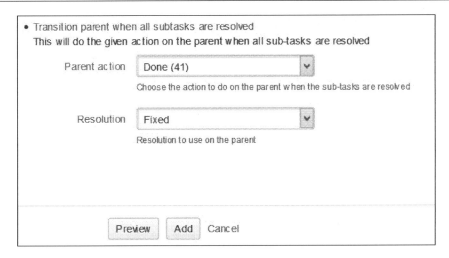

Select **Parent action** as **Done (41)** and **Resolution** as **Fixed**. Click on the **Add** button to add the post function.

There are numerous other post functions that can be used in the workflow. Using the Script Runner add-on, a lot of flexibility and control can be added in the workflow to perform actions that were not possible earlier.

Accessing powerful JQL functions

We have already discussed searching issues in JIRA with the basic and advance search using JQL. However, there are some limitations of JQL. JIRA administrators often try to fetch the information directly from the database, which is difficult to do because it requires a good knowledge of the JIRA database schema.

Script Runner introduces new JQL functions. You can use these functions in your instance. After installing this add-on, just perform the re-indexing to enable the new JQL functions.

Let's discuss some of these JQL functions.

Returning issues with a number of comments

Use the following JQL queries to return issues with the exact number of comments:

```
issueFunction in hasComments(3)
```

The following query will return an issue with more than four comments:

```
issueFunction in hasComments('+5')
```

Returning issues based on comments attributes

Use the following query to return issues commented on by project role administrators:

```
issueFunction in commented("role Administrators")
```

This query returns issues with comments from a specific user in the past 7 days:

```
issueFunction in commented("after -7d by ravisagar")
```

Returning issues based on attachments

Use the following query to fetch issues with PDF as an attachment:

```
issueFunction in hasAttachments ("pdf")
```

This query finds issues in the file that was attached by a specific user in the past 7 days:

```
issueFunction in fileAttached("after -7d by ravisagar")
```

Comparing dates

Issues can also be fetched by comparing their date fields, such as resolution date and due date.

Use this query to return issues that were resolved later than their due date:

```
issueFunction in dateCompare("", "resolutionDate > dueDate")
```

The following query finds issues that were resolved within 1 week of their creation:

```
issueFunction in dateCompare("", "created +1w > resolutionDate ")
```

These are just some of the examples of additional JQL functions that you can use. For the full list, I recommend you to refer to https://jamieechlin.atlassian.net/wiki/display/GRV/Scripted+JQL+Functions.

Script Runner is personally my favorite add-on that I use with all of the JIRA instances that I manage. It just gives so much power and control to effectively manage various administrative tasks in JIRA. Apart from various built-in scripts, which give administrators access to ready-to-use features, one can also write his/her own script and use it to perform more advanced and complex tasks. This ability to write scripts opens up a lot of possibilities to enhance the workflow and to add more features in JIRA without developing an add-on.

Summary

In this chapter, we discussed Groovy Script Runner, which is an amazing add-on to perform complex customizations in the workflow, access powerful JQL functions, and run various scripts that can be used by JIRA administrators to maintain the instance efficiently. Script Runner is by far the most popular admin tool used by JIRA administrators.

In the next chapter, we will discuss how to access the JIRA database directly to fetch data. JIRA offers lots of good reports, but sometimes they are not good enough and more insight is required. If you know the JIRA database schema and how to access the database, then any data can be retrieved for further reporting purposes.

12
Accessing the Database

JIRA offers a lot of project reports to keep track of the project progress, analyze trends over the past few months, and make decisions based on various statistics on time estimates, status, and workload. In most cases, these reports are enough to reach conclusions, but there are times when desirable information cannot be fetched from the existing JIRA reports; however, it's possible to generate complex reports directly from the database. In this chapter, we will discuss common databases that JIRA can use and the schemas these databases use. We will take a look at some reports that can only be generated by querying the database directly.

JIRA's database schema

JIRA stores its configuration and data in a database; if you are evaluating JIRA, then it's possible to use the embedded **Hyper SQL Database (HSQLDB)** written in Java. It's suitable for small applications and JIRA uses it only in its evaluation version. HSQLDB is not recommended for production usage. For that, JIRA recommends **MySQL** or **PostgreSQL**.

No matter what type of database is used, the database scheme, that is, the tables and the relationship between them is the same. If you want to take a look at the schema, then you can refer to `JIRA_HOME/WEB-INF/classes/entitydefs/entitymodel.xml`.

The contents of the file are as displayed in the following screenshot:

```xml
<?xml version="1.0" encoding="UTF-8"?>
<!DOCTYPE entitymodel PUBLIC "-//OFBiz//DTD Entity Model//EN" "http://www.ofbiz.org/dtds/entitymodel.dtd">

<!--

Are you going to add a new column?

Check fieldtype-postgres.xml and others to know exactly what given type means, and you could be surprised!

For example long-varchar is not very long :-)

-->
<entitymodel>
    <title>Entity Model for JIRA</title>
    <description>None</description>
    <copyright>Copyright (c) 2002-2006 Atlassian</copyright>
    <author>The Atlassian Dev Team</author>
    <version>1.0</version>

    <!-- sequence generator table -->
    <entity entity-name="SequenceValueItem" table-name="SEQUENCE_VALUE_ITEM" package-name="">
        <field name="seqName" type="id-long-ne"/>
        <field name="seqId" type="numeric"/>
        <prim-key field="seqName"/>
    </entity>

    <!-- User implementation -->
    <entity entity-name="User" table-name="cwd_user" package-name="">
        <field name="id" type="numeric"/>

        <field name="directoryId" col-name="directory_id" type="numeric"/>
        <field name="userName" col-name="user_name" type="long-varchar"/>
```

This is an XML file that contains the definition of all the tables in JIRA and its relationship with other tables.

Alternatively, you can also check the database schema on the Atlassian website at https://developer.atlassian.com/display/JIRADEV/Database+Schema.

Accessing HSQLDB

As we just mentioned that HSQLDB is used only for evaluation purpose and it should not be used for production instances; you may however want to run queries to generate reports from the database. Luckily, HSQLDB comes with a built-in console that can be invoked by performing the following steps:

1. Shut down your JIRA service.

2. Use the following command to start the HSQLDB console:

```
java -cp JIRA_INSTALL/lib/hsqldb-1.8.0.5.jar org.hsqldb.util.
DatabaseManager -user sa -url jdbc:hsqldb:JIRA_HOME/database/
jiradb
```

In the preceding command, replace `JIRA_INSTALL` and `JIRA_HOME` with the directory locations as per your installation. If you have installed JIRA using the Windows installer, then the following procedure should work.

Firstly, navigate to `C:\Program Files\Atlassian\Application Data\JIRA\ database` directory.

Then, run the following command:

```
java -cp ../../../JIRA/lib/hsqldb-1.8.0.5.jar org.hsqldb.util.
DatabaseManager -user sa -url jdbc:hsqldb:jiradb
```

The HSQLDB database manager will be displayed on your screen now:

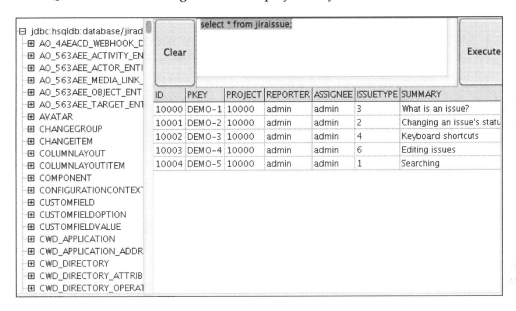

You can now run SQL queries in the HSQLDB database manager and check the output too in the same window.

Accessing MySQL

The HSQLDB database manager should never be used in the production instance because it's prone to data loss. The recommended database is either MySQL or PostgreSQL. Earlier in this book, we have discussed how to create a database in MySQL to store JIRA's data and configure it during the setup phase. To access your database in order to run SQL queries, you can either use the MySQL console, which comes with the MySQL server, or you can use **phpMyAdmin**.

phpMyAdmin

The phpMyAdmin application can be downloaded from `http://www.phpmyadmin.net/`.

This is a great web-based tool to manage your MySQL database and it's usually accessed using `http://localhost/phpmyadmin/`. The exact URL can be different based on your installation.

Perform these steps:

1. Open the previous URL in your browser to launch **phpMyAdmin**:

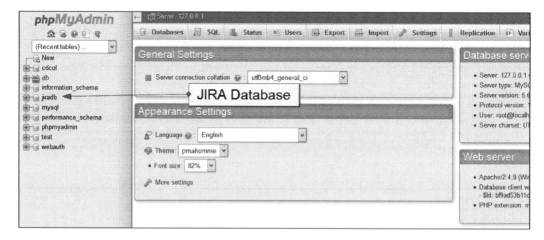

   You will notice that the list of databases appear on the left-hand side. Our **jiradb** database also appears in this list. We created this database for our JIRA instance.

2. Click on the plus (+) sign before the database name to expand the table in this database.

3. Now, you can click on any table to browse its content:

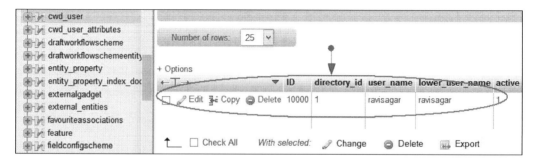

As you can see, we clicked on the `cwd_user` table and on the right-hand side, we have the list of users in our JIRA instance.

Similarly, you can browse any table you want for your JIRA instance. You should have some knowledge of JIRA's database schema to make some sense out of this data. Also, if you want to generate complex reports that involve more than one table, then you can write SQL queries as well.

1. Click on the **SQL** tab in the top navigation bar:

2. To execute your query, perform the following steps:

    1. In the preceding screenshot, you can enter your SQL queries under **Run SQL query/queries on database jiradb:**.

    2. Click on the **Go** button to run the SQL query.

The MySQL console

When you install the MySQL server on your machine, it comes with the MySQL console. This console can also be used to manage your database. It's not very user friendly compared to phpMyAdmin, but once you remember the basic command, then you will prefer the MySQL console for quick access to the database.

Run the following command to enter the MySQL console:

```
mysql -u USERNAME -p
```

In the preceding command, replace USERNAME with your username. In our case, it's root. The command will ask you to enter your password and you enter the MySQL console:

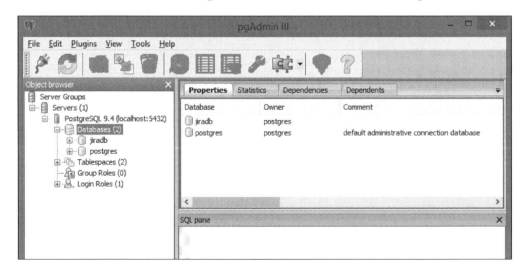

In the MySQL console, you can enter your commands and run queries.

Let's take a look at the structure of a few common JIRA tables and generate reports combining these multiple tables. For the following example queries, you may use either phpMyAdmin or the MySQL console depending on your comfort level.

Accessing PostgreSQL

When you install PostgreSQL using the Windows installer, it comes with **pgAdmin III,** which is another tool for PostgreSQL's administration and management:

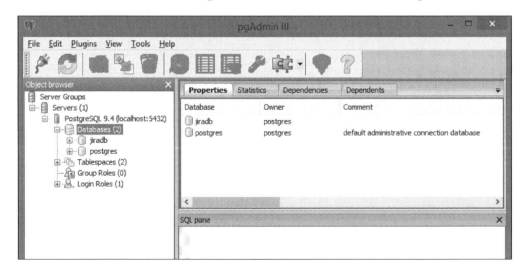

Let's take a look at some JIRA database tables that store useful information.

User table

The `cwd_user` table is used to store a user in the system. Let's check the structure of this table.

The table structure

Run the following query:

```
desc cwd_user;
```

The output of the query is as follows:

```
mysql> desc cwd_user;
+---------------------+---------------+------+-----+---------+-------+
| Field               | Type          | Null | Key | Default | Extra |
+---------------------+---------------+------+-----+---------+-------+
| ID                  | decimal(18,0) | NO   | PRI | NULL    |       |
| directory_id        | decimal(18,0) | YES  |     | NULL    |       |
| user_name           | varchar(255)  | YES  |     | NULL    |       |
| lower_user_name     | varchar(255)  | YES  | MUL | NULL    |       |
| active              | decimal(9,0)  | YES  |     | NULL    |       |
| created_date        | datetime      | YES  |     | NULL    |       |
| updated_date        | datetime      | YES  |     | NULL    |       |
| first_name          | varchar(255)  | YES  |     | NULL    |       |
| lower_first_name    | varchar(255)  | YES  | MUL | NULL    |       |
| last_name           | varchar(255)  | YES  |     | NULL    |       |
| lower_last_name     | varchar(255)  | YES  | MUL | NULL    |       |
| display_name        | varchar(255)  | YES  |     | NULL    |       |
| lower_display_name  | varchar(255)  | YES  | MUL | NULL    |       |
| email_address       | varchar(255)  | YES  |     | NULL    |       |
| lower_email_address | varchar(255)  | YES  | MUL | NULL    |       |
| CREDENTIAL          | varchar(255)  | YES  |     | NULL    |       |
| deleted_externally  | decimal(9,0)  | YES  |     | NULL    |       |
| EXTERNAL_ID         | varchar(255)  | YES  | MUL | NULL    |       |
+---------------------+---------------+------+-----+---------+-------+
18 rows in set (0.02 sec)
```

Finding the list of inactive JIRA users

One of the main responsibilities of JIRA administrators is user management. Let's say you want to find the list of inactive users along with their directory information. In big JIRA instances, it may be possible that there are users in JIRA's internal directory as well as users from corporate LDAP.

The following query will return the list of inactive users in JIRA:

```
SELECT u.user_name,u.first_name,u.last_name,u.email_address,d.directory_
name from cwd_user u join cwd_directory d on u.directory_id = d.id where
u.active = 0;
```

The preceding query relies on another table called `cwd_directory`. This directory stores the user directory information, whereas whether the user is active or not is stored in the `cwd_user` table under the `active` table field.

The jiraissue table

The `jiraissue` table is used to store JIRA issues. Let's check the structure of this table.

The table structure

Run the following query:

```
desc jiraissue;
```

The output of the query is as follows:

```
                                                                    C:\WINDOWS\sys

Oracle is a registered trademark of Oracle Corporation and/or its
affiliates. Other names may be trademarks of their respective
owners.

Type 'help;' or '\h' for help. Type '\c' to clear the current input statement.

mysql> use jiradb;
Database changed
mysql> desc jiraissue;
+----------------------+--------------+------+-----+---------+-------+
| Field                | Type         | Null | Key | Default | Extra |
+----------------------+--------------+------+-----+---------+-------+
| ID                   | decimal(18,0)| NO   | PRI | NULL    |       |
| pkey                 | varchar(255) | YES  |     | NULL    |       |
| issuenum             | decimal(18,0)| YES  | MUL | NULL    |       |
| PROJECT              | decimal(18,0)| YES  | MUL | NULL    |       |
| REPORTER             | varchar(255) | YES  | MUL | NULL    |       |
| ASSIGNEE             | varchar(255) | YES  | MUL | NULL    |       |
| CREATOR              | varchar(255) | YES  |     | NULL    |       |
| issuetype            | varchar(255) | YES  |     | NULL    |       |
| SUMMARY              | varchar(255) | YES  |     | NULL    |       |
| DESCRIPTION          | longtext     | YES  |     | NULL    |       |
| ENVIRONMENT          | longtext     | YES  |     | NULL    |       |
| PRIORITY             | varchar(255) | YES  |     | NULL    |       |
| RESOLUTION           | varchar(255) | YES  |     | NULL    |       |
| issuestatus          | varchar(255) | YES  |     | NULL    |       |
| CREATED              | datetime     | YES  |     | NULL    |       |
| UPDATED              | datetime     | YES  | MUL | NULL    |       |
| DUEDATE              | datetime     | YES  |     | NULL    |       |
| RESOLUTIONDATE       | datetime     | YES  |     | NULL    |       |
| VOTES                | decimal(18,0)| YES  |     | NULL    |       |
| WATCHES              | decimal(18,0)| YES  |     | NULL    |       |
| TIMEORIGINALESTIMATE | decimal(18,0)| YES  |     | NULL    |       |
| TIMEESTIMATE         | decimal(18,0)| YES  |     | NULL    |       |
| TIMESPENT            | decimal(18,0)| YES  |     | NULL    |       |
| WORKFLOW_ID          | decimal(18,0)| YES  | MUL | NULL    |       |
| SECURITY             | decimal(18,0)| YES  |     | NULL    |       |
| FIXFOR               | decimal(18,0)| YES  |     | NULL    |       |
| COMPONENT            | decimal(18,0)| YES  |     | NULL    |       |
+----------------------+--------------+------+-----+---------+-------+
27 rows in set (0.01 sec)
```

Finding issues of a specific project

It's quite easy to find the list of issues of a specific project using the JIRA Issue Navigator, but as we are exploring the database schema and its various tables, let's fetch the issues of a specific project directly from the database:

```
SELECT p.id AS project_id, p.pname AS project_name, CONCAT("GJA-",ji.
issuenum)  AS issue_id, ji.reporter AS issue_reporter FROM project p LEFT
OUTER JOIN jiraissue ji ON ji.project = p.id WHERE p.pkey = 'GJA' ORDER
BY ji.issuenum;
```

The preceding query will display the list of issues of the project with the DP key. You can replace the project key with yours and try the previous query. The project name and a few other fields are fetched from the project table.

The customfield table

The customfield table is used to store all the custom fields. Let's check the structure of this table.

The table structure

Execute the following query:

```
desc customfield;
```

The output of the query is as follows:

```
mysql> desc customfield;
+-----------------------+---------------+------+-----+---------+-------+
| Field                 | Type          | Null | Key | Default | Extra |
+-----------------------+---------------+------+-----+---------+-------+
| ID                    | decimal(18,0) | NO   | PRI | NULL    |       |
| CUSTOMFIELDTYPEKEY    | varchar(255)  | YES  |     | NULL    |       |
| CUSTOMFIELDSEARCHERKEY | varchar(255)  | YES  |     | NULL    |       |
| cfname                | varchar(255)  | YES  |     | NULL    |       |
| DESCRIPTION           | text          | YES  |     | NULL    |       |
| defaultvalue          | varchar(255)  | YES  |     | NULL    |       |
| FIELDTYPE             | decimal(18,0) | YES  |     | NULL    |       |
| PROJECT               | decimal(18,0) | YES  |     | NULL    |       |
| ISSUETYPE             | varchar(255)  | YES  |     | NULL    |       |
+-----------------------+---------------+------+-----+---------+-------+
9 rows in set (0.08 sec)
```

The customfieldvalue table

The customfieldvalue table is used to store custom field values. Let's check the structure of this table.

The table structure

Run the following query:

```
desc customfieldvalue;
```

The output of the query is as follows:

```
mysql> desc customfieldvalue;
+--------------+---------------+------+-----+---------+-------+
| Field        | Type          | Null | Key | Default | Extra |
+--------------+---------------+------+-----+---------+-------+
| ID           | decimal(18,0) | NO   | PRI | NULL    |       |
| ISSUE        | decimal(18,0) | YES  | MUL | NULL    |       |
| CUSTOMFIELD  | decimal(18,0) | YES  |     | NULL    |       |
| PARENTKEY    | varchar(255)  | YES  |     | NULL    |       |
| STRINGVALUE  | varchar(255)  | YES  |     | NULL    |       |
| NUMBERVALUE  | decimal(18,6) | YES  |     | NULL    |       |
| TEXTVALUE    | longtext      | YES  |     | NULL    |       |
| DATEVALUE    | datetime      | YES  |     | NULL    |       |
| VALUETYPE    | varchar(255)  | YES  |     | NULL    |       |
+--------------+---------------+------+-----+---------+-------+
9 rows in set (0.01 sec)
```

Some useful SQL queries

We will list a few useful SQL queries here that can help JIRA administrators quickly find the information they are looking for. It's important to mention that a new version of JIRA is released quite regularly with new features and bug fixes. The database schema may change slightly in the new versions. Therefore, verify your SQL queries on the new version of JIRA before using them.

List of shared filters

The following SQL query will list the filters created in the JIRA instance that are shared with others:

```
SELECT sr.filtername, sr.authorname
FROM searchrequest sr
LEFT JOIN sharepermissions sp ON sp.entityid = sr.ID
WHERE sp.entitytype = "SearchRequest" AND sp.sharetype != "global";
```

Fetching users of a specific group

It's quite easy to find users of a specific group from the JIRA interface, but you should know how to fetch this information using SQL. The following query will list the users of the `jira-users` group. You can change it to any group in your instance:

```
SELECT cu.user_name, cu.display_name, cu.email_address
FROM cwd_user AS cu
INNER JOIN cwd_membership AS cm
ON cu.directory_id=cm.directory_id
AND cu.lower_user_name=cm.lower_child_name
AND cm.membership_type='GROUP_USER'
WHERE cm.lower_parent_name='jira-users';
```

List of users with count of comments

One of the main responsibilities of JIRA administrators is to find users that are either inactive or not using JIRA a lot in a given month. The next query will fetch the list of users along with the number of comments they posted in a particular month. This will be useful in cases when it's necessary to find users who are active in system, but not performing much activity:

```
SELECT author, count(author) as comments
FROM jiraaction j
WHERE UPDATED > "2014-12-01 00:00:00"
group by author
ORDER BY author ASC;
```

Fetching the count of issues per component

Let's say you want to find the list of not only all the components in the system, but also the number of issues they are connected to, then the following query will give you that information quickly:

```
SELECT count(ji.id), c.cname FROM jiraissue ji
INNER JOIN nodeassociation na ON ji.id = na.source_node_id
INNER JOIN component c ON na.sink_node_id = c.id
GROUP BY c.cname;
```

Listing projects of a specific project category

If you want to retrieve the list of projects of only a specific category, then use the following query:

```
SELECT p.pname, p.LEAD, p.pkey

FROM project p

JOIN nodeassociation na ON (p.ID = na.SOURCE_NODE_ID AND na.ASSOCIATION_
TYPE = 'ProjectCategory')

JOIN projectcategory pc ON (na.SINK_NODE_ID = pc.ID)

WHERE pc.cname like 'Category';
```

Summary

In this chapter, you learned how to retrieve information directly from the database. This is quite useful when information cannot be easily fetched from the JIRA interface. We discussed some common JIRA tables and also looked at some example queries on how to find useful information. The ability to access the database directly empowers JIRA administrators to generate complex reports and seek information faster.

In the next chapter, you will learn how to customize the look and feel of JIRA by inserting the custom CSS code. Also, you will learn how to modify the behavior of HTML elements of the JIRA interface using JavaScript. We will take a look at some examples to show/hide JIRA fields based on the user selection of a specific value of a select list and to modify the values of text fields to insert text-based templates.

13
Customizing Look and Feel and Behavior

JIRA offers a simple functionality in its UI to change the colors of various sections and elements, such as header, footer, and links; you can also upload your custom logo. However, if you want to change the width of a certain section or the whole body element, then you can't do it from the UI. It's possible to include your custom CSS to make changes in the look and feel. It's also possible to load custom JavaScript in a JIRA instance; this enables changes in the behavior of various HTML elements, for example, you can selectively show or hide a field on other field's values and insert text-based templates in JIRA fields. In this chapter, we will take a look at such customizations.

How to add your own CSS

The JIRA Administration interface allows you to change the look and feel of various elements in JIRA and change the default logo. Perform these steps to customize your JIRA interface:

1. Navigate to **JIRA Administration | System | Look and Feel** (under **USER INTERFACE**).

2. The first option on this page is to change the **Logo,** click on the **Browse** button and then click on the **Upload Logo** button to upload your own custom logo:

3. The second option is to display **Site Title** located next to logo. Tick the **Show Site Title** checkbox and click on the **Update** button:

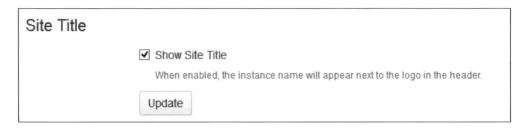

You will notice that the name of your instance that you entered while installing JIRA will now appear right next to the JIRA logo. In our example, it's **JIRA Demo**, which now appears next to the JIRA logo:

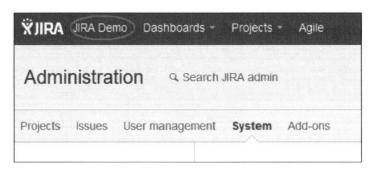

4. The third option is to update **Favicon,** which appears in the browser tab when JIRA is opened. Click on the **Browse** button to select the new **Favicon** image and then click on the **Upload Favicon** button:

5. The fourth option is to change the color of various sections of JIRA's web interface. For instance, click on any color in the box for **Header Background Color**. In the popup window, select the new color or you can directly enter the color's hexadecimal value. Let's change this color to red with a hexadecimal value of #ff0000. Click on the **Update** button to continue:

You will now notice that the color of the main navigation bar is red.

You can change the color of various sections that are available from this interface and match it with your company's color scheme, but JIRA's interface is only limited to changing colors. If you want to change the width of the body element or give extra padding and margins to certain sections, then it's now possible to do it through this interface.

However, it's possible to insert your own custom CSS in JIRA that can override the default look and feel. Perform these steps:

1. Go to JIRA **Administration | System | Announcement Banner** (under **USER INTERFACE**).

2. 2. In the **Announcement** text area, copy `<LINK href="http://localhost:8080/includes/custom_css/custom_style.css" rel="stylesheet" type="text/css">` and click on the **Set Banner** button:

The announcement banner is used to display a common text to all the users in JIRA in all the pages in JIRA; the good thing is that it supports HTML tags as well. In our case, we want to load a custom CSS code in all the pages. The `LINK` tag mentioned previously specifies the path where our custom CSS will be found. Perform these steps:

1. Create a `custom_css` folder in the following directory in your JIRA installation directory:

    `atlassian-jira\includes\`

2. Navigate to the `custom_css` folder and create a `custom_style.css` file; the location of the file should be `atlassian-jira\includes\custom_css\custom_style.css`.

When you save the announcement banner, nothing will be displayed to the user, but this CSS file will be loaded on all the pages. You can also verify this by viewing the source code of any page in JIRA and search for the filename:

```
269
270  <div id="announcement-banner" class="alertHeader">
271      <LINK href="http://localhost:8080/includes/custom_css/       style.css" rel="stylesheet" type="text/css">
272  </div>
273
274
```

In the preceding screenshot, you can see that our custom CSS file is loaded.

Now, it's time to add some CSS code in this file and change the look and feel of our JIRA instance. Open the `custom_style.css` code in your favorite editor and enter the following code snippet:

```
body {
  background-color: #e0e0e0;
  padding: 0 70px;
}
#content {
  box-shadow: 0px 0px 5px #232323;
}
#footer {
  background-color: #232323;
  box-shadow: 0px 0px 5px #232323;
}
```

Then, refresh your JIRA instance in your browser. You should now see that the preceding CSS code is applied and the changes will appear, as shown in the following screenshot:

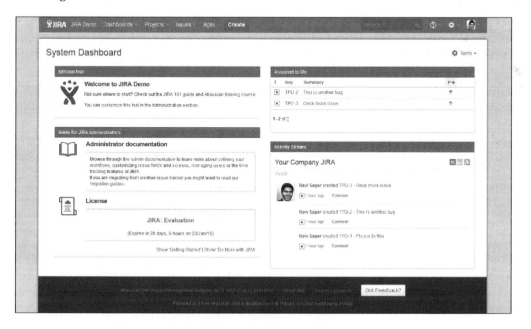

You can further customize the look and feel of the web page by adding your own CSS code. This will be loaded on every page; just make sure that the code in the announcement banner is not removed.

We have added an additional file to the JIRA file system. It's very important to keep a note of this file and save it separately too; when you upgrade your JIRA instance to a new version or migrate to a new server, the JIRA administrator should make sure that this file is not removed; otherwise, the customizations in the look and feel of the web page will not appear.

Adding JavaScript to show/hide a field

JIRA comes with tons of functionalities and customizations; however, there are times when you want more control over the behavior of HTML fields. For instance, if you want to show or hide a particular custom field on the basis of a value of another custom field, then you can use custom JavaScript to do this.

Let's take a scenario where users who create the ticket in JIRA need to enter their analysis in one of the text areas based on the custom field, but they only need to fill it when the priority of the issue is critical. Now, in order to achieve this, we want to completely hide the **Analysis** field first and display it only when users select **Priority** as **Critical**.

Unlike the preceding example to insert custom CSS, the custom JavaScript can be added directly from the JIRA interface. Perform these steps:

1. Go to JIRA **Administration | Issues | Custom Fields** (under **FIELDS**).

2. Click on the **Add Custom Field** button at the top-right corner and select **Field Type** as **Text Field (multi-line)**.

3. On the next screen, enter `Analysis` as **Name** and enter the JavaScript code (`analysis_js.css`) in the **Description** field of the custom field, as shown in the following screenshot:

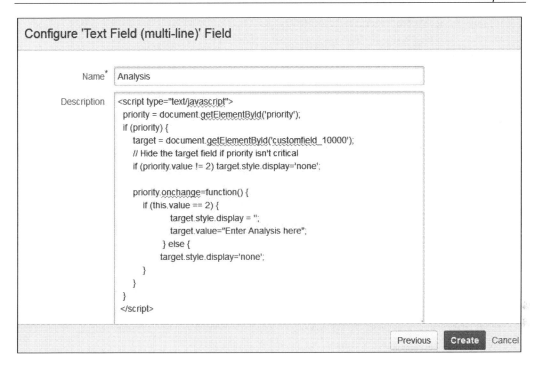

Configure 'Text Field (multi-line)' Field

Name* Analysis

Description
```
<script type="text/javascript">
    priority = document.getElementById('priority');
    if (priority) {
        target = document.getElementById('customfield_10000');
        // Hide the target field if priority isn't critical
        if (priority.value != 2) target.style.display='none';

        priority.onchange=function() {
            if (this.value == 2) {
                target.style.display = '';
                target.value="Enter Analysis here";
            } else {
                target.style.display='none';
            }
        }
    }
</script>
```

Previous | **Create** | Cancel

4. Click on the **Create** button to continue.

5. Add this field in the **Create Issue Screen** just after the **Priority** system field.

Note that the field description of custom fields can also be controlled by Field Configurations. In *Chapter 4, Customizing JIRA for Test Management*, we discussed the purpose of Field Configurations. In the previous example, we added the JavaScript code in the field description while creating the custom field; it will be overwritten if Field Configurations are used in the project.

Let's understand the important section of this JavaScript code.

The analysis custom field ID is equal to `10000` and we assigned a target variable to this field:

```
target = document.getElementById('customfield_10000');
```

Then, for the **Priority** field, we check whether its value is Critical, which is a select list with different numeric values for **Major**, **Blocker**, **Critical**, **Minor**, and **Trivial** (**Critical** being numeric value 2). For every other value, the **Analysis** field is hidden:

```
if (priority.value != 2)
  target.style.display='none';
priority.onchange=function() {
  if (this.value == 2) {
    target.style.display = '';
    target.value="enter message here";
  } else {
    target.style.display='none';
  }
}
```

When users select the **Priority** as **Critical**, the **Analysis** field is displayed again.

Creating the issue

After creating the **Analysis** field, just add one more issue in JIRA to test it. By default, the **Analysis** field is not displayed to the user:

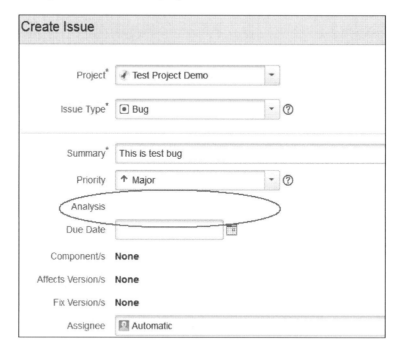

The moment you select **Priority** as **Critical**, the **Analysis** text area will be visible to the user:

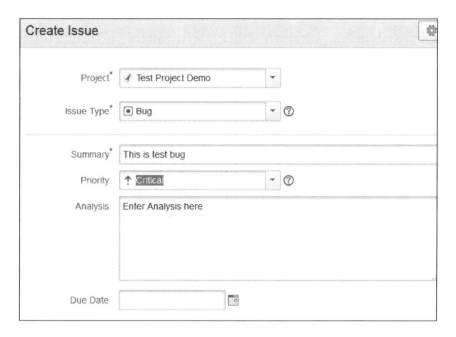

This example is just to give you an idea of how to use JavaScript to control the behavior of HTML elements.

Velocity templates

Velocity is a Java-based server-side template engine used to render page content that allows Java objects to be used along with HTML elements. As JIRA has been written in Java, it utilizes Velocity templates to display the content. These template files can be modified by the user; however, Atlassian will not provide any support on such changes in the template files; therefore, I recommend taking the backup of the original file before making any changes in them.

In this section, let's discuss a few examples where we will make changes in these templates.

Modifying the description system field with predefined text

JIRA allows you to add a description for every custom field, where some instructions on how to enter the data can be given to the end user. However, sometimes it's useful to present the user with a predefined text, which is like a text-based template. In this example, we will add some default text in the JIRA description system field. Perform these steps:

1. Edit the following file in your JIRA Installation directory:

   ```
   atlassian-jira\WEB-INF\
     classes\templates\jira\issue\field\description-edit.vm
   ```

2. Enter the following code just before the `$rendererDescriptor.getEditVM()` function:

   ```
   #set ($description = "Please enter the details in steps.\
   \
   Step 1:\
   \
   Step 2:\
   \
   Step 3:\
   \
   Issue Recurrance: Once or Always\
   Current Status: Working or Not Working
   \
   ")
   #set ($description = $description.replace('\',''))
   ```

3. The final code is shown in the following screenshot:

```
#customControlHeader ($action $field.id $i18n.getText($field.nameKey) $fieldLayoutItem.required $displayParameters $auiparams)
## setup some additional parameters
$!rendererParams.put("class", "long-field")
$!rendererParams.put("rows", "12")
$!rendererParams.put("wrap", "virtual")
#if ($mentionable)
    $!rendererParams.put("mentionable", true)
    #if ($issue.project.key && $issue.project.key != "")
        $!rendererParams.put("data-projectkey", "$!issue.project.key")
    #end
    #if ($issue.key && $issue.key != "")
        $!rendererParams.put("data-issuekey", "$!issue.key")
    #end
#end
#set ($description = "Please enter the details in steps.\

Step 1:\

Step 2:\

Step 3:\

Issue Recurrance: Once or Always\
Current Status: Working or Not Working
\
")
#set ($description = $description.replace('\','''))

## let the renderer display the edit component
$rendererDescriptor.getEditVM($!description, $!issue.key, $!fieldLayoutItem.rendererType, $!field.id, $field.name, $rendererParams, false)
#customControlFooter ($action $field.id $fieldLayoutItem.getFieldDescription() $displayParameters $auiparams)
```

4. Restart your JIRA instance.

5. Once the JIRA instance is restarted, click on the **Create** button to create an issue.

6. You will notice that the default text now appears in the **Description** field:

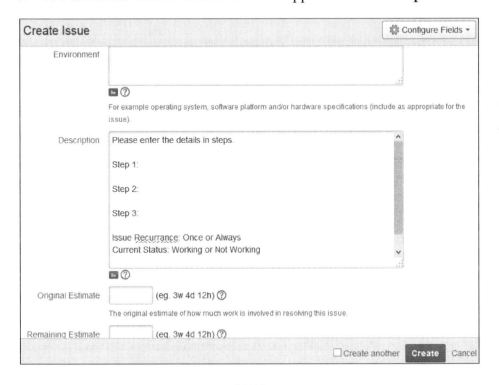

You can use the same method to add custom predefined text to other fields as well.

However, after modifying the description field template using the previous code, this predefined text will be added to the description field for all the projects and issue types in your JIRA instance, but it's possible to restrict it to a specific project and issue type. Instead, use the following code:

```
#if ($issue.getProject().getString("key") == 'TDP')
  #if(($description == "") && ($issue.getIssueTypeObject().getName()
== "Bug"))
    #set ($description = "Please enter the details in steps.\
      \
    Step 1:\
      \
    Step 2:\
      \
    Step 3:\
      \
    Issue Recurrance: Once or Always\
    Current Status: Working or Not Working
      \
      ")
    #set ($description = $description.replace('\',''))
  #end
#end
```

To define the default value of a custom field, the context can be used, which is discussed in *Chapter 14, JIRA Best Practices*.

In the preceding code, we just added two lines at the top to restrict **Project Key** to TDP and Issue Type to Bug. Make sure that you restart your JIRA instance before making any changes in the template file. If you don't want to restart your instance, then it's also possible to disable the caching of velocity templates by following these steps in your JIRA Installation directory:

- Open `/atlassian-jira/WEB-INF/classes/velocity.properties`
- Change `class.resource.loader.cache` from `true` to `false`
- Uncomment (remove the # sign from `#velocimacro.library.autoreload=true`)

  Now, any change in velocity templates will be reflected in your instance without restarting JIRA. Do this only on your development environment.

As we mentioned earlier for custom CSS, keep track of any changes you make in the template file and always keep a backup of the original template file. It's important to note that Atlassian will not provide any support for customizations done on the template files.

Modifying the footer

There are various template files that you can customize in JIRA and for various sections of the web page. Let's take a look at another example where we will add a custom text to the footer section. Perform these steps:

1. Edit the following file in your JIRA installation directory:

   ```
   atlassian-jira\WEB-INF\classes\templates\plugins\footer\footer.vm
   ```

2. This file has a lot of content; just navigate to the bottom of the file and add the following lines before #end:

   ```
   <ul>
       <li>This is a Test JIRA Instance and we are adding text in the
   footer.</li>
   </ul>
   ```

   The file looks like this:

   ```
   92      <ul>
   93          <li>This is a Test JIRA Instance and we are adding text in the footer. </li>
   94      </ul>
   95  #end
   ```

3. Restart your JIRA instance.

4. Once the JIRA instance is restarted, you will notice an additional text before the Atlassian logo:

Displaying a custom field in e-mails

It's also possible to customize e-mails sent to the users. The e-mail content is also generated using velocity templates. Let's now customize the template for e-mails that are sent when an issue is created. The custom fields that are created in the system are not included in the e-mail content, but we will modify the Velocity template of the issue creation e-mail and include the **Analysis** field (which we added earlier). Perform these steps:

1. Edit the following file in your JIRA installation directory:

   ```
   atlassian-jira\WEB-INF\classes\templates\email\html\issuecreated.
   vm
   ```

2. Add the following code at the end of the file:

   ```
   #if ($issue.getCustomFieldValue("customfield_10000"))
   <tr valign="top">
     <td >
       #text("Analysis"):
     </td>
     <td>
       $issue.getCustomFieldValue("customfield_10000")
     </td>
   </tr>
   #end
   ```

3. Save the file and restart JIRA.

4. Once the JIRA instance is restarted, create one issue in JIRA and fill the **Analysis** field.

5. Check the e-mail that you receive; the e-mail content should look similar to the following screenshot:

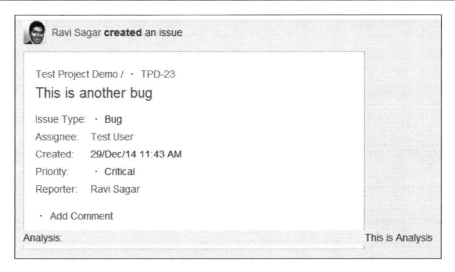

There are templates for similar events and system fields. You can explore them and make changes in them once you get comfortable with Velocity templates.

Summary

In this chapter, you learned how to customize the look and feel of JIRA by inserting custom CSS codes. We also modified the behavior of HTML elements of the JIRA interface using JavaScript to show/hide JIRA fields based on the selection done by the user of specific value of a select list. Finally, we explored velocity templates and how to modify the displayed content. We also discussed how to insert custom field values in e-mails.

In the next chapter, we will discuss best practices that need to be employed to use JIRA effectively, especially in Enterprise installation with thousands of users and multiple customizations. These best practices and standardized procedures will help administrators to maintain and support JIRA for a long time.

14
JIRA Best Practices

JIRA can become cumbersome to manage when used by many users for different use cases, especially custom schemes that are shared among projects. Imagine a case when a project manager asks you to remove a certain custom field from one of his project's screens, but you accidently remove it from other projects too. In this chapter, we will discuss the best practices that JIRA administrators can employ to maintain their instances.

A note of caution before modifying default schemes and configurations

A newly installed fresh JIRA instance comes with a lot of default schemes for issue types, workflows, field configurations, and permissions. These default configurations are suitable for simple bug tracking and have a process that is applicable to any generic project. Don't be tempted to start customizing the configurations too soon. If JIRA is used for the first time in the company, then it's a good idea to pilot it with default configurations. This will give users a good idea of what JIRA has to offer and collect feedback from the users.

When you are ready to customize configurations, either start with the blank configuration or create a copy of the default configuration and then make your changes in that.

The JIRA customization process

Customizing JIRA should be considered as a project in itself. It's quite easy to start making changes while configuring JIRA, but you should always plan your customizations first and document them.

You can perform these steps to begin the customization process:

1. Pilot JIRA with default configurations.
2. Gather feedback.
3. Document the proposed configurations.
4. Test the configurations on sandbox.
5. Implement it on production.
6. Standardize the configurations.
7. Set up a Change Control Board.

Piloting JIRA with default configurations

Moving to a new tool always faces resistance from users. JIRA is no exception; however, JIRA has the advantage of being intuitive and it allows you to have a clear distinction between usage and administrative sections. When deploying JIRA for the first time, always use the default configurations and ask users to test it for a few days. This will make sure that users first get comfortable with the features that come with JIRA out of the box. This piloting should ideally be done for at least one candidate from each team, consisting of a project manager, project lead, developer, and tester.

Gathering feedback

At the end of the pilot phase, ask the users to give their feedback. The following questions can be asked in the feedback form:

- Were the default Issue Types sufficient for your project?
- What changes would you like to perform in the workflow?
- Were the default fields enough to capture the information?
- Do you want e-mail notifications?
- How many types of users will be using JIRA?
- Do you want some users to have restricted access?
- Do you want e-mail notifications?
- What kind of reports would you like to have?

The answers to these important questions will give you a very good understanding of desired customizations from various stakeholders in the project.

Documenting and finalizing the proposed configurations

Merely collecting the feedback is not enough to start the customizations. It's very important to first document these customizations in a document to describe the requirements.

We discussed in detail how to gather the requirements in *Chapter 5, Sample Implementation of Use Cases*. Ideally, a separate document for each use case should be prepared. This document should be updated before making any changes in the system. This will ensure that if a new JIRA administrator joins the company, he/she will not have any problem understanding JIRA's customizations.

Once this document is prepared, share it with the stakeholders and ask them to give their inputs. Organize a meeting with them to fine-tune the requirements and make necessary changes in this document. Eventually, this document should have the details of all the actual customizations that will be performed in JIRA. What new issue types need to be created, workflows should be visualized in the documents along with the new states that need to be created, and permission schemes and notification schemes should also be mentioned.

Testing configurations on the sandbox

Once the requirements are finalized, you should test them on a test environment first. For this, set up a sandbox JIRA instance (which is an exact copy of your production). All the new and old changes in the existing configuration should first be tested on the sandbox. It's really important to have the sandbox for cases when JIRA needs to be upgraded to a new version and when you want to evaluate a new plugin.

The sandbox, which is an exact copy of production, will give the stakeholder a chance to test their requested customizations without worrying about any damages that they could have done on production.

During this testing phase, the stakeholders will surely give you a lot of feedback and ask you to improvise certain customizations that they earlier couldn't perceive. Note down all these changes and make necessary amendments in the document.

Implementing JIRA on the production stage

Once the implementation is successful on the test environment, you can then perform the customizations manually on production. At this time, the JIRA administrator will have all the information in front of him in the JIRA configuration document. Making actual implementation on production will not take much time.

However, if you are making any changes in the JIRA instance, which is already being used by several users, then it's a good idea to first notify them with the change. You can write a short release note and mention the changes that are done. This will not surprise the users with unexpected changes. Applying changes in the configurations usually doesn't require any downtime, but sometimes if you make changes in the workflow, then it's always a good idea to do it when no one is using the instance. For this matter, notify users of a downtime well in advance.

Standardizing configurations

JIRA has a wide range of applications. It's an issue tracking and project management tool. This tool can be used not only for bug tracking, but also for test management, helpdesk, requirement management, and Agile tracking.

Now, initially when JIRA is implemented, it will be customized for a specific use case for one or more projects, but eventually as more teams start using JIRA, they will request for more customizations. JIRA allows you to use the same configurations in multiple projects, but when the number of projects grows, the same schemes cannot be used for all. So, it becomes very important to standardize your configurations in JIRA and ask the new teams to follow it.

Let's take a look at the following scenario in JIRA with three different use cases:

Use case	Number of projects
Test management	10
Helpdesk	5
Requirements management	2

As you can see in the preceding table, there are multiple projects using the same configuration. Now, one of the project managers using the test management scheme may request you to add a new custom field in his/her project or to make one of the existing fields mandatory. Now, these minor customizations will affect all the other projects using the same configurations. We can limit these customizations to a single project by creating a new set of schemes, but this will lead to more maintenance for a JIRA administrator.

Avoid creating multiple schemes for the same use case, and before accepting any change in the existing configurations, discuss with the stakeholders of all the projects using that configuration. If one project manager requests for an additional custom field, then discuss this with other project managers and make the changes after confirmation from all the stakeholders.

So, it's very important to standardize your configurations as much as possible and reuse these configurations in other projects.

In *Chapter 4, Customizing JIRA for Test Management*, and *Chapter 5, Sample Implementation of Use Cases*, we discussed how to customize JIRA in detail along with various examples.

Setting up Change Control Board

JIRA administrators have the responsibility of implementing customization requests. As discussed in the previous section, configurations should be standardized as much as possible, but sometimes changes need to be done in JIRA to support JIRA's requirements; any change, be it small or big, needs to be analyzed first because it may lead to further issues. I recommend a **Change Control Board** whose job is to study the customizations before implementing them.

I recommend the following process:

1. Create a project in JIRA for support requests with various issue types, bug, improvements, and new feature.

2. Ask your users to raise a ticket in this project for any JIRA support.

3. Once the ticket is created, analyze the requested customizations and perform an impact analysis.

4. If there is no impact, then implement the changes directly in JIRA.

5. If there is any impact on other projects, then discuss the changes with the stakeholders of other projects.

6. On the basis of your discussion with stakeholders, make a decision on whether or not to implement the change in JIRA.

Various scenarios for impact analysis

Let's take a look at some of the customization requests from users and their possible impact on the instance:

Request	Used by other projects?	Impact	Conclusion
Addition on a new custom field	Yes	Minor	This confirms with other stakeholders first
Addition of new values in a select list custom field	Yes	Minor	This either confirms with other stakeholders or uses context to create a different set of values for that project
Change the workflow condition	Yes	Major	This is a major change and should be discussed with all stakeholders
Addition of a new workflow state	Yes	Major	This is a major change and should be discussed with all stakeholders
Create a mandatory custom field	Yes	Major	This is a major change and should be discussed with all stakeholders
Installing a new plugin	Yes, applicable globally	Major	This installs the plugin first on sandbox and asks the stakeholders to evaluate
Creation of new issue type	Yes	Major	This discusses the need of this new issue type with all stakeholders

These are some examples of requests that JIRA administrators will receive. For each request, analyze the impact first before implementing it in the system.

Using the project context to assign different options in multiple projects

Let's say we have a custom field called **Customer**. This is a select list with different values that users can select while creating an issue. If JIRA is used by multiple teams, each working on a different project, it's quite possible that the customer list will be different. One project may cater to a different set of customers than others. One approach to deal with this situation is to enter all the customers in a single list, but this will lead to confusion among the team members who raise the tickets and it will also lead to errors because users might select wrong customers.

A different custom field can be created for each project to deal with this problem (each having its own list of customers), but this leads to redundancy as we will store the same type of information.

JIRA's custom fields offer a solution to this problem using context. Perform these steps to create a new context:

1. Go to **JIRA Administration | Issues | Custom Fields** (under **FIELDS**) and you will see the list of all the custom fields in your system.

2. Click on the gear icon for your custom fields and select **Configure**:

3. On the next screen for **Configure Custom Field: Customer,** click on the **Add new context** link.

4. On the next screen for **Add configuration scheme context,** enter the **Configuration scheme label** and **Description.** Under **Choose applicable context,** select the name of the project for which this context will be available:

5. You will now have a new **Context for Demo project**, but there are no options yet. Click on the **Edit Options** link:

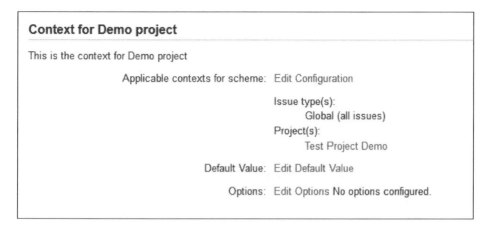

6. On the next screen, enter the customer names that are only relevant to a particular project:

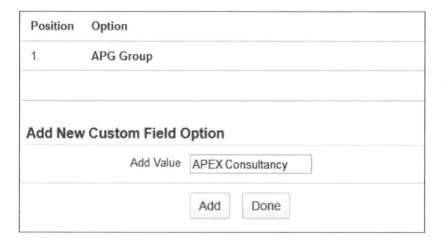

7. Finally, you will have two set of options for this custom field. One is default and the other is for a specific project:

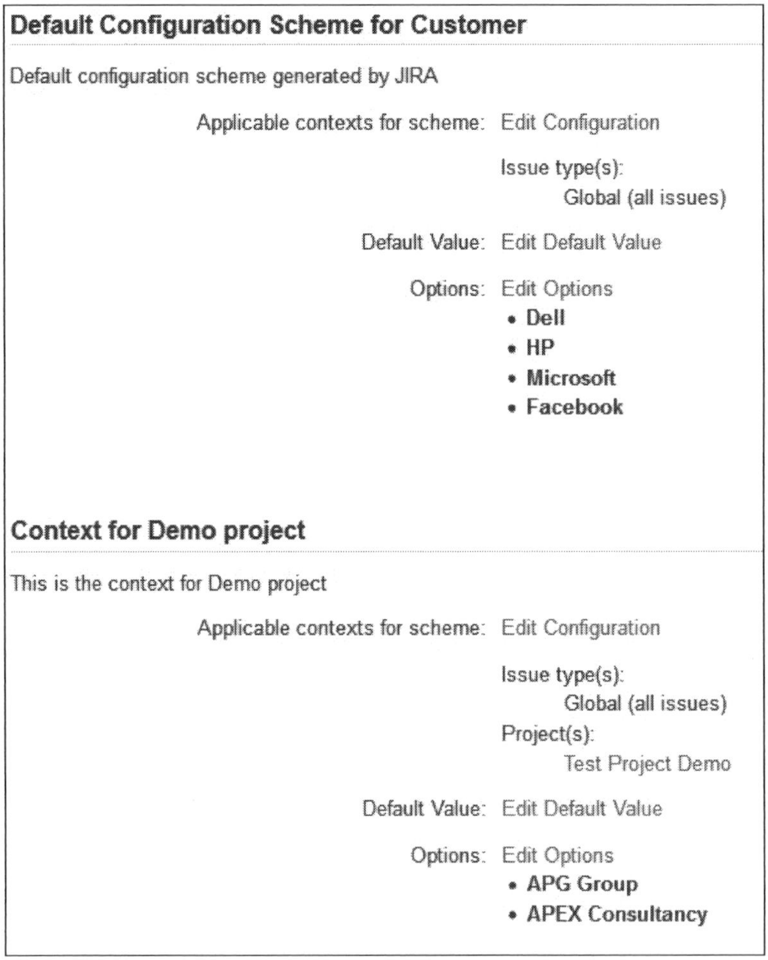

Default Configuration Scheme for Customer

Default configuration scheme generated by JIRA

Applicable contexts for scheme: Edit Configuration

Issue type(s):
Global (all issues)

Default Value: Edit Default Value

Options: Edit Options
- **Dell**
- **HP**
- **Microsoft**
- **Facebook**

Context for Demo project

This is the context for Demo project

Applicable contexts for scheme: Edit Configuration

Issue type(s):
Global (all issues)
Project(s):
Test Project Demo

Default Value: Edit Default Value

Options: Edit Options
- **APG Group**
- **APEX Consultancy**

Creating too many custom fields – a factor in slow performance

We just discussed that companies should devise a process to manage their customizations in their JIRA instance. As the JIRA instance grows in terms of number of issues, projects, and users, the performance of the instance will start degrading over a period of time. One of the major factors that leads to slow performance is a lot of custom fields.

JIRA administrators create custom fields to store data that can be filtered out in the reports. This is fine, but an attempt should be made to reuse the existing custom field. For this reason, create fields with generic names so that they can be reused easily in different projects.

Let's take a look at some generic custom fields that can be created in JIRA instances:

Custom field	Type	Description
Client/Customer	Select List	This uses **Project Context** to create different options for multiple projects
Category	Select List	These labels and components should be used in most cases, but this generic field can be used in many projects with different options using Project Context
External ID	Text Field	This field will be used to store the ID of issue, which is stored in some external tool
Type of testing	Select List	This field can be used when JIRA is used for test management
Start date	Date Picker	JIRA does come with a due date, but the start date of a task is not available

Think twice before adding new custom fields in the system. Your users will request you to create many fields, but remember several custom fields can cause performance issues. Always try to optimize the use of custom fields. For instance, before creating custom fields for **Text Field (multiline)**, try to reuse the **Description** field; if you want users to fill in the details using a template with a predefined text template, then use the method described in *Chapter 13*, *Customizing Look and Feel and Behavior*.

Choosing a custom field type wisely

When you are gathering the requirements from various stakeholders, they will ask you to create new custom fields to capture a specific piece of information. We have discussed in the previous section that you should always try to optimize the usage of these fields. However, once you have decided on the custom fields that need to be created, before creating them in the instance, spend some time working with the types of custom fields. Once created, the type of fields cannot be changed easily.

For instance, if you want to store a single value, then use Select List (single choice), whereas to select multiple values, use Select List (multiple choices). To capture dates, there is a date picker and to store lengthy text, **Text Field (multiline)** can be used.

Defining permissions

It's very important to secure your data stored in JIRA. There could be several client projects in JIRA whose information cannot be shared with other teams. JIRA can also be accessed by your clients and it becomes more important to hide other projects from your clients and only give them access to the projects relevant to them. In *Chapter 4, Customizing JIRA for Test Management*, we discussed how a project can be accessed only by users of a specific group.

JIRA comes with an amazing permission system that allows configuration at a granular level. JIRA has three types of permissions. These are:

- **Global permissions**: These permissions apply to the whole JIRA instance. Permissions such as who can log in and who will be the JIRA administrator can be configured here.
- **Project permissions**: These permissions apply to a specific project. Permissions such as who can access the project, create issues, and close issues can be configured here.
- **Issue security levels**: These permissions apply to the issues of a specific project to control who can view the issues.

The permissions need to be defined at all these levels, so make sure that people with the right access can view the data in JIRA.

JIRA's Audit Log

There is an **Audit Log** in JIRA that keeps track of all the configuration changes that happen in JIRA. This log is quite useful to track any changes in the schemes; the best part is that this log is available through the JIRA administrative interface.

Let's access JIRA's Audit Log.

Navigate to **JIRA Administration | System | Audit Log** (under **TROUBLESHOOTING AND SUPPORT**):

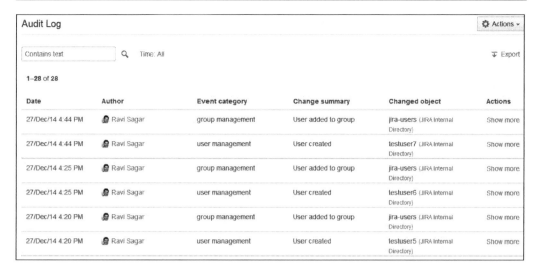

As you can see in the preceding screenshot, events such as a new user creation and modifications in the user group are recorded. The list of changes that is tracked by **Audit Log** is mentioned as follows:

- User management
- Group management
- Project changes
- Permission changes
- Workflow changes
- Notification scheme changes
- Custom field changes
- Component changes
- Version changes

JIRA administrator can refer to this audit log for troubleshooting purposes.

Adding the Announcement Banner

JIRA is a critical part of the software development life cycle and is used to store any kind of issues. Users rely on JIRA to check whether their daily tasks and managers use JIRA to keep track of their projects. JIRA administrators sometimes need to perform some maintenance activities that require downtime for users. As good practice, all the users, or at least the stakeholders, should be notified, but to avoid any surprises for the user, it's a good idea to give them an indication of any planned downtime.

JIRA has an option to add an Announcement Banner, which is visible all across the JIRA instance just after the main navigation. Perform these steps to add the announcement banner:

1. Navigate to **JIRA Administration | System | Announcement Banner** (under **USER INTERFACE**).

2. In the **Announcement** text area, enter your message and click on the **Set Banner** button. You can also include HTML tags. Select **Visibility Level** as **Public** to show this announcement to users who are not even logged in:

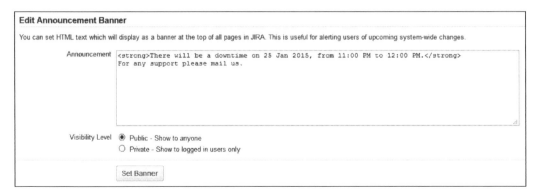

3. The following screenshot displays the announcement:

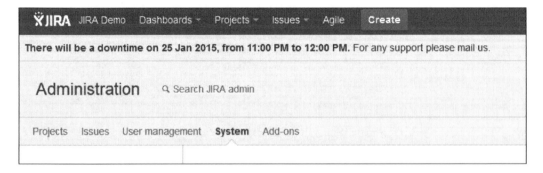

Adding an introduction

When you deploy new JIRA instances, users need to be trained; however, JIRA doesn't require in-depth training to start the basic usage and it's good practice to give useful introductory information to the users. This introduction will be visible not only to the users who are logged in, but also to the users who are logged out.

Perform these steps to add the introductory text:

1. Navigate to **JIRA Administration | System | General Configuration** and click on the **Edit Settings** button at the top-right corner:

2. On the new screen that opens up, scroll down until you see the text area for **Introduction**. Mention the instructions for the users and click on the **Update** button.

3. Now, visit your dashboard and note the **Introduction** box that is updated with your message:

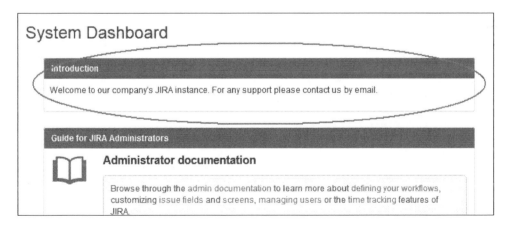

Performing indexing from time to time

In *Chapter 2, Searching in JIRA*, we discussed in detail the searching capability of JIRA and how to find the information that you are looking for. JIRA maintains and builds an internal search index, which is important for fast retrieval of data. However, after making configuration changes, such as creation of new field configuration schemes, adding new custom fields, and installing new plugins, the search index becomes out of sync. It's important to rebuild this search index from time to time so that users experience a fast search and can find the information they are looking for easily.

Whenever you make configuration level changes that involve the search index (such as creation of a new custom field), JIRA will prompt administrators to perform the search and you will get a message similar to this in the administration section:

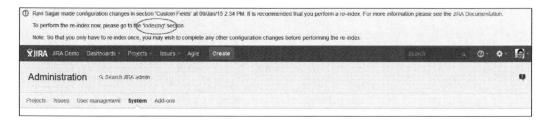

You can either click on the **Indexing** link that appears along with this message or navigate to JIRA **Administration | System | Indexing** (under **ADVANCED**) to perform the indexing process.

You will get two options to perform **Re-Indexing**. The first option is **Background re-index**, which doesn't lock the JIRA instance and users can continue working on the JIRA instance, but takes more time. The second option is **Lock JIRA and rebuild index**, which locks the instance and users can't access JIRA, but is quite fast:

Click on the **Re-Index** button to start the re-indexing process. Depending on the size of your instance, this process may take a few seconds, or it may be a few hours for big instances.

So, plan your indexing every 15 days during the period when there is less number of users accessing the instance.

Summary

In this chapter, we covered some of the best practices that JIRA administrators should follow to maintain their instances. We discussed the customization process that they should employ in their company to ensure that their JIRA instance doesn't get messed up with tons of configurations. We also covered some important aspects related to house-keeping and regular maintenance activities that good JIRA administrators follow.

What to do when JIRA is running slow or not working at all? As JIRA administrators, it's important to make sure that the JIRA service is not impacted. JIRA is a critical tool as it's a part of the development process. Developers rely on it to check their day-to-day tasks. In the next and final chapter, we will cover some common problems that may arise in your instance and most importantly, how to troubleshoot these issues.

15
Troubleshooting JIRA

One of the most important responsibilities of JIRA administrators is to provide support to the users who rely on JIRA for their daily work. As JIRA administrators, it's important to make sure that the service is not impacted. In this chapter, we will cover common problems that may arise in your instance. Most importantly, we will cover how to troubleshoot these issues.

Atlassian support

When you purchase JIRA, you are entitled to get official support from Atlassian and they are quite responsive when you raise a support request. You can raise a support ticket with Atlassian when you are not able to find the solution yourself.

Atlassian Answers

We all learn with our experiences and it takes time to become an expert on a specific tool or technology. Atlassian has a great online community of fellow JIRA administrators and users. Here, they share knowledge with each other and also seek help. I recommend that before raising a support ticket with Atlassian, you should always try to find the possible solution on the Atlassian Answers online portal at `https://answers.atlassian.com/`.

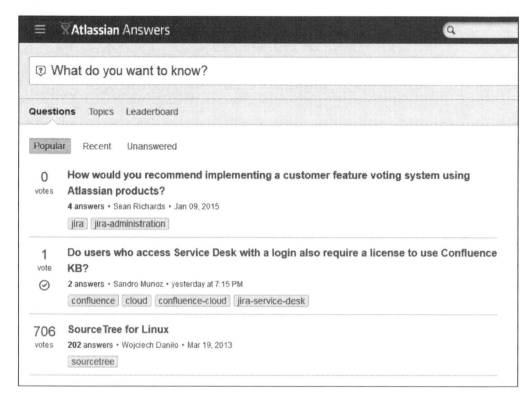

In this portal, you can see the questions that other users have posted. You can go through these questions and also respond to them if you want to contribute and help others. Each question is usually marked with tags (such as jira, jira-administration, and confluence). You can click on any of these tags and find all the questions related to a specific tag. Atlassian Answers is a wonderful online portal to seek help.

How to report a problem?

Raising a support request with Atlassian is quite easy. Atlassian has a support portal where you can raise your tickets. Depending on the urgency, you will get your response from Atlassian. In my experience, the support provided by Atlassian is quite good and they respond in a timely manner. If you have further queries on your ticket, then you can post a follow-up comment and close the ticket only when you are satisfied with the solution provided.

Perform these steps to raise a support request ticket:

1. Enter `https://support.atlassian.com/` in your browser and click on **JIRA** from the list of tools and then click on **JIRA Support**:

2. On the next screen, click on **Submit a problem report to us**:

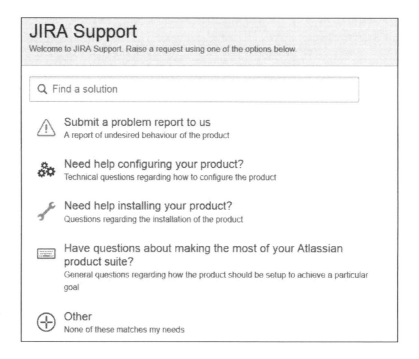

3. On the next screen, you will be presented with a form. This form contains various fields where you can explain the issue. You will notice that based on your issue details, suggestions will also come up on the right-hand side. These suggestions come from users who might have similar issues:

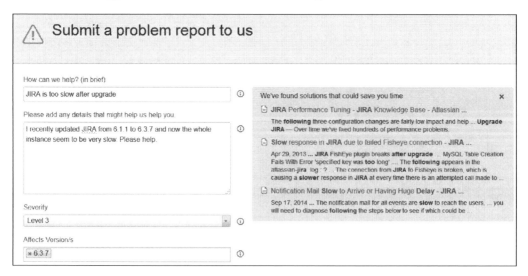

4. After the issue is created, you can also upload the screenshots, if any, or attach the log files:

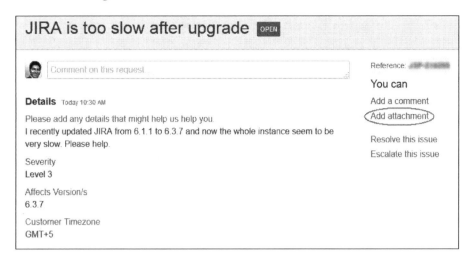

Log Scanner

If you ever run into an issue of any kind, you should first check the log file located at `home/log/atlassian-jira.log` under your `JIRA HOME` directory.

All internal error messages are logged in this file and it provides very useful information on the possible source of the problem. You will get good clues on where to start your troubleshooting. You can search the respective error message from your log file on **Atlassian Answers**.

If you find looking into the log files daunting at the beginning, then you can also use **Log Scanner** option that comes with JIRA. Perform the steps to run **Log Scanner**:

1. Go to JIRA **Administration | Atlassian Support Tools** (under **ATLASSIAN SUPPORT TOOLS**):

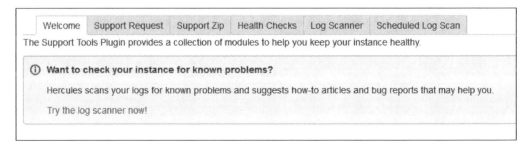

2. Click on the **Try the log scanner now!** link to run the scanner. You will get the option to either run the scanner on the standard log file or any other log file whose location you can enter. We will select the standard log file. Click on the **Scan** button to continue:

3. The scanner will run and look into the log file for error and warning messages; the good thing about log scanner is that it will also provide various links to Atlassian Answers and JIRA issues based on similar error messages that other users might have faced. As a JIRA administrator, you should run this scanner regularly, read these recommendations, and take appropriate action:

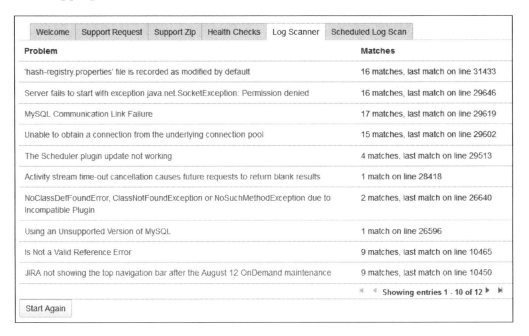

Support Zip

When you raise the support request ticket with Atlassian support, it's always a good idea to attach the log files. You can manually copy the whole log folder in your JIRA HOME directory and send Atlassian the compressed version of this folder; however, JIRA also makes the job easier for you. You can generate the **Support Zip** file. This not only contains the log files of your instance, but also contains **Application Properties**, **JIRA Configuration Files**, and a few other important files that give Atlassian a very good idea about your instance, which will enable them to give you better answers for your issues.

Under **Atlassian Support Tools**, click on the third tab called **Support Zip**. Here, you will have the option to select the file to include in the support zip file. Then, click on the **Create** button to generate the support ZIP file:

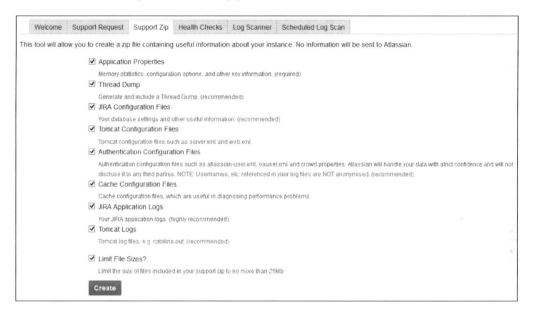

The support zip will be suffixed with a timestamp and its zipped version will be placed in your home\export folder under the JIRA HOME directory. You can copy this file and attach it to your support ticket.

Common configuration issues

In *Chapter 14, JIRA Best Practices*, we discussed various best practices that you can employ in your organization to implement customizations in JIRA. We also described the process (from gathering the requirement to testing new configurations) to perform customizations. If testing is not done properly, then it's quite possible to have issues later on and users will complain. Let's go through some common configuration-related issues and their possible causes.

User is not able to log in

Let's say that you receive a request to create a new user account in JIRA. You create the account manually and assign appropriate groups to the user to provide access to the relevant projects, but you receive the complaint that the user is not able to log in at all in JIRA.

Solution

First, check in your JIRA instance's global permissions, whose groups are part of the JIRA users permission. In the default JIRA configuration, the **jira-users** group is part of this permission. Just check whether this user is part of the **jira-users** group or not.

Users don't see the project

If you are using different permission schemes in your projects to hide specific projects from everyone, then it's possible that users will not be able to see the projects they want to work on.

Solution

In *Chapter 4, Customizing JIRA for Test Management*, we discussed how to limit the visibility of a project to a certain group. The **Browse Projects** permission in the project permission scheme decides who will see the project or not. Just check which group or project role is part of this permission and add the user to this group or project role.

User complains about e-mails not being received

JIRA has the capability to send e-mail notifications to relevant users on various events, such as issue creation, resolutions, and workflow transitions.

If the user is not able to receive e-mails, then seek more clarification based on the following questions:

E-mail not received	Solution
E-mail not working for some events or not working at all	If e-mails are not working at all, then check the outgoing mail configuration. It can be an issue with the SMTP mail server.
E-mails are not received for changes in a particular issue	Check whether the user is either the reporter, assignee, watcher, component lead, or project lead. Then, check whether the project notification scheme is configured to send e-mails on issue events.
E-mails are not received on state transition	If a custom workflow is used, then check whether the post function on any custom event is triggered or not. Then, in the project notification scheme, check whether any user, group, or role is configured to receive e-mails on this custom event.

Workflow buttons are missing

Customized workflows have the ability to add conditions on various transitions and a common usage is to limit who can perform these transitions. For instance, in the default workflow, once the issue is created, only the assignee of the issue can move it to the **In Progress** state. In a customized workflow, you have to be very careful about these conditions because users might not be able to move the issues in the workflow if these conditions are not met.

Solution

If users complain about not being able to perform workflow transitions, then check the condition for that transition. Either modify or remove the condition if it's not required or add the user to the relevant group or permission to be able to make the transition.

The options in the select list suddenly changed

In *Chapter 14, JIRA Best Practices*, we discussed using the same custom field of the type select list in multiple projects by using context to create a different set of options that appear in the field. The request to add a different set of options for individual projects is quite common and the same can be easily done using the context. However, if two or more projects are using the same context, then it's equally easy to make a mistake by not selecting the project name.

While configuring **Choose applicable context**, the project names are available in the list, and to select multiple projects, you need to click on the *Ctrl* key.

The custom field disappears from the project

Working with context can be tricky at the beginning. Another common problem that JIRA administrators face is that users complain about a custom field, which suddenly went missing from the project, although this custom field is present on the screen.

While creating the context, as discussed in *Chapter 14, JIRA Best Practices*, there is an option to **Choose applicable issue types**. By default, **Any issue type** is selected, but if you mistakenly select a specific issue type (such as **Bug**), then this issue type should be present in the project and the content will be limited to this issue type only. Unless there is a specific request to limit the custom field for a particular issue type, it's better to select **Any issue type**.

Increasing memory

As your JIRA instance grows both in terms of the number of users and data, you will need to keep track of how much memory is consumed by your instance. In *Chapter 1, Planning Your JIRA Installation*, we discussed hardware recommendation, where we mentioned how much the minimum amount of RAM and CPU is required based on the usage; there are times when JIRA will consume more memory than usual (such as taking XML backup), which consumes lot of memory, so make sure that not many people are using the instance before performing these activities. However, when your instance grows, it will consume a lot of memory and you might get degraded performance. It's quite possible that due to lack of sufficient memory, your JIRA instance might stop working.

Perform these steps to check the consumption of memory:

1. Go to **JIRA Administration | System | System info** (under **TROUBLESHOOTING AND SUPPORT**).

2. Scroll down until you see **Java VM Memory Statistics**:

⌄ Java VM Memory Statistics	
Total Memory	683 MB
Free Memory	372 MB
Used Memory	311 MB
Total PermGen Memory	384 MB
Free PermGen Memory	201 MB
Used PermGen Memory	182 MB
Memory Graph	**54% Free** (Total: 683 MB) (Force garbage collection)
PermGen Memory Graph	**52% Free** (Total: 384 MB)
Non-Heap Memory Graph (includes PermGen)	**53% Free** (Used: 203 MB Total: 432 MB)

In this section, you can see how much memory your instance has and how much is currently free. To free up some memory, you can also click on the **Force garbage collection** link.

If you notice degraded performance or *Java Heap Out of Memory* errors in your log file, then you can increase the available memory for JIRA. Follow these instructions to modify it:

1. Open `setenv.bat` in your JIRA Installation Directory (`/bin`).

2. Increase the JVM Maximum memory from 768 MB to 1024 MB or more depending on the number of issues in your instance:

   ```
   set JVM_MAXIMUM_MEMORY=768m
   ```

Atlassian recommends that JVM maximum memory of 1 GB is enough to handle 5000 issues. You can increase it appropriately for your case, making sure that you have enough physical RAM on your server.

Integrity Checker

Whenever there is an issue with the instance, any experienced JIRA administrator will always have clues on where to look first to fix these problems; however, there is a built-in tool called **Integrity Checker** that can be used to identify any possible problems with the tool. Perform these steps to use **Integrity Checker**:

1. Go to **JIRA Administration | System | Integrity Checker** (under **TROUBLESHOOTING AND SUPPORT**).

2. Tick the **Select All** checkbox:

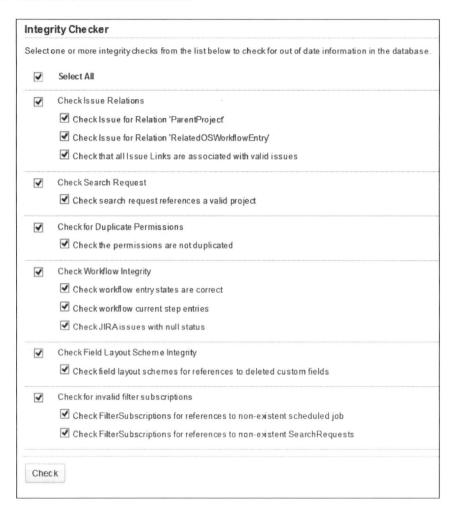

3. Click on the **Check** button to continue.

☐	**Fix All**

☐	Check Issue Relations

PASSED: Check Issue for Relation 'ParentProject'

PASSED: Check Issue for Relation 'RelatedOSWorkflowEntry'

☑ Check that all Issue Links are associated with valid issues

ERROR: The following Issue Link will be removed due to a related invalid issue: IssueLink (ID:10025)

ERROR: The following Issue Link will be removed due to a related invalid issue: IssueLink (ID:10026)

ERROR: The following Issue Link will be removed due to a related invalid issue: IssueLink (ID:10027)

ERROR: The following Issue Link will be removed due to a related invalid issue: IssueLink (ID:10200)

ERROR: The following Issue Link will be removed due to a related invalid issue: IssueLink (ID:10201)

ERROR: The following Issue Link will be removed due to a related invalid issue: IssueLink (ID:10202)

ERROR: The following Issue Link will be removed due to a related invalid issue: IssueLink (ID:10203)

ERROR: The following Issue Link will be removed due to a related invalid issue: IssueLink (ID:10204)

ERROR: The following Issue Link will be removed due to a related invalid issue: IssueLink (ID:10300)

ERROR: The following Issue Link will be removed due to a related invalid issue: IssueLink (ID:10400)

ERROR: The following Issue Link will be removed due to a related invalid issue: IssueLink (ID:10401)

ERROR: The following Issue Link will be removed due to a related invalid issue: IssueLink (ID:10402)

ERROR: The following Issue Link will be removed due to a related invalid issue: IssueLink (ID:10403)

ERROR: The following Issue Link will be removed due to a related invalid issue: IssueLink (ID:10404)

ERROR: The following Issue Link will be removed due to a related invalid issue: IssueLink (ID:10500)

Check Search Request

PASSED: Check search request references a valid project

☐	Check for Duplicate Permissions

☑ Check the permissions are not duplicated

ERROR: Duplicate Permission: SchemePermissions (ID:10003)

ERROR: Duplicate Permission: SchemePermissions (ID:10032)

ERROR: Duplicate Permission: SchemePermissions (ID:10100)

ERROR: Duplicate Permission: SchemePermissions (ID:10101)

Check Workflow Integrity

PASSED: Check workflow entrystates are correct

PASSED: Check workflow current step entries

PASSED: Check JIRA issues with null status

☐	Check Field Layout Scheme Integrity

☑ Check field layout schemes for references to deleted custom fields

ERROR: The field layout item with id 11934 has a reference to the deleted custom field with id customfield_10200. (JRA-4423)

Check for invalid filter subscriptions

PASSED: Check FilterSubscriptions for references to non-existent scheduled job

PASSED: Check FilterSubscriptions for references to non-existent SearchRequests

Fix	Back

On the next screen, the system will display the list of problems with the configurations found in the instance. You can tick the **Fix All** checkbox and click on the **Fix** button to resolve these issues. Alternatively, if you know the actual reason behind these problems, then you can resolve them manually and run **Integrity Checker** again.

Summary

In this chapter, we discussed the various problems that may arise in the JIRA instance. Most importantly, we discussed how to handle these issues. If the configurations are not tested properly, then users will complain about usage-related issues, which can be fixed by making appropriate changes in the configurations. In this chapter, we discussed such configuration-related issues and their solutions.

This is the last chapter of this book. I hope you enjoyed reading these chapters and I am sure you must have learned a lot of interesting things that JIRA has to offer. In the last section of this book is the *Appendix, Integrating JIRA with Other Tools*, where we will discuss integrating JIRA with other Atlassian tools, such as Crowd, Confluence, Fisheye, Crucible, and Git version control.

Integrating JIRA with Other Tools

One of the best features of JIRA is its ability to integrate with a variety of tools from Atlassian and other third-party companies. In this appendix, let's take a look at some of the common integrations that you can perform with JIRA.

JIRA with the Subversion plugin

Subversion is a popular and widely used version control software. JIRA has an add-on called **JIRA Subversion plugin** that can be used to integrate JIRA with SVN:

1. Navigate to JIRA **Administration | Add-ons | Find new add-ons** (under **ATLASSIAN MARKETPLACE**), enter `subversion` in the search box, and click on the *Enter* key:

2. The **JIRA subversion plugin** will appear in the list. Click on the **Install** button to continue.

3. This add-on will then be downloaded and installed in your JIRA instance. Once installed, you will get a message confirming the installation:

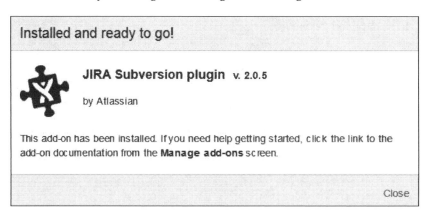

4. Click on the **Close** link to close the popup.

5. Navigate to **JIRA Administration | Add-ons | Subversion Repositories** (under **SOURCE CONTROL**):

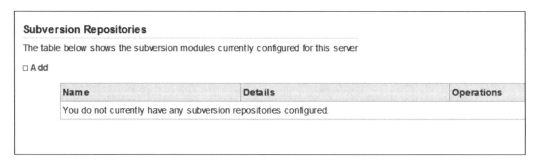

6. Now, you will have the option to add SVN repositories in your JIRA instance. Click on the **Add** link. On the next screen, enter **Display Name** and **Repository Root**; if your SVN repository requires authentication, then enter username and password. Select **Web Link** as **WebClient for SVN** if your repository can be browsed through a browser. Finally, click on the **Add** button:

Add Repository

Use this page to add a new Subversion repository.

* Display Name: `Tomato SVN`

Subversion Repository Details

* Repository Root: `http://tomatocart.googlecode.com/svn/trunk/`
Full path to the Subversion root - at the moment svn://, svn+ssh://, http://, https:// and file:// are supported. Note: when using file: protoco

* Revision Indexing: ◉ Index and link to any mentioned issue keys in the revision history ○ Do not index and link to the revision history

* Revision Cache Size: `10000`
The number of revisions to keep cached in memory for quick retrieval. Note: this number does not affect the speed with which revisions which the full content of those revisions are retrieved from SVN.

Username: ``

Password: ``

Private key file: ``
Please note: The passphrase for the private key file is the password above.

Web Linking

Web Link: `WebClient for SVN ▾`
If you are not sure what to enter for the web links, you may select from one of the more popular options provided. We'll make a "best gu
to customize these for your specific configuration.
Note: If Fisheye web link is selected, you need to replace ${repository} with the Fisheye repository key/name.

View Format: `http://tomatocart.googlecode.com/svnwebclient/changedResource.jsp`

Changeset Format: `http://tomatocart.googlecode.com/svnwebclient/revisionDetails.jsp?lo`

File Added Format: `http://tomatocart.googlecode.com/svnwebclient/changedResource.jsp`

File Modified Format: `http://tomatocart.googlecode.com/svnwebclient/changedResource.jsp`

File Replaced Format: `http://tomatocart.googlecode.com/svnwebclient/changedResource.jsp`

File Deleted Format: `http://tomatocart.googlecode.com/svnwebclient/changedResource.jsp`

`Add` `Cancel`

The SVN repository will be added in your instance and whenever some user includes the ticket ID such as KEY-1 in the SVN commit message, this specific file will be listed in the JIRA view issue operation under the **Subversion** tab.

JIRA with Bitbucket and GitHub

JIRA comes with a built-in functionality to connect with Bitbucket and GitHub repositories. Perform these steps to integrate JIRA into Bitbucket and GitHub:

1. Navigate to JIRA **Administration | Add-ons | DVCS Accounts**.

2. On the next screen, click on the **Link Bitbucket or GitHub account** button:

DVCS Accounts

Connect your Bitbucket and GitHub accounts to JIRA and link every commit with a bug or development task. Once configured, JIRA will query the repository searching commits for issue keys.

`Link Bitbucket or GitHub account`

3. In the popup that appears, select either **Bitbucket** or **GitHub** from the **Host** drop-down list, enter your username in the **Team or User Account** text field, and enter **OAuth Key** and **OAuth Secret**, both of which you can generate from your Bitbucket or GitHub account. Click on the **Add** button to continue:

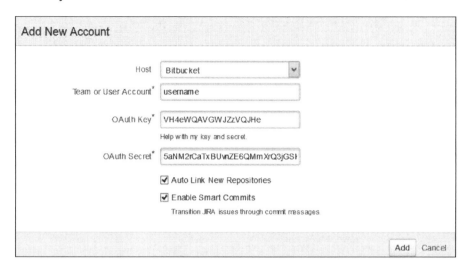

4. After the configuration is complete, the JIRA instance will list the available repositories:

Once the repositories are listed in the instance, the Git commit messages can include the JIRA issues ID and these files will be displayed in the JIRA view issue **Source** tab.

JIRA with other Git repositories

It's also possible to connect your JIRA instance with any Git repository and not just Bitbucket and GitHub. There is an add-on called Git Integration plugin for JIRA that can be installed for such integrations. Perform these steps:

1. Navigate to **JIRA Administration** | **Add-ons** | **Find new add-ons** and search for `git` in the search box.

2. In the search result that appears, select **Git Integration Plugin for JIRA**. Click on the **Free trial** button to install and evaluate this add-on:

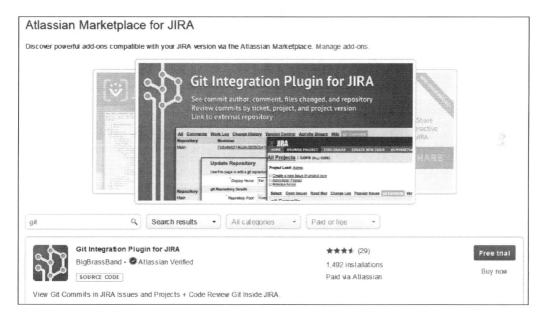

3. Once the add-on is installed, navigate to JIRA **Administration** | **Add-ons** | **Git Repositories** (under **GIT INTEGRATION PLUGIN**).

4. Click on the **Add Git Repository** button:

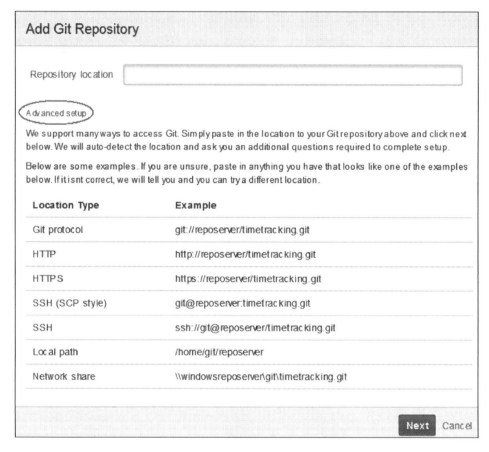

5. In the popup window, click on the **Advanced setup** link to add a Git repository with more configuration options. On the next screen, enter the **Display Name** of the Git repository and provide **Repository Root** of your Git repository. In our example, we will use a local Git repository hosted and located at the c:\git-repo location. In the **Enable Fetches** radio button, select **Git repository hosted on same server as JIRA**. Also, from the **Smart Commits** drop-down list, select **Enabled** and click on the **Add** button to continue:

Add Git Repository

Use this page to add a new git repository.

Display Name Local Git Repo

Repository Root c:\git-repo   ⓘ

Full path to the Git root on same local machine as JIRA.

Enable Fetches ○ Git repository hosted on remote server

○ Git repository hosted on same server as JIRA

Revision Indexing ● Index and link to any mentioned issue keys in the revision history

○ Do not index and link to the revision history

Revision Cache Size 10000

The number of revisions to keep cached in memory for quick retrieval. Note: this number does not affect the speed with which revisions are looked up from the index (to get revisions for a given issue). This affects the speed at which the full content of those revisions are retrieved from Git.

Main Branch

Specify branch if your repo has no master branch. Leave blank if master branch is present.

Repository Browser

Disabled   ⓘ

Project Permissions

Associate Project Permissions

☐ Associate with all projects

Restrict access to the Repository Browser for the repository by associating the project permissions. Remember — the **View Development Tools** permission must be granted to Users / Group / Project Roles.

Smart Commits

Enabled

What is Smart Commits?

Web Linking [OPTIONAL]

Web linking allows JIRA users to click on changeset and file links to web server capable of showing changes and files.

Web Link

View Format

Changeset Format

File Added Format

File Modified Format

File Deleted Format

[Add] Cancel

6. The Git repository will be added and visible in the list:

Also, click on the **Reindex All** button in the top-right corner to perform the indexing of the Git repository. As we have enabled the smart commits while configuring the repository, developers can also transition the JIRA issues while they commit the code in Git. To know more about smart commits, read the document at `https://confluence.atlassian.com/display/BITBUCKET/Processing+JIRA+issues+with+commit+messages`.

Although not free, this add-on opens up a lot of possibilities to use any Git repository in your JIRA instance.

JIRA with Confluence

Confluence is another popular tool from Atlassian used widely for online collaborations. Users can use it to prepare documentation, tutorials, articles, blogs, project reports, and various other types of documents. Integrating JIRA with Confluence allows users to create real-time JIRA reports in Confluence. Let's take a look at the steps to set up this integration:

1. Go to **Confluence administration | Application Links** (under **ADMINISTRATION**). The link to JIRA can be created here. Enter your JIRA instance URL in the **Application** textbox and click on the **Create new link** button:

2. On the next screen, you will be asked to confirm the link for your JIRA instance. Click on the **Continue** button:

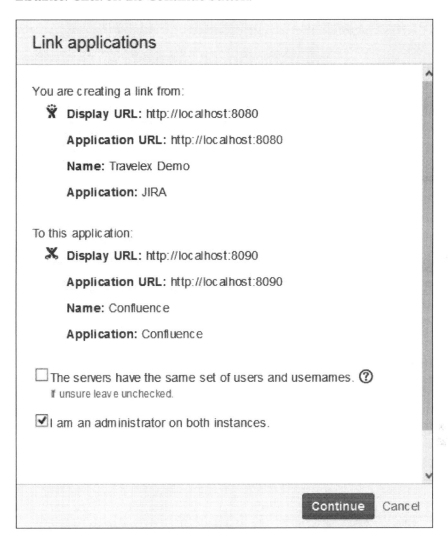

3. You will then be directed to your JIRA instance to create a reciprocal link in JIRA to Confluence. Click on the **Continue** button and you will be redirected back to Confluence. It's also possible to synchronize the user base of JIRA and Confluence. In that case, select **The servers have the same set of users and usernames**:

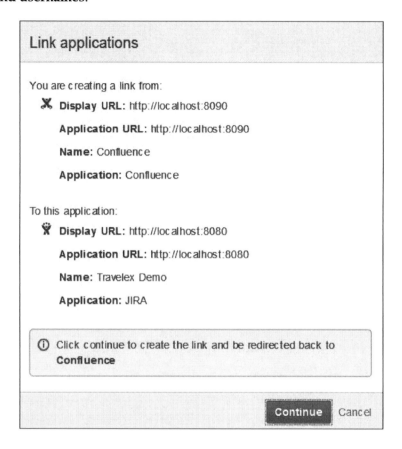

Finally, you will have the application link created both in Confluence and JIRA. After this integration, you will be able to embed JIRA issues in the Confluence page and generate charts as well.

 The integration of JIRA with other Atlassian products, such as Fisheye/Crucible, Crowd, Fisheye, and Stash is usually performed by creating application links only.

Summary

In this appendix, you learned how JIRA can be integrated with other common tools used in software development processes. Integration with version control software enables developers to associate the code file with the JIRA ticket. Most of the other tools from Atlassian can also be integrated into JIRA by either installing an add-on or by configuring application links.

Index

D

dashboards
  configuring 62-64
  sharing 62-64
data
  visualizing, add-on charts used 69
database schema
  about 229, 230
  HSQLDB, accessing 230, 231
  URL 230
default configuration modification
  tips 257
default scheme modification
  tips 257
description system field
  modifying, with predefined text 250-252
directory structure
  about 14
  JIRA Home Directory 14
  JIRA Installation Directory 14
directory, Atlassian plugin SDK
  apache-maven-3.2.1 143
  bin 144
  repository 144
documentation, for requirement management 117

E

Eclipse IDE
  configuring 148
  downloading 147
  functionality, adding to Helloworld plugin 152
  Helloworld plugin, importing 152, 153
  installed JREs, updating 149, 150
  Maven plugin, installing 150, 151
  setting up 147
  URL, for downloading 147
e-mails
  custom field, displaying 254
Excel
  issues, exporting in 37
external system import
  CSV, using 176, 177

F

fallback method
  for mission-critical applications 16
  reference link 16
fields
  for bug tracking 120
  for requirement management 116
filters
  about 30
  sharing 32, 33
footer
  modifying 253
functions, for advance search
  currentLogin() 35
  currentUser() 35
  endOfDay() 35
  endOfMonth() 36
  endOfWeek() 36
  endOfYear() 36
  lastLogin() 36
  membersOf() 36
  now() 36
  reference link 36
  startOfDay() 36
  startOfMonth() 36
  startOfWeek() 36
  startOfYear() 36
  using 35

G

gadgets, for reporting
  about 64
  Activity Stream 65
  Created vs. Resolved Chart 65
  Issue Statistics 67
  Pie Chart 66
  Two Dimensional Filter Statistics 67, 68
GitHub
  JIRA, integrating 291, 292
Git repositories
  JIRA, integrating 293-296
global permissions 268
groups
  adding, in project role 129
  creating 126, 127

information, synchronizing 139
managing 123

H

Helloworld plugin
  creating 145
  functionality, adding 152
  importing, in Eclipse IDE 152, 153
  loading, in JIRA 146, 147
  menu, creating in top navigation
    bar 153, 154
  organization details, adding in
    pom.xml file 146
HyperSQL Database (HSQLDB)
  about 9, 229
  accessing 230, 231

I

indexing
  performing 272
installation, JIRA
  as service 5
  from archive file 6
  on Linux 5
  on Windows 4
  planning 1-4
Integrity Checker
  about 286
  using 286, 287
introduction
  adding 271
Issue Navigator window 25
issue security levels 268
Issue Statistics 67
issue types
  best practices 110
  creating, for test campaign 74, 75
  creating, for test cases 74, 75
  for bug tracking 119
  for requirement management 115
  requisites 110
Issue Type Schemes
  creating 75-78
issues
  creating, JavaScript used 248, 249
  exporting, in Excel 37

exporting, in RSS 37
exporting, in XML 37
searching 26-29
searching, text used 29

J

Java Developers Kit (JDK)
  about 6
  installation, on Linux 7
  installing 6
  URL 6
Java Runtime Environment (JRE) 6
JavaScript
  used, for creating issue 248, 249
  used, for displaying custom field 246-248
  used, for hiding custom field 246-248
JDK 7
  URL 6
JIRA
  applications 19-21
  applications, connecting to 139
  architecture 22
  authentication mechanism 133
  core concepts 22
  examples 19-21
  Helloworld plugin, loading 146, 147
  integrating, with Bitbucket 291, 292
  integrating, with Confluence 296-298
  integrating, with GitHub 291, 292
  integrating, with other Git
    repositories 293-296
  integrating, with Subversion
    plugin 289-291
  uses 19-21
JIRA add-ons development
  reference link 155
JIRA Administrator 132
jira-administrators 130
JIRA Agile
  about 185
  configuration 188
  installing 185-187
  overview 185
  project, setting up 188
JIRA configuration document
  data, capturing 110

W

Waiting for Client state 212
Web Application Archive (WAR) 17
Windows
  Atlassian plugin SDK, installing 143
  JIRA installation 4
workflow
  customizing 79
  for bug tracking 119, 120
  for requirement management 115
  for test campaign 79
  for test case 94
  modifying, with conditions 214, 215
  modifying, with Post Functions 222, 223
  modifying, with validators 219

X

XAMPSERVER package
  URL 160
XML
  issues, exporting in 37

Thank you for buying
Mastering JIRA

About Packt Publishing

Packt, pronounced 'packed', published its first book, *Mastering phpMyAdmin for Effective MySQL Management*, in April 2004, and subsequently continued to specialize in publishing highly focused books on specific technologies and solutions.

Our books and publications share the experiences of your fellow IT professionals in adapting and customizing today's systems, applications, and frameworks. Our solution-based books give you the knowledge and power to customize the software and technologies you're using to get the job done. Packt books are more specific and less general than the IT books you have seen in the past. Our unique business model allows us to bring you more focused information, giving you more of what you need to know, and less of what you don't.

Packt is a modern yet unique publishing company that focuses on producing quality, cutting-edge books for communities of developers, administrators, and newbies alike. For more information, please visit our website at www.packtpub.com.

About Packt Enterprise

In 2010, Packt launched two new brands, Packt Enterprise and Packt Open Source, in order to continue its focus on specialization. This book is part of the Packt Enterprise brand, home to books published on enterprise software – software created by major vendors, including (but not limited to) IBM, Microsoft, and Oracle, often for use in other corporations. Its titles will offer information relevant to a range of users of this software, including administrators, developers, architects, and end users.

Writing for Packt

We welcome all inquiries from people who are interested in authoring. Book proposals should be sent to author@packtpub.com. If your book idea is still at an early stage and you would like to discuss it first before writing a formal book proposal, then please contact us; one of our commissioning editors will get in touch with you.

We're not just looking for published authors; if you have strong technical skills but no writing experience, our experienced editors can help you develop a writing career, or simply get some additional reward for your expertise.

[PACKT] enterprise
PUBLISHING professional expertise distilled

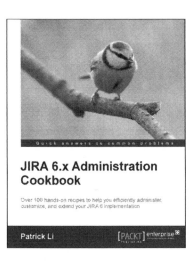

JIRA 6.x Administration Cookbook

JIRA 6.x Administration Cookbook

Over 100 hands-on recipes to help you efficiently administer, customize, and extend your JIRA 6 implementation

Patrick Li

[PACKT] enterprise

ISBN: 978-1-78217-686-2   Paperback: 260 pages

Over 100 hands-on recipes to help you efficiently administer, customize, and extend your JIRA 6 implementation

1. Make JIRA adapt to your organization and process flow.

2. Gather and display the right information from users with customized forms and layouts.

3. Extend the capabilities of JIRA with add-ons, scripts, and integrations with other popular applications and cloud platforms.

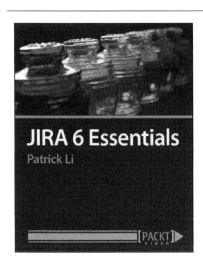

JIRA 6 Essentials
Patrick Li

[PACKT] VIDEO

JIRA 6 Essentials [Video]

ISBN: 978-1-84968-924-3   Duration: 02:17 hours

Design a successful project and issue tracking implementation for your organization through a series of hands-on exercises and live examples

1. Comprehensive coverage of important features and updates in JIRA 6.

2. Step-by-step instructions to deal with real-world situations.

3. Illustrations straight from the application to help visualize issue tracking.

Please check **www.PacktPub.com** for information on our titles

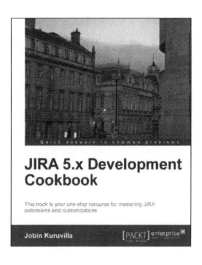

JIRA 5.x Development Cookbook

ISBN: 978-1-78216-908-6   Paperback: 512 pages

This book is your one-stop resource for mastering JIRA extensions and customizations

1. Extend and customize JIRA; work with custom fields, workflows, reports, gadgets, JQL functions, plugins, and more.

2. Customize the look and feel of your JIRA user interface by adding new tabs, web items and sections, drop down menus, and more.

3. Master JQL (JIRA Query Language) that enables advanced searching capabilities through which users can search for issues in their JIRA instance and then exploit all the capabilities of the issue navigator.

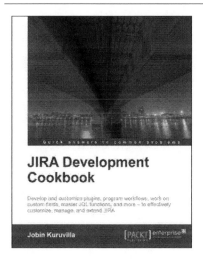

JIRA Development Cookbook

ISBN: 978-1-84968-180-3   Paperback: 476 pages

Develop and customize plugins, program workflows, work on custom fields, master JQL functions, and more - to effectively customize, manage, and extend JIRA

1. Extend and Customize JIRA--Work with custom fields, workflows, Reports & Gadgets, JQL functions, plugins, and more.

2. Customize the look and feel of your JIRA User Interface by adding new tabs, web items and sections, drop down menus, and more.

3. Master JQL - JIRA Query Language that enables advanced searching capabilities through which users can search for issues in their JIRA instance and then exploit all the capabilities of issue navigator.

Please check **www.PacktPub.com** for information on our titles

Made in the USA
San Bernardino, CA
01 September 2016